Jehovah's Witnesses

ALSO AVAILABLE FROM BLOOMSBURY

The Bloomsbury Companion to New Religious Movements, edited by
George D. Chryssides and Benjamin E. Zeller
The Bloomsbury Handbook to Studying Christians, edited by
George D. Chryssides and Stephen E. Gregg
The Study of Religion, George D. Chryssides and Ron Geaves

Jehovah's Witnesses

A New Introduction

GEORGE D. CHRYSSIDES

BLOOMSBURY ACADEMIC
LONDON • NEW YORK • OXFORD • NEW DELHI • SYDNEY

BLOOMSBURY ACADEMIC
Bloomsbury Publishing Plc
50 Bedford Square, London, WC1B 3DP, UK
1385 Broadway, New York, NY 10018, USA
29 Earlsfort Terrace, Dublin 2, Ireland

BLOOMSBURY, BLOOMSBURY ACADEMIC and the Diana logo are trademarks of
Bloomsbury Publishing Plc

First published in Great Britain 2022

Cover design: Tjasa Krivec
Cover Image: Photodrama of creation © Alamy

A catalogue record for this book is available from the British Library.

A catalog record for this book is available from the Library of Congress.

ISBN: HB: 978-1-3501-9088-7
PB: 978-1-3501-9089-4
ePDF: 978-1-3501-9091-7
eBook: 978-1-3501-9090-0

Typeset by Newgen KnowledgeWorks Pvt. Ltd., Chennai, India

To find out more about our authors and books visit www.bloomsbury.com
and sign up for our newsletters

Contents

Preface

When Bloomsbury first received my proposal for this book, I had been invited to a conference in Wuhan, China, but had to decline. Shortly after, news began to break about a virus there, and I felt pleased that I would avoid its effects. Little did I know that it would soon overtake the world and have a huge impact on religious life, including Jehovah's Witnesses. At an early stage, Kingdom Halls were firmly closed, and physical gatherings for congregational worship and conventions were cancelled. Jehovah's Witnesses proved extremely efficient at swiftly transforming the events to online meetings, including their annual Memorial service, which took place very soon after the lockdown in the UK. While it was interesting to see these transformations, it had obvious implications for the research that went into this book. On the one hand, my experience of the organization was atypical; on the other hand, attending events online was easier than making the effort to travel to a Kingdom Hall or a convention centre. We have all learned to make changes during the pandemic, and most people have become more technologically competent and are seeing the benefits of conducting many of our affairs online rather than in person. At the time of submitting my manuscript, the world was only beginning to see some hope of regaining normality, and it is difficult to know which changes will become permanent features among Jehovah's Witnesses and which will be abandoned when some form of normality returns. Jehovah's Witnesses have made frequent changes in their teachings and ways of worship, and it is therefore a likelihood that I have provided no more than a snapshot of the Watch Tower organization at this point in its history.

A few mundane points should be mentioned at the outset. Presenting a religious organization that is not one's own presents inevitable problems. For example, Jehovah's Witnesses not only hold that the Bible is inerrant but also do not accept the views of many mainstream scholars that Paul did not write the book of Hebrews, or some of the letters that are attributed to him. Rather than enter into a debate about biblical authorship, I have tended to explain their faith as they would and follow their own practice of speaking about Paul writing to Timothy. Likewise, it should not be assumed that when I use the expression 'the truth' I am endorsing the religion. The word 'pagan' also deserves explanation: Jehovah's Witnesses use it to refer to any form of religion that deviates from what they regard as the truth. It should not be confused with Paganism as a living religion, and Jehovah's Witnesses always spell the word entirely in lowercase.

Apart from instances where I am obviously expressing my own opinion, it should be assumed that I am using *oratio obliqua* – indirect speech. It would be tedious to keep inserting expressions like 'supposedly', or 'Jehovah's Witnesses believe that' throughout. Jehovah's Witnesses prefer to describe themselves without the definite article, on the grounds that they are Witnesses by dedication, not by membership of an organization. I have followed this practice, but not the convention of describing themselves as 'one of Jehovah's Witnesses' (which I think is slightly cumbersome) rather than 'a Jehovah's Witness'. I have used the expression 'Watch Tower Society' throughout the text, although, strictly speaking, there is no organization that goes by that name. There are two incorporated organizations in the United States – the Watch Tower Society of Pennsylvania and the Watchtower Society of New York – as well as other associated bodies with names like International Bible Students Association and the Christian Congregation of Jehovah's Witnesses. My abbreviation, I hope, makes the text more readable, while indicating that I am referring to beliefs and practices that ultimately emanate from the Governing Body. All biblical quotations, except where indicated, are taken from the Society's 2013 edition of the New World Translation.

It has not always been possible to explain in detail the underlying rationale for some of Jehovah's Witnesses teachings or to indicate that some are not necessarily unique to the organization. Inevitably, authors cannot cover every aspect of the subject matter, and some readers may feel that I have omitted or glossed over important topics. If I have done this, it is not in any attempt to cover up potentially sensitive material. Readers who wish to explore such topics further may consult some of my earlier publications, or those of the Watch Tower Society.

Acknowledgements

This book could not have reached its present form without the help and encouragement of others. I am particularly indebted to Don Allen, Emily Baran, Donald Jacobs, Zoe Knox, Hege Rignes and Bruce Schulz for commenting on earlier drafts of the manuscript. Grateful thanks are also due to Bill Thompstone of the Wednesbury Congregation and to staff at the Office of Public Information at the Society's headquarters at Wallkill, New York. There are those who have asked not to be named, but their help and support are highly appreciated, nonetheless. Finally, my thanks are due to my wife Margaret, who has accompanied me for some thirty years on various Jehovah's Witnesses' events, including online meetings during the recent Covid lockdown. She has read and discussed numerous drafts, and also deserves thanks for compiling the index.

List of acronyms

AJWRB	Advocates for Jehovah's Witness Reform on Blood
ASV	American Standard Version
BCE	Before Common Era
CE	Common Era
CIAOSN	Centre for Information and Advice on Sectarian Organizations
FECRIS	Féderation Européen des Centres de Recherche et d'Information sur le Sectarisme (European Federation of Centres of Research and Information on Sectarianism)
HLC	Hospital Liaison Committee
IP	internet provider
IUD	intrauterine device
JW	Jehovah's Witness
KJV	King James Version
MAN	Maschinenfabrik Augsburg-Nürnberg
NRM	New Religious Movement
NWT	New World Translation
QR	Quick Response
RTO	Remote Translation Office
USB	Universal Serial Bus

1

Researching Jehovah's Witnesses

Jehovah's Witnesses and academia

When I was a student many years ago in a Scottish theological college, Jehovah's Witnesses and Mormons were never mentioned in class sessions. Teaching mainly focused on Christianity, and 'comparative religion', as it was then called, had only begun to take off. We had one lecture per week on the subject, and our lecturer, who obviously felt the need to start at the beginning, began with ancient Egyptian religion, moving on to the archaeological finds that were believed to be the origins of Hinduism. Although the classes were mildly interesting, they did little to prepare budding ordinands, who were much more likely to encounter a pair of Jehovah's Witnesses at the door than someone seeking to revive the worship of Horus or Osiris. Occasionally one would hear a preacher launching a tirade against Jehovah's Witnesses from the pulpit, and we gained a small amount of knowledge about the Watch Tower Bible and Tract Society through our extracurricular reading of Walter Martin's *Kingdom of the Cults*, which was first published in 1965.

The relative lack of academic study of Jehovah's Witnesses is no doubt due to a number of factors. Until around the 1960s the teaching of other major world religions had barely commenced, and in the mid-1960s and early 1970s the mainstream churches were only beginning to define their attitudes to other religions. The Second Vatican Council (1962–5) expressed a desire to develop relationships with other traditional religions, and it was only in 1967 that the World Council of Churches began to expand its ecumenical agenda beyond Christianity, and serious consideration was not given to new religious movements (NRMs) until around fifteen years later.

The serious academic study of NRMs only began when newer groups gained public attention in the West, notably the Unification Church, the Children of God (subsequently The Family International), the Church of Scientology and the Hare Krishna movement. The neglect of NRMs in theology faculties was no doubt due to the contempt with which their ideas were held, and it was left to sociologists to treat them as social phenomena. As a result, the older minority religions, sometimes called the 'old new religions', were left behind, and attention tended to be focused on societal issues, often at the expense of beliefs and practices. For those who belong to a minority religion, its teachings and lifestyle are of much greater importance than societal issues such as demographic factors, members' socio-economic background and patterns of conversion and disaffiliation.

Of all the 'old new' religions, Jehovah's Witnesses have probably given rise to the largest quantity of published literature, quite apart from their own in-house material. Almost from the inception of the Watch Tower Bible and Tract Society, its detractors put their criticisms into print. The first critiques were written mainly by clergy, who were offended by founder-leader Charles Taze Russell's departures from mainstream Christian doctrine, and this marked the beginning of countercult Christian literature – a genre which continues to the present day. Some of these books specifically targeted Jehovah's Witnesses, while others included the Watch Tower organization among chapters addressing a variety of new – and not quite so new – forms of spirituality. The aim of Christian critique was to rebut the doctrinal claims of groups such as Christian Science, the Church of Jesus Christ of Latter-day Saints (the Mormons), Jehovah's Witnesses and more recently the Unification Church, comparing their doctrines with those of mainstream Christianity, or suggesting what one might say to a Mormon or Jehovah's Witness who called at the door. It is difficult to evaluate the effectiveness of such literature either in discouraging seekers or persuading existing members to leave; for Jehovah's Witnesses, such comparisons with the rest of Christianity serve to reinforce their conviction that they are 'in the truth' and that Christendom is in error.

As time progressed, a number of Jehovah's Witnesses became disenchanted with the Society and wrote about their experiences, adding a further category of literature to mainstream Christian apologetic – ex-member testimony. This genre has proliferated recently for a variety of reasons: evangelical publishing houses had become saturated with countercult critique, and the decline of mainstream Christianity resulted in diminished interest in doctrinal deviations; also, the ease of self-publishing provided a relatively easy platform for ex-members to tell their story, although the frequent absence of a refereeing process has caused such works to vary considerably in standard. Many such accounts are written as autobiographies, while other ex-members' experiences have been transformed into works of fiction and others have combined fact and fiction in a way that is impossible to disentangle. Although a number of scholars have disparaged ex-member testimony (e.g. Wilson 1994; Kliever 1995), these writings frequently give valuable insights into aspects of the organization to which the average researcher cannot be party. Particularly in the case of authors such as William J. Schnell (1959), Raymond V. Franz (2000) and William and Joan Cetnar (1983), all of whom attained high positions of responsibility – including membership of the Governing Body (the Society's central authority) in the case of Franz – we have insider testimony about the Society's organization and history which could not otherwise be obtained.

In contrast to this proliferation of negative accounts, a small number of faithful Watch Tower members have written about the society. A. H. Macmillan (1877–1966), one of Russell's early disciples and a director of the Society, wrote a history of the organization, and journalist Marley Cole's (1916–2009) writings included two introductions to the Watch Tower organization, as well as an autobiography (Cole [1955] 1985; 1957; 1966; Macmillan 1957). Although the Society invariably promotes its own writings, it took the unusual step of advertising Cole's *Jehovah's Witnesses: The New World Society* (1955). Max and Simone Liebster each told their stories of their experiences during the Third Reich (Liebster, M. 2003; Liebster, S. 2000), and Bernhard Rammerstorfer's *Unbroken Will* (2004) is a remarkable account of Leopold Engleitner (1905–2013), an Austrian Bible Student who refused military service and was the oldest male concentration camp survivor. Jehovah's Witnesses typically focus on the Society's own accounts of its history and teachings, which they often call 'spiritual food'. Since its inception, the Watch Tower organization has published more than a hundred books, as well as yearbooks, songbooks and smaller booklets and pamphlets, with at least some of its material available in over a thousand different languages, making it probably the world's most prolific religious publishing house. It is also one of the world's largest religious organizations, claiming 8.47 million followers who were actively engaged in its evangelizing work in 2019 and over 20.5 million attendees at its annual Memorial service in that year. (This exceeds the number of Jews worldwide, for example.)

One factor that militated against scholarly publication on Jehovah's Witnesses was the lack of cooperative relationships between scholars and the Watch Tower Society. Anyone who writes to the organization will usually receive a reply, but the communication will be unsigned by any identifiable individual, bearing only the Society's official stamp. Establishing personal contacts with workers in branch offices and in the Society's headquarters can prove difficult. The Society's prime interest is its evangelizing work, coupled with the belief that Armageddon will come soon, thus diminishing the value of academic study. When H. H. Stroup began his research for *The Jehovah's*

Witnesses, which was published in 1945, he initially approached Nathan H. Knorr, who was the Society's president at the time, seeking cooperation, only to find that it was denied.

The first scholarly publication was Milton Stacey Czatt's *The International Bible Students: Jehovah's Witnesses* (1933), originally a thesis in part-fulfilment of a PhD degree at Yale University: it is a short dissertation of less than 15,000 words. Stroup's 1945 volume was more substantial, being a full-length book, and was followed almost a decade later by Royston Pike's *Jehovah's Witnesses: Who They Are, What They Teach, What They Do* (1954). Pike's brief volume is written as short encyclopaedia-style entries, but while he attempts to be objective, he tends to present Jehovah's Witnesses as the religion of the dispossessed. He writes:

> The gospel of the Jehovah's Witnesses ... is highly material – and most people find it distinctly difficult to imagine the spiritual. The heaven that is preached in Kingdom Hall [*sic*] is the sort of place that may well appeal to the man who knows what unemployment means, who has had to tighten his belt, who works at a monotonous job, who has tried to bring up a family in a smelly little box of a house. It is the sort of place that will appeal to the woman who has had to share a kitchen and has had too many children when she didn't want them, and has had to nurse a girl with polio or mourn a baby that hardly lived to breathe. (Pike 1954: 134–5)

A small number of academic studies followed: Alan Rogerson's *Millions Now Living Will Never Die* (1969), James A. Beckford's *The Trumpet of Prophecy* (1975) and Melvin D. Curry's unduly neglected *Jehovah's Witnesses: The Millenarian World of the Watch Tower* (1992). Until recently, the most oft-quoted studies have been M. James Penton's *Apocalypse Delayed* ([1985] 2019) and Andrew Holden's *Jehovah's Witnesses: Portrait of a Contemporary Religious Movement* (2002). A prominent Witness until 1981, Penton was disfellowshipped, and his hostility towards the Society is evident. Holden's study is based on a doctoral thesis and focuses on one single congregation in Blackburn, England. The twenty-first century brought about an increase in serious scholarly study, and in 2016 the organization CESNUR (Center for Studies on New Religions) convened a conference in Antwerp, attended by over thirty scholars with a professional interest in Watch Tower Studies. This was followed up by the creation of an online network called JW Scholars, which continues to serve as a forum for discussion and exchange of information on the organization.

If one were merely to read the popular Christian critiques and the ex-member accounts, one might readily draw the conclusion that Jehovah's Witnesses suffer deprivation and pursue a lifestyle based on a naive understanding of the Bible. Undoubtedly there are those who have had bad experiences while they belonged, but they form part of a spectrum: while the more highly committed members are the most visible to a researcher, there are those who are less enthusiastic and those who have doubts and who are wavering. However, if everyone shared the experiences described by the ex-member testimonies, the organization would now be well and truly defunct. Instead, it continues to grow, and hence it is important to examine the beliefs and the lifestyle that continue to appeal to those who remain insiders. What follows therefore aims to focus on what it means to be a Jehovah's Witness. Previous publications on the organization have addressed its history or selected themes such as political opposition or legal challenges. The ensuing chapters explore the lifestyle of those who belong to the Watch Tower Society: how one becomes a Witness, what kind of everyday life is expected, how they worship, how they celebrate life cycle events and what happens if a member fails to live up to the Society's expected standards. The present study is not based on defined sampling or systematic interviewing: formalizing the scholar-practitioner relationship can often cause subjects to be nervous, and answers obtained can be confined to limited interview situations. Instead, it is the result of nearly three decades of a continuing relationship with Jehovah's Witnesses.

Becoming acquainted with Jehovah's Witnesses

It may be helpful to mention something of the history of my acquaintance with the Watch Tower organization. Initially, like most people, I encountered Jehovah's Witnesses who came to our door, accepting their literature, but paying only cursory attention to their work. In 1992, on taking up a post in Religious Studies at the University of Wolverhampton, I initiated a module on new religious movements. This had three consequences. First, there was insufficient material in the library to sustain the topic, so a quick temporary solution involved writing around various minority religious groups to ask if they would donate some of their literature which we could use as primary source material. Several organizations sent books and pamphlets directly, but someone from the Watch Tower branch office telephoned to say that this was not their normal policy and that they preferred to initiate personal contact first, asking if the City Overseer might call at my office. I agreed to this, and this began a continued relationship with Bill – the overseer – and his family. The second consequence, resulting from this relationship, was that Bill was invited to talk to our students. In teaching traditional religions in higher education it is common practice to invite adherents to speak to students, and I saw no reason why more controversial newer religions should be different.

One problem about inviting a religion's exponents to speak to students is that they do not always cover the tutor's agenda, and some visiting speakers are not so accustomed to speaking in public. Not quite knowing what to expect from our informant, I suggested that I should introduce the topic in the first half of the session, and then Bill would take over in the second. As things turned out, Jehovah's Witnesses are well trained in public speaking: it was a normal expectation that members undergo training at the Theocratic Ministry School (now called Christian Life and Ministry), which takes place weekly on a designated evening. My own attempt to explain Jehovah's Witnesses in Bill's presence was a valuable exercise, making me realize that what I might have said in their absence could be inadvertently disparaging or inaccurate. The third consequence was that it became apparent that there was no good academic book in the early 1990s either on minority religions generally, or Jehovah's Witnesses in particular, and this gap in the market prompted me to author *Exploring New Religions* (1999), which contained a modest amount of material on the Watch Tower Society, and later my *Historical Dictionary of Jehovah's Witnesses* ([2012] 2019) and *Jehovah's Witnesses: Continuity and Change* (2016).

At an early stage in our relationship, Bill informed me that his wife and daughter ran a haberdashery stall in the Dudley market; he jokingly said that they were following in the footsteps of Charles Taze Russell (1852–1916), the founder of the Watch Tower organization, whose family ran a haberdashery business. He suggested that my wife and I should look out for them when we were next in Dudley and introduce ourselves. We were slightly hesitant about presenting ourselves at a stand at which we had no intention of buying their merchandise, but out of politeness we complied, and we found his wife and daughter very friendly and welcoming. Being new to the area, we needed tradespeople to carry out work on the property we had recently bought. Bill had remarked to the students that Jehovah's Witnesses 'come from all walks of life', and we enquired whether that included window cleaners, scaffolders, builders and painters. Window cleaning, as we discovered, is a popular occupation for Jehovah's Witnesses, who often elect to run small businesses, allowing themselves flexibility to pursue their house-to-house work when needed, as well as other commitments that membership entails. Predictably, we were invited to Kingdom Hall meetings, particularly to their Memorial service – the Lord's Evening Meal – which commemorates the last meal that Jesus celebrated with his disciples in the upper room in Jerusalem and is held annually in the spring.

A short time after my initial acquaintance with the local Jehovah's Witnesses, a colleague who specialized in Holocaust Studies had independently been in touch with the Watch Tower organization, who were seeking appropriate locations to mount an exhibition highlighting their situation during the Third Reich in Germany. The exhibition took place in 1997, and guest speakers included Max and Simone Liebster, who recounted their experiences under the Nazi Regime to our students. The historian Christine King also delivered a lecture, and one of the Society's researchers from Brooklyn, New York (the Society's world headquarters at that time), was also present. This was particularly useful for my own research purposes, being an identifiable human contact, affording a direct link for directing questions and discussing issues at a later stage. The Holocaust exhibition was being taken to other countries, and in 1997 I was invited to Toronto to give a lecture at the university there as part of this event. This enabled me to meet Canadian 'brothers' and 'sisters' (their names for baptized members) and also to discover that there was actually a Jehovah's Witnesses' student society. Jehovah's Witnesses are often criticized for discouraging higher education, and, while most young people who remain in the organization tend to follow trades rather than professions, the Society has seen the advantages of having members with professional skills: knowledge of languages and IT expertise are particularly important in the twenty-first century for promoting their work worldwide.

Methodology

The contacts I have made with Jehovah's Witnesses over nearly thirty years have enabled the present study of what has come to be described as 'lived religion'. The study of 'lived religion' contrasts with the more traditional approach to religious communities, which tended to presuppose a normative version of a religious community, defined by its leaders, scholars and key historical figures. It has been customary to write about mainstream Christianity, for example, by examining its origins, its canon of scripture, its official creeds and its historical turning points. This approach has tended to focus on beliefs rather than practices, on texts rather than people and on leaders rather than the rank and file. It presented a 'top-down' version of the faith, and, since leaders have tended to be male rather than female, scholarly accounts tended to be male-dominated – written by men about men, and from a western standpoint. While it would be an exaggeration to claim that laypeople, especially women, do not receive mention, their role is certainly diminished in scholarly literature. Discussion of beliefs has tended to focus on historical controversies and abstract theology, the meaning of which is not substantially understood by the average layperson. How many practising Christians could explain what it means to say that Christ is 'eternally begotten of the Father' or that the Holy Spirit 'proceeds from the Father and the Son'?

When illustrating to students the distinction between these top-heavy accounts and a 'lived religion' approach, I have sometimes used the analogy of driving a car. When I drive my car I have limited understanding of how its engine works, and when my mechanic talks about crankshafts, differentials and head gaskets, I have no more than a vague layperson's understanding of what he means. I can, however, give a somewhat different description of my car by offering a driver's point of view. I can talk about its reliability, its petrol consumption, its manoeuvrability and perhaps some intermittent fault that always seems to elude the mechanic. These two ways of describing the vehicle are not contradictory but reflect different perspectives, and numerous aspects of our descriptions will overlap. The mechanic's understanding draws on the kind of detail to be found in a technical owner's manual, while the driver's understanding is more at home with a consumer's magazine. By analogy, 'lived religion' more closely reflects the 'consumer' of religion, while the historian and theologian analyse its more technical aspects. Like all analogies, however, there are points at which such parallels break down: for example, the mechanic identifies faults and makes improvements, whereas as scholars of religion we aim, as far as we can, to leave the phenomenon as it is, rather than to criticize or to suggest changes. This is not to suggest that there is no place for the critic or the reformer, but this is not the role for the scholar of religion, who aims, as far as possible, to achieve neutrality.

The issue of neutrality, of course, poses problems. Can any writer be totally neutral and objective? The manner in which we describe a set of beliefs and practices can itself indicate our standpoint; indeed, even the selection of material betrays what the author believes to be important and what is not worthy of mention. There has been much discussion of the concept of neutrality by scholars of religion, and I cannot do justice to it here. It is sufficient to say that in what follows my aim is neither to criticize nor commend the Watch Tower organization but to describe and explain what Jehovah's Witnesses believe, how they live and why they do so. Inevitably, authors who write on any religious community are subject to limitations and must select their material from what is available to them. Choice is inevitable, and there will always be those who question an author's judgement on what to include. In writing a book of this kind, I am conscious that there is a tension between what Jehovah's Witnesses themselves might want me to tell, what critics would like me to highlight, what the media like to publish and the account that I would ideally like to give. I have tried to balance these four perspectives, although this will no doubt fail to satisfy every reader. The media and the Society's critics would probably want me to give more coverage to the issue of sexual abuse within the organization, while the Watch Tower organization would no doubt prefer me to draw a veil over it. The fact that something has received considerable media attention obliges the author to take it on board, despite the fact that sexual abuse is, fortunately, only experienced by a small proportion of members. This is not to recommend passive acceptance of malpractices but rather to note what has happened, what some of the consequences have been and how the Society intends to respond to its critics and to the authorities on such issues.

It might be suggested that, since strict neutrality is unachievable, at least the author ought to declare his standpoint. Being married has been a considerable advantage in researching Jehovah's Witnesses, and my wife has accompanied me to Watch Tower events on many occasions. Not only was it beneficial to have a second observer, but Jehovah's Witnesses respond positively to happily married couples. Arriving at a Kingdom Hall as a couple conforms much more closely to the congregation's expectations, and it allowed us to blend more readily. However, belonging, as we do, to a mainstream Christian denomination, which Jehovah's Witnesses would regard as Babylon the Great, I am writing very much as an outsider. This raises a further issue which has elicited much discussion in the study of religion, namely the insider-outsider debate. Despite being an outsider, I have been drawn into numerous activities of Jehovah's Witnesses, and this inevitably raises the question of how close researchers should get to their subjects. One author talks about 'going native' in connection with a small-scale study of a Jehovah's Witness congregation (Holden 2002: 4), but to describe the relationship in this way is not only inaccurate but also offensive, suggesting a colonialist-style superiority to a less advanced community. If the expression implies that the researcher adopted the Jehovah's Witnesses' lifestyle in its entirety, that is an impossibility, unless he underwent the instruction needed to become a baptized member and to enter into all their expected activities. This author does not mention whether he engaged in house-to-house field ministry, whether he attended family Bible studies or whether he carried a 'No Blood' card to prevent the health professionals from using blood transfusion as a medical procedure.

How far the researcher goes in researching his or her subject matter is a matter of judgement. In pursuing my study of Jehovah's Witnesses I have been willing to attend Kingdom Hall meetings – the Sunday service and the mid-week meeting – and the annual Memorial service, as well as assemblies and conventions. All of these are open to the public, although it is unusual to find casual attendees who have simply walked in off the streets. I have also been a guest at two Jehovah's Witness weddings, attended one funeral and been present at a memorial service for a prominent member who had recently died. I have also visited a number of Bethels – national headquarters where Watch Tower materials are printed and distributed – and spoken to several workers there. Time permitting, I try to make a point of talking to those who staff the literature carts, both in this country and abroad. At meetings I have been happy to join in the worship, even to the extent of attempting to learn their songs in advance (for reasons that will be explained, none of them are likely to be familiar to those outside the organization), and I ensure that I comply with the dress code: in the West, suits and ties are expected for men, and modest dresses that come below the knee for women. Jehovah's Witnesses even take the trouble to ensure that their cars are clean when arriving at a Kingdom Hall, and I have learned to comply with this custom also. All this ensures that I am as much of a participant-observer as possible, rather than looking like an obvious outsider.

During the course of writing this book the Covid epidemic swept the world, causing all Kingdom Halls to close. While this made conventional participant-observer research impossible, it added a new dimension to my acquaintance with the organization. Their activities swiftly went online, and we were able to receive invitations from two congregations – one local and the other in England's Lake District – to attend meetings. While the obvious drawback was being unable to meet people physically, it had the advantage of convenience, since one could 'attend' such gatherings without leaving one's home. Unlike regular Kingdom Hall meetings, they were not directly open to the public, since it would have been all too easy for opponents to disrupt, and we had to be given meeting numbers and passwords for Zoom and Teams. The lockdown in the UK occurred shortly before the date of the annual Memorial service, and it was particularly instructive to see how the Society organized in cyberspace a rite which by its very nature involves handling the physical substances of bread and wine. Even in cyberspace, Jehovah's Witnesses made a point of ensuring that their demeanour and behaviour reflected normal practice in a Kingdom Hall; for example, all were expected, especially at the Memorial service, to conform to the normal dress code.

The Covid crisis afforded other insights into congregational life. Jehovah's Witnesses have recreational activities as well as religious ones, and one congregation devised online quiz nights, to which we were invited. Apart from their entertainment value, they offered insights into the range of Jehovah's Witnesses' knowledge and interests: although Watch Tower literature cautions against listening to certain varieties of pop music, most of the congregation left us far behind in terms of their acquaintance with popular culture. It was reassuring, however, that we could match them on the round on biblical knowledge. Under normal circumstances, some congregations organize special guided tours to places of interest, often to museums where there are artefacts of particular relevance to studying the history of the Bible and the events it describes. One of the congregations extended an invitation for us to take part in online 'tours', focusing on, but not confined to, Oxford's Ashmolean Museum: two of these focused on John Wycliffe and William Tyndale, and their contribution to Bible translation, while two others addressed the themes of biblical symbolism in the first eleven chapters of Genesis. These were led by two members who had particularly researched this material, and the online delivery enabled participants to see more of Oxford than would have been possible if we had been led around the city on foot.

One effect of going online during the pandemic is that a group can extend beyond a single congregation, and a small online group we recently attended featured an Australian sister who had researched the life and work of Isaac Newton. Although Newton is primarily known for his scientific achievements, he also wrote extensively on religious themes and is noted for his apocalyptic writings, focusing on the book of Daniel. His ideas therefore were perceived as having strong affinities with those of the Society, and there was speculation as to whether he was 'one of Jehovah's witnesses' and might even belong to the 144,000. (Jehovah's Witnesses hold that there are 144,000 who will rule with Christ in heaven, while the majority will live on the everlasting paradise on earth.) Those who belong to the Society will typically say that they are 'one of Jehovah's Witnesses' rather than 'a Jehovah's Witness': Jehovah's Witnesses are not merely those who belong to the present Watch Tower organization but also include those of the past who have 'come into the truth' and accepted Jehovah's rule. For similar reasons, Jehovah's Witnesses will never ask, 'Are you saved?', since belonging to Jehovah's kingdom by undergoing baptism and perseverance in the faith is more important than the instantaneous personal salvation that is sometimes offered by mainstream evangelicals.

My involvement with Jehovah's Witnesses is best understood not in terms of an anthropologist temporarily becoming 'native' but rather, as Graham Harvey (2003) expresses it, the 'guest'. I believe this is a much more appropriate metaphor for describing the researcher-subject relationship, since guests are people who have their own residence, who visit from time to time and, while having their own independent lifestyle, observe the house rules during their visits. Guests are not family members who have full access to all of the host's accommodation and facilities but are there by invitation and know where they are permitted to go and what is out of bounds. Considerate guests do not help themselves to the contents of the refrigerator, play the piano uninvited or criticize domestic arrangements; similarly, researchers find that there are aspects of an organization to which they are privy but others that cannot be accessed. In the course of my research, I would not expect to sit in on an elders' meeting or to have an automatic right to go on an organized congregational study tour, or even to know the local Kingdom Hall's Wi-Fi password.

Critics might suggest that my degree of closeness precludes critical distancing and makes me a 'cult apologist', to use the phrase employed within the anticult movement. This expression, so frequently used by critics of new and minority religions, is a misnomer. An apologist is someone who defends the beliefs and practices of a religion: when the early scholar Tertullian wrote his *Apology*, his aim was to commend the Christian faith to its critics and in the process to clear up some popular misunderstandings. While this present volume aims to correct some misapprehensions about the Watch Tower organization, my aim is certainly not to commend or endorse its beliefs and practices.

The root meaning of 'apology' is to speak on behalf of someone or something, and in the sense of speaking on their behalf as an outsider, my aim is to give a neutral account of the Watch Tower Society, as far as that is possible. I am happy to speak on behalf of Jehovah's Witnesses by setting the record straight where they are misunderstood or misconstrued. In September 2020 all the speakers at a conference on Jehovah's Witnesses, myself included, signed a petition urging President Putin to cease the systematic persecution of Witnesses in Russia. Whether or not this compromises academic neutrality, I do not believe a scholar can simply stand by and observe armed police raids, confiscation of property, arrests and prison sentences imposed against a peace-loving community.

One of the hazards of researching a religious community is that one can be regarded as a target for proselytizing, and from time to time Witnesses have said that they cannot understand how someone can come to know so much about them and not yet be tempted to join. I always note the word 'yet' in their invitation, which is given with every good intention: they genuinely hope that I will survive Armageddon with them. However, increased knowledge about a spiritual community can also have the reverse effect; as well as seeing the positive aspects, one can become more acquainted with less appealing ones.

There is sometimes an expectation that, when writing about Jehovah's Witnesses, one must mention their deficiencies. For those who want to find critiques of the Watch Tower Society, there is certainly no shortage of material, and there is no need for me to add to it, although in what follows I shall indicate some common criticisms that Witnesses have encountered. However, for any critique to be effective, critics have an obligation to ensure that their facts are correct and to present their criticisms in an appropriately measured way. While what follows does not attempt to conceal popular concerns about the organization, an accurate understanding of members' beliefs and lifestyle should at least help to raise the current level of debate about the Society.

Although I have contrasted 'lived religion' with more traditional approaches, my extended acquaintance with Jehovah's Witnesses has revealed that there is less of a gap between the ideal and the real than one might find in mainstream Christian denominations. The concept of 'the truth' entails that beliefs are important, and much emphasis is given to the teaching of biblical doctrines and the Society's interpretation of them. Those who disseminate views that are in conflict with the organization's official teachings risk being disfellowshipped, thus ensuring a high degree of uniformity of belief. If what follows substantially includes men rather than women, this is because women are not involved in the Society's governance: the Governing Body has always been exclusively male; only men can hold office as elders or ministerial servants, and only men are allowed to address the congregations at the Kingdom Hall meetings and at conventions.

However, in what follows, I have tried to reflect something of the diversity that exists within the Watch Tower organization, commenting on the lifestyle and spiritual obligations that are expected of its members, what is involved in undertaking 'publishing' work, the steps that are involved in becoming one of Jehovah's Witnesses and the lifestyle they have outside congregational activities, including the role of women. It is more difficult to note the degrees of commitment that exist among members, however. The researcher inevitably sees the regular attendees, not those who are absent, and it is therefore harder to include reference to the non-active members, those who are 'fading' (a term frequently used by ex-members for those who are about to exit from the organization) and those who have stopped attending but have not formally disassociated or been disfellowshipped. Since spreading divisive teachings is considered unacceptable, it is not so easy, although not completely impossible, to encapsulate those who think differently from the organization's official teachings and policies. There is evidence that there exist those who question the Society's teachings on blood; there are waverers who are unsure of where they stand with regard to the organization; and there are those who are sometimes described, mainly by ex-members, as 'PIMOs' – Physically In, but Mentally Out – who remain inside the organization, with varying degrees of attendance and commitment, but nonetheless remain inside, not wishing to lose contact with family and friends. There are some who are known to me who still remain Jehovah's Witnesses but have sufficient curiosity to attend other places of worship – for which they might risk judicial action if this were known to their congregation's elders. In common with the traditional approach to studying religious communities, my account of Jehovah's Witnesses starts at the beginning, with the early founder-leader Charles Taze Russell. Not every Witness is necessarily familiar with the Society's history; nonetheless, I believe it is important to contextualize today's Watch Tower organization, and the three official publications *Jehovah's Witnesses in the Divine Purpose* (1959), *Jehovah's Witnesses: Proclaimers of God's Kingdom* (1993a) and *God's Kingdom Rules* (2014b) all place today's organization within its historic context.

In giving an account of a lived religion, there is a further problem. Whose version am I describing? One method is to select a small community, such as a local congregation, attending events and speaking to members, but such an approach merely gives a small slice of an organization that is considerably larger. Life as Jehovah's Witnesses in the English Midlands is very different from those in Russia or China. Focusing on congregational life leaves out living in a Bethel, life as a pioneer, family life and much more. However, the Watch Tower Society has been prolific in its publications, which provide many more insights than limited fieldwork can achieve. The Society is also well known for its considerable worldwide uniformity. The organization takes great care to ensure that all its meetings follow the same prescribed pattern and that consistency is maintained regarding the beliefs and practices of its members. Virtually all the Society's past publications are available online and can be readily accessed, although the researcher has to bear in mind that some of these have undergone changes after their initial publication.

Jehovah's Witnesses typically describe themselves as being 'in the truth' (John 8.32) and make a clear separation between their own way of life and that of unbelievers. I am therefore writing as an outsider, and, when it comes to religious literature, members tend to confine themselves to the Society's own publications, which they believe to offer the one true interpretation of the Bible and contain all that is needed for everlasting life. My position as an author, writing about Jehovah's Witnesses, inevitably encounters the question of how outsider interpretation should be regarded. There continues to be much debate about the insider-outsider relationship and who understands their religion better. One way of bridging the gap between the insider and outsider is to write in dialogue with the community that is being studied. Accordingly, it has been my practice to allow Jehovah's Witnesses themselves to have the opportunity of commenting on draft material, and this volume is no exception. The scholar Wilfred Cantwell Smith (1916–2000) once wrote that 'no statement about a religion is valid unless it can be acknowledged by that religion's believers' (Smith 1959: 42). It should be noted that Smith uses the word 'acknowledged' rather than 'accepted': in other words, an author's account of another religious community should be recognizable as an accurate portrayal, not necessarily that the community should accept all that an author writes. Dialogue is not negotiation or an attempt to produce an agreed text. In subjecting my material to scrutiny by some of the Society's researchers, it has always been clear that, as the author, I must make the final judgement regarding the content, and the principle of authorial control has always been accepted. This book does not contain the Watch Tower Society's endorsement and, while many of their comments have been taken on board, for various reasons I have not always accepted suggestions.

2

Historical background

History and faith

A number of years ago a law firm asked me to prepare an expert report on an Eritrean woman who had come to the UK seeking asylum. She claimed to be a Jehovah's Witness, but the authorities were suspicious and had interrogated her about her knowledge of the Watch Tower Society. Among their questions were 'When did Charles Taze Russell die?' and 'What was the date of Jesus' birth?' I later put these same questions to a long-standing elder: he was a year adrift on his answer to the first question but pointed out that the second had no certain answer.

The incident raises the question of how much knowledge is reasonable to expect of a religious believer. Adherents to a religion can often be surprisingly ignorant of its history and basic teachings, and it can be unreasonable to expect a Jehovah's Witness to know details either about its founder-leader or how the organization's interpretation of Christian history differs from the mainstream. In writing about religious communities, scholars are accustomed to starting at the beginning, commencing with the historical background and the biography of early leaders. Until recently, many Kingdom Halls in the West had a small library containing the writings of the Society's first two presidents, Charles Taze Russell and his successor Joseph Franklin Rutherford. Their books are now seldom read, however, and many of their teachings have now been superseded. A new enquirer would certainly not be directed to them and would have been more likely to have studied a more recent, shorter single book like *What Can the Bible Teach Us?*

Inside a Kingdom Hall one will find no portraits of Russell, Rutherford or any other historical figure, no monuments commemorating worthy benefactors and certainly no statues. The fact that the location of Rutherford's burial place is uncertain is not a matter of concern, and Russell's monument in

Pittsburgh, Pennsylvania, erected by the Society in 1921 is occasionally visited by Witnesses who are interested in the Society's history, but such visits are not particularly encouraged. To pay tribute to anyone other than Jehovah is to be avoided. When candidates for baptism receive instruction, the somewhat lengthy list of questions that are put to them makes no reference whatsoever either to the Society's history or to the history of Christianity: in coming to know the truth, the key consideration is whether they accept Christ's ransom sacrifice, and whether their lifestyle matches the organization's expected standards (Watch Tower 2019a: 193–207).

For most people, history is not the gateway to the Watch Tower organization. Most readers will have answered their doors to Jehovah's Witnesses, or seen them standing with their literature carts in public places. The majority shut their front doors with varying degrees of politeness, and relatively few engage in conversation in the street. They make few converts; according to David Voas (2008: 121), a lifetime of publishing work in the United States on average is likely to bring only two additional people to baptism. Nevertheless, their congregations expect members to undertake 'field ministry' (or 'field service') – their terms for evangelizing – and even during the recent Covid lockdown they have found ways of disseminating their beliefs.

What happens when someone shows an interest at the door or the cart? The ensuing chapters will outline the various stages of engagement with a 'publisher' (someone who undertakes field ministry), through receiving instruction, baptism, active membership and finally exiting, which occurs either through death, if one remains within the community for the rest of one's lifetime, or else by leaving the organization, which can occur in a number of ways.

Charles Taze Russell

Before discussing initial encounters with Jehovah's Witnesses, however, it is necessary to provide some background to the Society's origins and developments over the years. The founder-leader of what later became known as Jehovah's Witnesses was Charles Taze Russell (1852–1916), who worked for his father's haberdashery business in Allegheny, Pennsylvania, and whose family were Presbyterians. As a young man, Russell had a keen interest in religious matters and was dissatisfied with mainstream Christianity on a number of grounds: he could not accept that a loving God would condemn most of humankind to the eternal torment of hell, and he could not accept his church's Calvinist doctrine of predestination – the belief that God had decided in advance who were the 'elect' and who were the 'damned'. Russell came in contact with a number of Adventist teachers and finally found a small group led by Jonas Wendell, which brought him back to the Christian faith and prompted him to get together a small group of men who met to study the Bible. Various Adventist teachers circulated journals, and Russell came to set up his own journal, which was named *Zion's Watch Tower*, the first edition of which appeared in 1879 and which has regularly appeared ever since, up to the present. The journal has undergone various minor name changes over the years and is well known today as *The Watchtower*. The first edition of *Zion's Watch Tower* bore the subtitle 'Herald of Christ's Presence', and underneath was a banner with an explanatory biblical verse: 'Watchman, What of the Night? ... The Morning Cometh' (Isaiah 21.11-12, KJV). Russell's editorial introduction warned that humanity was living in the last days and that the journal's purpose was to prepare its readers for Christ's return. He alluded to one of Jesus' parables – the parable of the 'chaste virgins' (Matthew 25.1-13) – ten bridesmaids who waited at night for the bridegroom's arrival, in accordance with ancient Middle Eastern custom. Five were wise and had brought sufficient oil for their lamps, while the other five were foolish and had omitted to do so; while the foolish bridesmaids went out to buy oil, the bridegroom arrived, and they found themselves too late to be admitted to the wedding banquet. As Russell explained, the Church is the bride of Christ, redeemed through Christ's ransom sacrifice on the cross, and therefore Christ's true followers will be ready for his imminent coming. The editorial mentioned two further points which have been important throughout the Society's history. Russell stated that the Society had 'no creed but the Bible'. Unlike some other religious founder-leaders, Russell did not receive any vision or special supernatural revelation from God; he only claimed to interpret the Bible, as he understood it. Despite the various changes in the course of the Society's history, the Bible has remained the final authority, with no additional creeds or confessions of faith, although it has occasionally produced short summary points of beliefs and practices for the benefit of enquirers. The second point was that readers could take out a year's subscription to *Zion's Watch Tower*, post-paid, for 50 cents (possibly the equivalent of £10 today), but those who could not afford that sum could have it free, on request. The practice of making 'spiritual food' (1 Corinthians 10.3) available free of charge has normally been the Society's policy. Russell's first congregation made a point of advertising that it was 'a church without a collection'.

A number of small congregations – ecclesias, as they were called – sprung up in several US states; they met together to study the Bible, using Russell's material, and Russell made a point of visiting them. Russell's publications were printed by commercial firms until 1889, when Bible House – a four-storey edifice in Allegheny – was completed. This building had its own printing facilities and accommodation for meetings. In 1884, Zion's Watch Tower Tract Society became legally incorporated and in 1896 registered under its present name, Watch Tower Bible and Tract Society of Pennsylvania. The various congregations that had grown up were autonomous, but Russell wanted to give them a sense of identity by inviting them in 1881 to come to Allegheny to celebrate the annual Memorial. Jehovah's Witnesses continue to celebrate the rite, which commemorates Jesus' final meal with his disciples, typically called the Last Supper by mainstream Christians. Russell and his supporters never celebrated Easter, partly because they regarded it as a pagan festival and also because they insisted on using the Jewish calendrical date of Nisan 14, which is a fixed date and which does not fall in line with the mainstream Christian practice of celebrating the event on Maundy Thursday, followed by Good Friday and then Easter Sunday. A further unifying factor was the practice of holding conventions (aka assemblies), which began in the 1890s and which found biblical precedent in Moses' instructing his people to assemble (Leviticus 8.4-5). In 1910 Russell devised the name 'International Bible Students Association' for his federation of Bible Student congregations.

Russell travelled widely throughout the United States as well as to foreign countries, including Britain, numerous European countries, Russia, the Middle East – including Egypt and Palestine – as well as Africa and the Far East, including Japan and China (Watch Tower 1975a: 56). In 1900 he set up a branch in London, and another in Germany in 1903, and conventions could now be held outside the United States. In 1909 the decision was taken to move the Society's offices from Allegheny to Brooklyn, New York, partly because the former premises were too small and also because New York was more prestigious, had a higher population density for evangelizing and afforded better transport facilities to distribute Watch Tower literature. The building was named the Brooklyn Bethel: the name 'Bethel' means 'house of God' and was the name the patriarch Jacob gave to the place where he had a dream of angels ascending and descending on a ladder reaching heaven (Genesis 28.19).

Russell was a prolific writer. Apart from his material in *Zion's Watch Tower*, he wrote a book entitled *Food for Thinking Christians*, which appeared in 1881. This book was distributed countrywide, first by boys, who often stood outside churches after morning services, and subsequently by colporteurs – itinerant evangelists who delivered books and tracts. Russell's major work, however, was his six-volume *Millennial Dawn*, subsequently retitled *Studies in the Scriptures*, the first volume of which appeared in 1886, titled *Divine Plan of the Ages*. This book provided an overview of biblical and post-biblical history, and purported to reveal God's overall plan for humankind. The plan outlined a number of 'ages', encompassing a Jewish Age, a Gospel Age and an imminent Millennial Age. Drawing on the book of Daniel, Russell identified a number of empires in human history – seven in all, the final one being the present Anglo-American system. This would be the last: like its predecessors it is part of a world ruled by Satan, and it would soon come to an end with Christ's return, when he would take his 'saints' up to heaven to reign with him. Jehovah's Witnesses are noted for setting dates for the end times, and their date-setting will be discussed later; Russell came to attach great importance to the year 1914, derived from somewhat complex calculations based on time periods mentioned by Daniel. This year was not only the one in which Christ's return was expected, but it also marked the end of the Gentile Times. The Jewish Age had begun when the patriarch Jacob established the nation of Israel and ended when the Jews were exiled in Babylon and subjected to Gentile rule. These Gentile Times were now about to end.

The year 1914 was not accompanied by any supernatural intervention to history, as the Bible Students expected. However, the First World War broke out in that year, and this was seen as confirmation that Satan had been cast out of heaven and hurled down to earth, as described in the book of Revelation (12.9). On 2 October, Russell entered the Brooklyn Bethel dining hall at breakfast, and instead of greeting the Bethelites with his usual 'Good morning', he simply stated, 'The Gentile Times have ended.' The fact that the saints were not taken up into heaven was explained biblically: as Russell pointed out, the Greek word *parousia* – often translated as 'coming' – was more properly rendered as 'presence' and signified that Christ had returned invisibly to begin the preparation of his kingdom.

Mention should also be made of Russell's *Photo-Drama of Creation*. This was an ambitious cinematic project, commenced in 1912, and receiving its premiere screening in New York on 4 January 1914, with an audience of 5,000 people. The production, screened in four instalments, lasted eight hours and covered biblical history, from Adam to Jesus, and subsequently the early Christian Church to the present time, culminating in the expected paradise on earth which the enthroned Christ would inaugurate. The Photo-Drama employed motion picture, coloured slides and vocal and musical recording, and was screened by technicians using a series of gramophone records and slides. The production was screened not only in various locations in the United States but also in Europe, Australia and New Zealand.

During his final years, Russell's health was deteriorating. On one of his preaching tours in 1916 he became seriously ill and was advised to return to Brooklyn. He was unable to survive the journey, however, and died on board a train at Pampa, Texas, on 31 October.

Joseph Franklin Rutherford

Russell's death inevitably raised the question of succession. Joseph Franklin Rutherford (1869–1941) was an attorney who had been introduced to the

Society's literature around 1894 and was baptized by A. H. Macmillan in 1906, soon becoming the organization's legal adviser. He is often referred to as Judge Rutherford, on account of serving as a special judge for four days in the Eighth Judicial Court Circuit in Missouri. When Rutherford came to office in 1917, the First World War was at its height. Russell had expressed concerns about his supporters' bearing arms but left it to their own conscience as to whether to offer themselves for non-combatant duties. A soldier who was opposed to killing might shoot with the deliberate intention of missing his target, or a conscript might volunteer for alternative service, perhaps working for the ambulance corps, with the aim of saving rather than destroying life (Russell 1904: 595; Watch Tower 1915: 5754–5). Rutherford, by contrast, came to adopt a stance that was totally opposed to any kind of participation in armed conflict, and his opposition marked the beginning of the Society's controversial anti-war stance.

During his lifetime, Russell had hinted that he would like to write a seventh volume in his *Studies in the Scriptures* series. Although the editors of *The Finished Mystery* declared in the preface that the book was 'a posthumous publication of Pastor Russell', this was far from the case. Russell had only expressed that he would like to write a commentary on Ezekiel and the Song of Solomon, stating that the task must be left for others to complete. Rutherford commissioned three other writers to produce the commentary, which also included the book of Revelation: Clayton J. Woodworth and George H. Fisher, together with Gertrude Seibert, compiled the volume. Seibert is seldom credited with her contribution, possibly because she was a woman: she had written poems and songs for the organization, and collated articles from *Zion's Watch Tower* for a small devotional book called *Daily Heavenly Manna* (1905) (see Chapter 7). *The Finished Mystery* was published on 17 July 1917, just over three months after America joined its allies and, as well as adopting a strident anti-war stance, accused the Christian clergy of being responsible for its outbreak. On 7 May 1918, Rutherford and seven other Watch Tower leaders were arrested and charged under the Espionage Act. All but one were sentenced to twenty years' imprisonment; the book was banned in Canada, and the US government required several pages to be removed. They only served a small portion of the sentence, their conviction being reversed by the Court of Appeals, and were released on 26 March 1919, with the US government officially dropping the charges early the following year. However, the appalling conditions of the penitentiary caused Rutherford to contract pneumonia, leaving him with a lung condition from which he never fully recovered.

Once out of prison, Rutherford organized a convention at Cedar Point, Ohio, in September 1919, attended by 7,000 people, 200 of whom were underwent baptism. During this assembly a banner was displayed bearing the letters 'GA'. This was one of a number of occasions on which a tantalizing banner was exhibited and whose meaning was only revealed later. On this occasion the congregation discovered that 'GA' meant *'Golden Age'*, which was the title of a new magazine to be launched and made available to the public. The name was later changed to *Consolation* in 1937, and in 1946 it was again retitled *Awake!*, which remains its present title. (Unlike *The Watchtower*, the articles in *Awake!* are often of secular rather than biblical interest.) Like Russell, Rutherford wrote prolifically, although his writings were somewhat shorter and more reader-friendly in style. He is particularly well known for his publication *Millions Now Living Will Never Die*, which was initially the title of a lecture that he gave and was expanded into a short book in 1920. The book's themes are biblical chronology – which was slightly different from that of Russell – and biblical prophecy, which he believed was now being fulfilled. Both Russell and Rutherford supported the Jews' return to Palestine, and *Millions Now Living* applauded the 1917 Balfour Declaration which permitted their return and heralded the establishment of the State of Israel.

Under Rutherford's leadership a number of distinctive features of the Society, as it is known today, were introduced. House-to-house evangelism became an expectation of all members and a *sine qua non* for holding office. Like his predecessor, he made use of technological innovation, encouraging members to use phonographs in their house-to-house work to play recordings of Rutherford's lectures. Rutherford also abolished the celebration of Christmas, which had been the occasion for an annual party at the Brooklyn Bethel but was discontinued after 1926, on the grounds that its celebration was unbiblical and that it had its origins in pagan Rome's Saturnalia. True Christians, he believed, should be kept pure and free of all pagan practices. Rutherford also held that the cross was a pagan symbol and that the Greek word *stauros* in the Bible was more correctly translated as 'torture stake'. In the Russell era, the Society had used a 'cross and crown' symbol – a laurel wreath, intercepted by a diagonal cross – which was displayed on editions of *The Watch Tower* and which some men wore as a lapel badge.

Rutherford was responsible for other major changes. Under Russell's leadership there was merely a federation of individual communities which met for worship, using Watch Tower materials, and were organized democratically. Rutherford wanted a more uniform 'theocratic' Society, contending that this was more in line with early Church practice, noting that the early disciples met together to decide on matters of policy. In place of elders and deacons, Rutherford wanted each congregation to have a Service Committee, coordinated by a service director and with a chairman, secretary and treasurer. While each local congregation had the right to elect their service director, the nomination had to be approved centrally. Not all of the ecclesias were amenable to Rutherford's changes, however, favouring Russell's arrangements, and a number of them formed their own organizations, some of which have continued to the present, although their membership is small.

Rutherford introduced two further important changes. At the convention in Columbus, Ohio, in 1931, banners were displayed bearing the letters 'JW'. The acronym was unknown at the time, and once again attendees wondered what it meant; on Sunday, the third day of the convention, Rutherford revealed that the initials stood for 'Jehovah's witnesses' – the name by which members of the Society are best known today. This was not exactly a name change: the name 'Jehovah's Witnesses' did not designate a legal entity, and the Society continued to be incorporated as the Watch Tower Bible and Tract Society of Pennsylvania, and the Watchtower Bible and Tract Society of New York. Rutherford's reason for introducing this new unofficial name may have been to distinguish his organization from the splinter groups, some of whom were continuing to use the expression 'Bible Students', for example, the Dawn Bible Students Association.

The second significant change occurred in 1935. During the 1930s, a large number of people had attended the Society's meetings and expressed an interest in its work, but were not totally committed. At the annual Memorial service, they would not partake of the bread and wine but merely passed the emblems on to their neighbours. They were known as Jonadabs – an allusion to an ancient foreigner who supported the Hebrew King Jehu and rode in his chariot: although he was not an Israelite, he nonetheless helped the king to fight against false religion (2 Kings 12.15-16). In addition to the 144,000, the book of Revelation mentions a 'great crowd', and there had been some uncertainty as to who this great crowd might be. Some thought it might have meant the 'ancient worthies' – leaders of ancient Israel – who would rise from the dead in the last days. At a convention in Washington in 1935, Rutherford elected to speak on Revelation 7.9-10:

After these things I saw, and, look! a great crowd, which no man was able to number, out of all nations and tribes and peoples and tongues, standing before the throne and before the Lamb, dressed in white robes; and there were palm branches in their hands. And they keep on crying with a loud voice, saying: 'Salvation we owe to our God, who is seated on the throne, and to the Lamb.'

At the climax of his address, Rutherford instructed the audience, 'Will all those who have the hope of living for ever on the earth please stand?' upon which more than half of the audience took to their feet, thus accepting that they had an 'earthly calling', as opposed to the 'heavenly calling' of the 144,000: the great crowd would live in an everlasting paradise on earth, while those with the heavenly calling – often referred to as the 'anointed class' – would rule with Christ in heaven.

The Second World War

The 1930s saw the rise of the Third Reich in Germany. Hitler's rise to power and the ensuing Second World War heralded a dark period for Jehovah's Witnesses. In Germany, the Bibelforscher (as Jehovah's Witnesses called themselves there) were banned from house-to-house evangelism. Their refusal to give the greeting 'Heil Hitler', to honour the national flag and to accept military service had serious repercussions, as will be discussed in a subsequent chapter, which led to many being sent to concentration camps. In the United States, Rutherford stridently opposed armed conflict, denounced patriotism and accused the churches – particularly the Roman Catholic Church – of exacerbating the conflict by colluding with Hitler and Mussolini.

An important issue that came to the fore during the war years was blood. Although blood transfusion had been a procedure at the time of the First World War, it was used almost exclusively for servicemen, but by 1948 it had become more widely available. The Watch Tower Society believes that the Bible identified the blood with the life (Genesis 9.4), and hence blood was sacred; accordingly, two articles appeared in *The Watchtower*, defining the Society's anti-blood stance (Watch Tower 1944b, 1945). Ever since 1945, Jehovah's Witnesses have refused the procedure, and the sanction for voluntarily accepting a blood transfusion was disfellowshipping. In 2000, voluntary acceptance of blood came to be regarded an indication of disassociation from the organization.

Nathan Knorr as president

Another important occurrence in the war years was Rutherford's death in 1942. His successor was Nathan H. Knorr (1905–1977), who had been baptized at the age of 18 and was almost immediately invited to the Brooklyn Bethel. He acquired a reputation for having excellent organizational skills, and in 1932 he was appointed factory manager of the Bethel, becoming a director of the Peoples Pulpit Association (the previous name of the Watchtower Bible and Tract Society of New York) in 1940 and vice president the following year. Knorr established the convention of anonymous authorship in all Watch Tower publications, the stated reason being that credit should only properly be given to Jehovah, not to individual contributors. The new president's organizational skills were employed in several important areas. Knorr wanted to ensure that the Society's overseas missionaries were properly trained, and in 1943 he set up the Gilead School in South Lansing, New York, for that purpose. The syllabus included knowledge of the Bible and proficiency in public speaking. The book *Course in Theocratic Ministry* was introduced in that year, with the aim of training speakers in how to prepare and deliver the talks at congregation meetings. The book '*Equipped for Every Good Work*' was issued in 1946 with the aim of ensuring that Witnesses were properly versed in scripture and able to answer questions in the course of their field ministry.

A further major achievement was the publication of the Society's *The New World Translation of the Holy Scriptures*. Knorr proposed the project in 1946, and translation began in the following year. The translation of the Christian Greek Scriptures – the Society's preferred term for the New Testament – appeared in 1950. In line with the organization's anonymity policy, the names of the translators remain officially undisclosed, although it is widely recognized that the translation committee consisted of Frederick Franz, A. D. Schroeder, George Gangas and Knorr himself. Translating the Hebrew-Aramaic Scriptures (their preferred name for the Old Testament) was a more substantial undertaking: work commenced in 1953, and the final publication saw the light of day in 1960. Since then, the translation has undergone several revisions.

Another major change under Knorr's presidency was an organizational one. The Society's existing structure had created blurred boundaries between its status as a legal entity and its role as a spiritual organization. Before 1971, the legally incorporated Society had a Board of Directors, whose period of office was technically only three years and who were elected to office by the organization's 450 voting members, most of whom now belonged to the great crowd rather than the anointed class. The Board of Directors had always belonged to the 144,000 anointed class, and it did not seem right that these anointed members should be voted into office by members of the great crowd, and it also seemed inappropriate that, as the organization's spiritual leaders, their period of office should be restricted to three years only. Knorr therefore introduced a new system, whereby the spiritual and the earthly leadership would be separated. There would be a Governing Body, which was not subject to election, and there would be a Board of Directors who would be elected for a three-year period; however, it was an expectation that the Governing Body would consist of Directors drawn from both the Watch Tower Bible and Tract Society of Pennsylvania and the Watchtower Bible and Tract Society of New York, and that their election would be ratified when their office as earthly directors periodically expired. The Governing Body would be self-perpetuating, and when new members were needed they would be co-opted by the Governing Body – a practice which continues today. Knorr believed that this was consistent with early Christian practice, as described in the Bible: the first apostles were not appointed by election, but by being called by Christ.

When Matthias was appointed to replace Judas Iscariot, he was not elected as his successor, but the apostles drew lots, relying on God to determine the appropriate candidate (Acts 1.15-26). Under Knorr's new system, eleven men were appointed to the Governing Body. The number had no particular significance; unlike the Church of Jesus Christ of Latter-day Saints, who maintain a fixed number of twelve apostles, Jehovah's Witnesses find no biblical injunction that stipulates the number of Governing Body members: at one time there were as many as eighteen, and the lowest number at one point was seven.

From 1976, the ongoing running of the Society was assigned to six committees: a Personnel Committee, a Publishing Committee, a Service Committee, a Teaching Committee, a Writing Committee and a Chairman's Committee (now called the Coordinators' Committee). Members of the Governing Body only sit on the Coordinator's Committee, which exists to deal with urgent matters, such as responses to persecution, and natural disasters such as earthquakes and famines; these committees now largely consist of members of the great crowd. Also worthy of mention during Knorr's period of office was the publication of the *Aid to Bible Understanding* in 1971. This is a substantial encyclopaedia of biblical and doctrinal topics, which evidently took six years to research and prepare, and was the work of 250 researchers in ninety different countries. It was used in the Watchtower Bible School of Gilead, until it was replaced in 1988 by the two-volume *Insight on the Scriptures*, which contains much of the material of the original volume, but updated.

Knorr died in 1977 and was succeeded by Frederick W. Franz (1893–1992). Unlike the Knorr era, there were no major changes under Franz's leadership, which may have been due to the fact that the Governing Body as a whole made decisions, rather than a single individual leader. Franz was baptized in 1923 and became part of the Brooklyn Bethel staff the following year, where he became in charge of the colporteur desk. Franz was also a singer and was part of a male quartet on the Society's WBBR radio station, and he occasionally conducted the Society's orchestra. After becoming vice president in 1945, he travelled widely and was a speaker at many conventions. During his presidency, there was some minor restructuring, and in 1987 the Ministerial Training School was set up as part of the Watchtower Bible School of Gilead. The School's purpose was to train elders and ministerial servants in teaching, public speaking and organizational matters, to serve congregations at home and abroad. Also of note was the publication of *Jehovah's Witnesses: Proclaimers of God's Kingdom* in 1993, which is a substantial history of the Society from its inception to the late twentieth century, written for a popular readership rather than an academic audience. The publication replaced *Jehovah's Witnesses in the Divine Purpose* (1959), which was a shorter volume written as a dialogue between two inquirers.

When Franz died in 1992 at the age of 99, he was succeeded by Milton G. Henschel (1920–2003). Henschel's father had served at the Brooklyn Bethel as a construction worker, and Milton had been brought up as a Bible Student. Knorr had appointed him as his assistant when he came to office in 1942, and, like all the other Watch Tower leaders, he had done much travel internationally and spoken at conventions. Henschel was 72 when he became president: this was young compared with the average age of the Governing Body at the time, which was 82. The requirement that the Governing Body must consist of members of the anointed class was beginning to present problems, since it was virtually closed in 1935, when Rutherford distinguished the 144,000 from the great crowd, and the Society was becoming increasingly dominated by its earthly class. As a means of solving this problem, Henschel took the unprecedented step in 2000 of resigning as president of both Watch Tower Societies, and all members of the Governing Body resigned en masse as directors of the Watch Tower Bible and Tract Society of Pennsylvania. No president had resigned before: all four of his predecessors had remained in office until their death. This did not bring the Governing Body to an end, however: the effect of Henschel's action was to separate the Governing Body from the directorship of the legally incorporated earthly Societies. Henschel explained that the move enabled the Governing Body to focus more on the spiritual leadership of the organization, while the physical running of the organization could be left to others. Don A. Adams (1925–2019) replaced Henschel as president of the Pennsylvania Society, and Max H. Larson (1915–2011) took over as president of the New York one. Neither Adams nor Larson were members of the anointed class: this was the first time that the two Societies have been headed by members of the great crowd. Three new bodies were created to oversee the earthly running of the organization: The Christian Congregation of Jehovah's Witnesses would oversee religious and educational affairs; the Religious Order of Jehovah's Witnesses would be responsible for personnel matters; and the Kingdom Support Services would look after the Society's physical resources, principally buildings and vehicles.

I stated above that the heavenly class was virtually closed in 1935. However, although most of the anointed class have tended to belong to the Society before that date, the possibility of a member becoming acknowledged as one of the 144,000 still remains. As those who belonged to the Governing Body at the time of these major changes grew older and died, a new generation of anointed ones came on board, and in 2018 the average age of Governing Body members was 68 – not exactly young, but certainly more youthful than when Henschel took office. No member of the Governing Body was born before 1935. Unlike the two incorporated societies, the Governing Body does not have a president but a rotating chairman, who is changed each year, in alphabetical order.

Technological innovation

Despite its conservative theology, and its attempts to return to first-century Christian practice, the Watch Tower Society has always made use of technological innovation, as was evidenced by Russell's 1914 Photo-Drama and the use of the phonograph. Unlike the Amish, Jehovah's Witnesses do not take the view that maintaining the practice of the early Church involves reverting to first-century technology. However, the advent of the internet presented Jehovah's Witnesses with the problem that 'surfing the web' would bring members into contact with unbelievers who might give rise to 'bad associations' – an expression used by Paul to highlight the hazards of mixing with those who were likely to lead one astray (1 Corinthians 15.33). In particular, the Society was concerned that some might gain access to pornographic material, or to ideas posted by critics, or become addicted to its use, which might lead them away from the truth. A 1995 comment in *Awake!* magazine described the internet as a 'moral minefield' (Watch Tower 1995b: 29), and subsequent *Watchtower* and *Awake!* articles warned of the dangers. However, by 1997 the Society decided that its own internet presence was desirable: entering the Society's name in a search engine only too often highlighted hostile material, and having one's own web pages ensured that Jehovah's Witnesses' own voice could be heard, unfiltered by antagonistic comments. Accordingly, in 1997 the Watch Tower Society launched its website with the domain name www.watchtower.org. In 2008 this was replaced by JW.org, and in 2014 there was a positive drive to encourage Witnesses and non-Witnesses alike to visit the Society's web pages. The literature carts, which were introduced in 2012, carried QR (quick response) codes, enabling those with smartphones to access the pages, and all Kingdom Halls were instructed to display the JW.org logo at their entrances. The content of the printed *Watchtower* and *Awake!* magazines was reduced in size, and readers were directed to additional online articles. The website became increasingly ambitious, with JW Broadcasting streaming videos and sound recordings, and the addition of Memorial talks began in 2020, since the coronavirus crisis prevented members from attending in person. The Society aims to make its material available in all languages, and although it is not possible to translate every publication, there is at least some material available in over a thousand different languages.

New headquarters in Warwick

The technological revolution had a further impact. The impact of the electronics revolution meant that it was no longer necessary to make the heart of New York the centre for printing and distributing literature. It was now more efficient and economical to send material electronically to various branch offices throughout the globe. The Brooklyn Bethel, at which the Society had been located since 1909, was expensive to maintain in the middle of New York City and had become quite antiquated. It consisted of six buildings that were connected by underground tunnels, with a further eleven that were scattered in different nearby locations. New premises were clearly needed, and in 1989 work began on the Watchtower Educational Center in Patterson, New York, around 70 miles north of Brooklyn. Gilead School was relocated there in 1995, and the work was finally completed and dedicated in 1999. In 2004 the Society had purchased two new MAN Roland Lithoman printing presses, which had proved too large to fit into the Brooklyn premises and had to be housed in purpose-built accommodation at the Wallkill complex. From that time, the printing and distribution of Watch Tower literature were handled at Wallkill.

The Society's work now operates from the three main sites. Wallkill was the location of Watchtower Farms: from 1963 the Society ran a number of farms, and owned 3,000 acres of farmland in the locality. Until recently they produced meat, poultry, milk and eggs to feed its many full-time workers, but the site is now largely used as a printery, and most food is purchased from outside sources. In 2017, the famous landmark Watchtower sign from the Brooklyn buildings was taken down, and the Society's headquarters were relocated to a newly designed 253-acre site at Warwick. The premises are open to visitors for tours and have attracted many visitors since opening.

Building these new premises was, of course, expensive, and recent rationalization of the use of local Kingdom Halls has helped to finance these projects. In previous years, congregations set up their own premises by appointing a building committee and raising the necessary funds through donations from their members and, where necessary, by obtaining loans from other nearby congregations or the branch office. It was not unusual for more than one congregation to share the same Kingdom Hall in order to optimize the use of resources. In 2014 arrangements changed, and congregations no longer had the autonomy to build their own Kingdom Halls; instead, the relevant branch office would make decisions about building new premises and which congregations should share buildings. A number of Kingdom Halls were sold off, with the proceeds going to the branch office, which would then be asked to make appropriate contributions to the worldwide organization.

It may be asked why such expensive building work and painstaking reorganization is needed if humankind is in the last days and Armageddon will occur very soon. However, as will be explained, Armageddon is not the end, and Jehovah's organization will continue to be needed for worship and teaching in the coming millennium.

3

Belonging

Demographics

According to the Watch Tower Society's 2019 report, there are 8,683,107 Jehovah's Witnesses worldwide, 119,712 congregations and 240 lands in which they preach their message (Watch Tower 2019g).[1] The membership statistic refers to the number of active baptized members who undertake house-to-house evangelism and staff their literature carts. This statistic relates to the aggregated highest monthly figure for each congregation worldwide. In 2019 a remarkable total of 2,088,560,437 hours of publishing was reported. There are others, of course, who attend congregation meetings but are not engaged in active field service, and, if one measures the annual Memorial attendance, the statistic is much higher: 20,919,041 worldwide in that year. In the United States, Jehovah's Witnesses are the most racially diverse of any Christian denomination: 36 per cent are white, 32 per cent Hispanic, 27 per cent black and 6 per cent mixed or other race. There are more women than men – 65 per cent to 35 per cent – and 65 per cent of adult members are converts (Lipka 2016). It is not surprising, given the statistics, that 90 per cent of Jehovah's Witnesses, when surveyed, stated that religion is very important in their lives and that they believe in God with absolute certainty, and 94 per cent believe the Bible to be the word of God. Eighty-three per cent stated that they believe their faith is the only true one. Eighty-five per cent stated that they attended services at least once a week (this compares with 47 per cent of Christians in the United States), 90 per cent said they prayed daily (compared with 68 per cent of US Christians) and 76 per cent share their faith with others at least once a week – only 26 per cent of the nation's Christians claimed to do so. However, Jehovah's Witnesses have the highest attrition

---

[1]Although 2020 figures are available, these may not be a realistic reflection of the Society's situation, on account of the Covid-19 pandemic.

rate of any denomination: of those who have been brought up in the faith, 66 per cent will leave during their lifetime.

The 35 per cent who are born into the organization, of course, have not been drawn into the organization through a knock on the door, although a significant proportion of those who have written on their experiences within the Society have recalled that this happened to their parents. Those who are brought up as Witnesses are normally expected to engage in all the meetings' activities. Kingdom Halls do not run Sunday Schools, and children are encouraged to take part in congregation meetings as far as they are able, even to the extent of making comments at the Watchtower Bible studies, and they often accompany their parents on house-to-house work.

The word 'publishing' is regularly used in the Society's Service Year Reports. Although the Watch Tower Society does much publishing in the sense of producing printed material, the word is applied to evangelizing more generally in the sense of 'publishing abroad' or proclaiming. It harks back to an occasion when Paul says to Barnabas, 'Let us return and visit the brothers in every one of the cities in which we published the word of Jehovah to see how they are' (Acts 15.36). The word tends not to be used in common parlance by Witnesses, who usually talk about 'field service' or 'field ministry', but it appears in the Society's reports. Other translations use the word 'preached' instead of 'published', but for Jehovah's Witnesses proclaiming is not simply something that is done by a preacher from a pulpit or platform but by everyone who is in the truth.

Field ministry is supremely important to Jehovah's Witnesses. In his gospel, Matthew records Jesus' final words to his disciples: 'Go, therefore, and make disciples of people of all the nations, baptizing them in the name of the Father and of the Son and of the holy spirit, teaching them to observe all the things I have commanded you. And look! I am with you all the days until the conclusion of the system of things' (Matthew 28.19-20). A number of points should be noted about this verse. It is a definite command given by Jesus, and Jehovah's Witnesses are not alone in viewing this as an instruction to preach the gospel. Jesus sent out seventy of his disciples in pairs to preach (Luke 10.1), which is why Witnesses come to people's doors in twos, rather than singly. The command to make disciples of all nations is important, causing Jehovah's Witnesses to venture into every possible country and make their literature available in so many different languages. The verse mentions the last days, and elsewhere Jesus suggests that the final eschaton cannot arrive until every nation has heard the gospel (Mark 13.10) The book of Revelation states that an innumerable great crowd who stand before God's throne, in front of the Lamb (i.e. Jesus Christ), consists of 'all nations and tribes and peoples and tongues' (Revelation 7.9). For this to be possible, no nationality must be left out of their evangelistic work.

Field ministry is carefully organized. A publisher is normally a baptized member, who is required first to meet with two elders and be approved and whose status as a new publisher is then formally announced to the congregation (Watch Tower 2019a: 73–4). Formerly, they were expected to undertake ten hours of field service each month, but the Society recognizes that members have different circumstances, and hence there is now no such target, publishers being encouraged to set their own goals. However, they are asked to report monthly the time spent on field service, using a record card. Those who give monthly returns are known as active publishers, while someone who undertakes field service but does not report monthly is classified as an irregular publisher. An inactive publisher is someone who has not reported during the previous six months, although they are still regarded as members of the congregation. There are four ways in which publishing is done: public preaching, house-to-house witnessing, staffing literature carts and 'informal witnessing'. A publisher can count hours spent in conducting a Bible study with a student or an unbaptized family member, or speaking about the faith to a fellow passenger on a train or a colleague at work.

There are opportunities to go beyond the Society's basic expectations of a publisher. One can become an auxiliary pioneer, which involves committing 30 or 50 hours to field ministry each month. A regular pioneer must have served as a baptized publisher for a minimum of six months and is expected to average 70 hours of field service per month. Special pioneers undertake to work in areas where there are fewer Witnesses per capita and spend 130 hours in field ministry; because this is not usually compatible with normal employment, special pioneers are paid a modest stipend. Those who work abroad for the Society are known as missionaries: in common with special pioneers, 130 hours per month is expected as the minimum, and they are also paid a stipend (Watch Tower 2014c: lesson 13).

Witnesses' children may accompany their parents in field ministry, and unbaptized publishers are allowed, subject to the elders' approval. It is envisaged that those who undergo Bible study with a Witness will come to attend congregation meetings and express a desire to engage in house-to-house field ministry. The Witness should first discuss the seeker's lifestyle, to ensure that it is appropriate; they should be working towards baptism and living up to the standards expected of Jehovah's Witnesses. A number of basic requirements are specified: for example, they must believe the Bible to be God's word and to have a good understanding of its contents; they must attend congregation meetings regularly and avoid 'bad associations' (undue contact with those who may lead them astray); they may not be living with a partner to whom they are not married; they must not be involved in political affairs; and they must have broken all contact with other forms of religion (Watch Tower 2019a: 74–5). A meeting with two elders will then be arranged, and once they are satisfied that they believe that the Bible is God's inspired Word and are living in accordance with Jehovah's standards, then they will announce to the congregation that they are new unbaptized publishers. They are given a Congregation's Publisher Record and included in the congregational file, and will report on their field service.

It should be mentioned that, while there are other forms of Kingdom service (as it is called), for example, helping to build a new Kingdom Hall, such work is not considered to be preaching the truth and hence is not clocked up as publishing, which consists exclusively of spreading the message. A small handful of publishers have questioned whether the practice of returning record cards is a scriptural requirement and whether this was indeed the early Church's practice. One publication refers to a somewhat obscure story involving the prophet Ezekiel, in which he has a vision of six men with deadly weapons, who have come to execute the people of Jerusalem because of their apostasy. These men are followed by a seventh man bearing an inkhorn, who puts an ink mark on those inhabitants who deplore the city's evil practices and are thus to be saved from execution, and he returns to make a report (Ezekiel 9.1-9). While this is not viewed as a direct instruction to keep records, Ezekiel was seeing part of Jehovah's heavenly organization, and the vision is a symbolic reminder that it is Jehovah who will require a final report of one's preaching work. The publication explains:

> We do not know what final report Jehovah will request regarding the grand preaching work accomplished in fulfilment of Matthew 24:14. However, we can demonstrate our appreciation for the small part we are allowed to have in the ministry by conscientiously reporting our field service regularly each month. (Watch Tower 2005a: 91)

Until the literature carts came into prominence, Jehovah's Witnesses were best known for ringing door bells, the rationale being their understanding of early Church practice: Paul mentions 'teaching you publicly and from house to house' (Acts 20.20). The expression 'house to house' is taken to mean systematically going from one door to the next, rather than – as the majority of Christians interpret the Bible – simply entering various homes, as one typically does. The Society attempts to ensure that all homes are visited, even in remote parts, to which publishers can be specially sent, so that no one is deprived of the opportunity of hearing the message. Each congregation has an assigned territory, and 'field service' meetings are held, at which prayer is offered, and morale boosted, before Witnesses work their designated territory.

During Rutherford's period of office, publishers used 'testimony cards' for house-to-house ministry: this was a card with an introductory message, which was committed to memory. This no doubt sounded somewhat wooden, and Nathan Knorr, in his eagerness to train publishers, encouraged them to prepare and practise their own short talks. Until around 2008 the key book in field ministry for publishers was *Reasoning from the Scriptures* ([1985] 1989). The book suggested a number of introductions the publishers might use when speaking to householders; topics included crime and safety, war and peace, family life, happiness and current events, as well as some more religiously orientated themes such as the Bible, old age and death, and Armageddon. Today, conversation openers tend to be more religiously slanted, inviting comments on questions like 'Who was Jesus?', 'Is the Bible compatible with science?' or 'Where can we find help to deal with grief?'

While some members of the public complain that Jehovah's Witnesses are 'always calling at the door', others affirm that they have never had a visit for years. Those in the former category may have unwittingly expressed more interest than they intended, causing publishers to call back, while others sometimes confuse Jehovah's Witnesses with Mormon missionaries or other secular canvassers. Those who claim to have been missed out may not have been at home when the publishers called: Jehovah's Witnesses do not normally leave calling cards or publications that may simply be discarded. Some of my acquaintances have claimed to have devised responses that have caused Witnesses not to return. One person suggested to me that informing them that a blood transfusion had saved his life would be a sufficient deterrent, while another – a proprietor of a Christian book store – insisted that her callers were unable to reconcile the Society's millions of members with their belief that only 144,000 would be in heaven. Numerous Christians claim to have found biblical passages that have floored Watch Tower publishers, and indeed entire books have been written suggesting conundrums that publishers allegedly cannot answer. It is unlikely that a Jehovah's Witness would be unable to respond to these questions about blood or about the heavenly class, otherwise they would not be authorized to undertake house-to-house work. For anyone who does not wish Jehovah's Witnesses to call, they will normally respect signs on doors that specify 'No religious groups'. According to one long-standing elder in my locality, the most effective way of persuading Jehovah's Witnesses not to call is simply to ask them to note that visits are unwelcome. However, he added that publishers may call back after a couple of years, to ascertain whether the household has had a change of heart, or whether new residents have moved in.

To the outsider it might seem incomprehensible that anyone should spend such a great proportion of their time ringing doorbells or standing at a literature cart, often faced with a lack of interest. Witnesses to whom I have spoken have told me that, perhaps unsurprisingly, they have a mixed reception. A typical response at the door is 'No thank you', while some who have gone pioneering have been overwhelmed by the hospitality they have sometimes been given. Others have experienced aggression, even physical violence, and one publisher has told me how his car was once smeared with dog excrement in east London. Some have found their experiences daunting, having to overcome shyness or being embarrassed when a door is answered by an acquaintance or a work colleague, who may not have known their religious affiliation. Some publishers, particularly younger ones, have recounted that at times they merely pretended to ring doorbells, so as to ensure that they did not have to engage with householders, or that they exaggerated the number of hours they reported. One informant told me that, to add interest to their doorstep conversations, he and his companion would give each other an improbable word, which had to be introduced in his introduction: examples were 'clown' and 'banana'! Nonetheless, Witnesses would scarcely be committed to investing so much time and effort if they did not find satisfaction in giving such service to Jehovah.

Informal witnessing

Change took place for a number of reasons. Although house-to-house field ministry continues, it became difficult to gain access to multistorey flats with security pads, and changing work patterns meant that people were not always at home when Jehovah's Witnesses called. Witnesses were encouraged to get out and about to proclaim the message whenever appropriate opportunities arose, and they were recommended to redouble their efforts at informal witnessing. Informal witnessing is not formally organized by the congregation but is done in a number of ways that do not involve house-to-house calling or staffing literature carts. This can be done simply by striking up casual conversations, and the time involved can be counted as publishing time when it comes to handing in one's monthly return. In some countries where evangelism is banned by law and subject to penalties, this is the only possible means of witnessing for pioneers, who may try to forge friendships with strangers and cautiously progress towards introducing the message and offering literature. Even in countries where religious freedom is the norm, some Jehovah's Witnesses will intentionally look for promising situations to speak to others. One Witness known to me makes a point of walking along the canal banks in the English West Midlands and tells me he has meaningful conversations about the truth with people he meets; he also strikes up conversations with fellow passengers on buses and trains when he travels. When his wife had to be admitted to a care home, she could no longer engage in the more usual methods of public ministry and saw this as an opportunity for informal witnessing to other residents.

Publishers who are incapacitated should look for opportunities for informal witnessing. Members who cannot get out and about are encouraged to write letters to friends, or even to strangers, for other able-bodied members to deliver. During the 2020–1 coronavirus epidemic, when house-to-house witnessing and staffing literature carts was disallowed, Witnesses did not abandon attempts to spread the truth but used their phones, wrote letters, sent emails and used whatever ways they could legitimately find.

Literature carts

Although Jehovah's Witnesses have emphasized house-to-house evangelism as an early Christian practice, the Bible also mentions that Paul 'began to reason in the synagogue with the Jews and the other people who worshipped God and every day in the marketplace with those who happened to be on hand' (Acts 17.17). From 2001, Jehovah's Witnesses in France, with the Governing Body's approval, began to explore new methods of witnessing in public, including the use of carts to display literature and to introduce their message. Some of the early displays were on ordinary tables, but in 2011 the first specially designed literature cart was approved in New York City. The carts are manufactured in China, having a standard design that enables them to be easily assembled and dismantled, and they usually display the current editions of *The Watchtower* and *Awake!* magazines, together with the favoured introductory book that is promoted at the time. Although the Bible is the cornerstone of Watch Tower teaching and practice, Bibles are not displayed on the stands but usually can be made available if an enquirer requests one. The stands are set up in places where there is high footfall, for example, railway stations and shopping centres. In cosmopolitan cities, some stands may be staffed by Witnesses who can speak another language, with literature available in that language. The Society makes a point of anticipating major forthcoming events that are likely to attract crowds, ensuring that literature carts are on display and adequately staffed. When thousands of visitors came to Smith's Rock State Park in Oregon in 2017 to view the solar eclipse, Jehovah's Witnesses organized multiple congregations to set up literature carts, involving some 200 publishers. The nature of the event enabled Witnesses to arouse interest in the origins of creation and the Bible's teaching on the subject.

Publishers who staff the literature carts are given careful instruction. They are not normally proactive in initiating conversations with passers-by, but wait to be approached, and they no longer hand out literature indiscriminately. In the past, when publishers distributed literature unduly liberally, it often ended up in trash cans or was thrown down on the pavement: 'spiritual food' should not be wasted. The literature is available without charge, and publishers at these stands do not accept money but will advise anyone who wishes to donate to visit the JW.org website for information on how to do so. Although the Bible states that Paul followed up his marketplace evangelism with a public debate with the Athenian philosophers, publishers on stands are not encouraged to debate the Society's teachings, although they are happy to answer questions posed in the spirit of enquiry rather than hostility. If a member of the public becomes unduly aggressive, the publishers are advised simply to move their stand elsewhere. After all, Jesus taught, 'Wherever anyone does not receive you or listen to your words, on going out of that house or that city, shake the dust off your feet' (Matthew 10.14). The main aim is not to score points in debate but to bring people into the truth, and the publishers' hope is that inquirers will be encouraged to pursue these teachings further and take the next step of accepting a Bible study.

The electronics revolution

The electronics revolution suggested new ways of evangelizing. Every literature cart displays a QR code, which leads the enquirer to the JW.org website. In recent years the Society has encouraged its members and the general public to use its web resources, for several reasons. The younger generation in particular are more at home with electronic resources rather than with solid printed text and are able to access much more material online than could realistically be made available in print form. The transition also saves print costs. Until 2008 *The Watchtower* was published twice monthly, but in 2008 it was split into two different monthly editions – Public and Study – produced alternately; the former consisted of items judged to be of public interest, while the latter contained material that was more relevant to congregation meetings. In July 2011 a Simplified Edition, additionally, was introduced as an experiment, aimed at readers whose first language was not English and younger readers who found the regular edition difficult: this was discontinued after 2018. *Awake!* magazine, formerly fortnightly, was reduced to six editions per year in 2016 and three editions in 2018. Readers of both magazines are directed to additional articles placed on the internet. Jehovah's Witnesses have also directed some of the material towards children: a series of animated videos entitled 'Become Jehovah's Friend' feature Caleb and Sophia – two Jehovah's Witness children, whose parents support them in their faith.

This shift towards the internet not only made the Society's material more user-friendly but also opened up new possibilities. Most publishers now go around with their smartphones and laptops, enabling them to show residents video items rather than printed text, and if they spoke a different language, the material could readily be made available by calling up the student's preferred language. The app JW Language facilitates communication in another language and enables the publisher to learn rudimentary expressions to use when communicating with a non-English speaker. Importantly, the use of visual material enables sign language to be seen, and Watch Tower material is now available in over 100 varieties of sign language. There are also unofficial apps, which some publishers find useful: one of these is JW Memory, which provides a list of themes, accompanied by relevant biblical quotations. Countries where internet access is limited are not neglected. One recent innovation is JW Box, which is an inexpensive router device which forwards data created by the Society's Computer Department – mainly publications and videos – which can be downloaded on to mobile phones. For congregations lacking internet access, their branch office periodically sends USB keys containing new data from JW.org. At the time of writing, some 1,700 JW Boxes have been sent to congregations in Africa, Oceania and South America (Watch Tower 2020c).

In the past, the usual pattern was for a Jehovah's Witness to place a copy of the most recent *Watchtower* or *Awake!* magazine, offering to make a return visit to enquire what the householder or family thought of its content. It is now possible to request a Bible Study online, and the electronics revolution permits a variety of options. The study need not take place at home; publishers can agree to meet students at their workplace, or in a cafe, or in any reasonable venue of their choice. Study can also take place over the telephone, or with video conferencing.

The Bible study

The Bible study which follows the publisher's house-to-house visits does not involve reading the Bible systematically but introduces a number of key themes on which the Bible sheds light, for example, whether the Bible is trustworthy, how it is possible to hope for the future and why people suffer. The Society has invariably used one favoured key book for its Bible studies. Until recently the favoured study book was *What Can the Bible Teach Us?*, introduced in 2015, but at the time of writing, this is being superseded by a multimedia package titled *Enjoy Life Forever!* (See Chapter 11.)

At an appropriate stage in their study, enquirers will be invited to attend a Kingdom Hall meeting, and they are encouraged to spread the message to friends and other family members. If interest continues, the next stage is preparation for baptism. Baptism is the public expression of one's commitment and marks the transition to full membership of Jehovah's organization.

Baptized members are referred to as 'brothers' and 'sisters'. These titles are not always used in regular conversation, but if they wish to make a comment at a congregation meeting, the presiding elder will address them as 'Brother Patel' or 'Sister Jones'. Conversationally, Witnesses will sometimes talk about a 'fleshly' brother or sister, if they wish to make it clear that they are talking about a family member, rather than a baptized Witness. Being a baptized Witness also confers certain benefits: they are eligible to be married in a Kingdom Hall and, at a later stage, men may be considered for offices such as ministerial servant and, subsequently, elder. Both men and women can apply for service at a Bethel. At the end of their life, baptized members can be given a Kingdom Hall funeral.

Congregational discipline

Baptism does not mark any substantial change in one's lifestyle, since candidates have already demonstrated that they are living up to Jehovah's expected standards. However, baptized members are now subject to congregational discipline, in which there are sanctions for transgressing Jehovah's law, as interpreted by the Society. These sanctions can include judicial reproofs and, at worst, disfellowshipping. Congregations ensure that strict discipline is maintained among their members, in accordance with Jesus' teaching. A member who becomes aware of another person's misdeed should talk to that person and point out their error, thus giving them an opportunity to repent and change their behaviour. If this proves ineffective, the accuser should bring in other members to speak to the offender. If the erring member continues, then the matter should be raised at congregational level by involving the elders, who will consider the accusation and determine how it should be dealt with and whether they should form a judicial committee (Matthew 18.15-17).

The most lenient stage of disciplining is 'marking', which is done by the congregation's elders when someone's lifestyle does not meet the expected standards of the Society but is not sufficiently serious to invoke judicial action. The biblical warrant for this is Paul's advice to the Thessalonians: 'Keep this one marked and stop associating with him' (1 Thessalonians 3.14). The type of offence that merits marking could be idleness, being overcritical, interfering in matters that should not be of concern to them (2 Thessalonians 3.11) or inappropriate dating. The effect of marking is that elders will counsel the erring member, then avoid social contact with that person; such avoidance should be carried out by anyone else in the congregation who knows about the matter. However, no public announcement is made at congregation meetings, although, if that member's lifestyle improves, then an elder may give a talk to the congregation about the type of misdeed, counselling members against it. When the member proves suitably repentant, the elders will lift the mark, and this is signalled by their resumption of social contact, enabling others to resume normal relationships.

The next stage of discipline occurs either if marking is ineffective or if a more serious offence is involved. A judicial committee of three elders is appointed and meets with the accused, who is unaccompanied. Witnesses may be summoned and, in accordance with biblical principles, two witnesses are needed before he or she can be found guilty and disciplined. Depending on the severity of the offence, the committee may issue a judicial reproof, which may either be private or public, or they may decide to disfellowship the offending member. A public reproof or a decision to disfellowship will be intimated to the congregation at its weekday meeting, but not the reason: only the member's name and the verdict are announced. A reproof is more than a reprimand but involves the withdrawal of 'privileges'; it is considered a privilege for an elder to give Bible talks, or for a ministerial servant to operate equipment or staff the bookstore, so he will no longer be allowed to perform these functions until the reproof is lifted. A rank-and-file member may be barred from making comments at the Watchtower studies or from role-playing in 'demonstrations' (see Chapter 5). Disfellowshipping is more serious: this involves being barred from any association with fellow members; the disfellowshipped person may attend congregation meetings but must have no social exchange with others, not even a simple greeting. At the end of the meeting, the disfellowshipped person must depart immediately.

Shunning

The practice of shunning those who have been disfellowshipped or who have dissociated from the Society has frequently attracted criticism. In earlier times, the congregation as a whole adjudicated on misdemeanours, but Nathan Knorr, the third president, argued that there was no biblical warrant for congregational voting and instituted judicial committees in 1944. Offences that merit judicial investigation and possible disfellowshipping now include 'disturbing the unity of the congregation' and not merely moral lapses. Paul's advice to the Corinthians was the following:

> But now I am writing you to stop keeping company with anyone called
> a brother who is sexually immoral or a greedy person or an idolater or a

reviler or a drunkard or an extortioner, not even eating with such a man. ...
Remove the wicked person from among yourselves. (1 Corinthians 5.11-13)

In 1952 it was made a requirement for congregations to disfellowship those who were guilty of serious offences, and in 1955 a *Watchtower* article went further, stating that even associating with a disfellowshipped person could itself be grounds for disfellowshipping. However, a 1974 *Watchtower* article urged readers to continue to show common acts of kindness to disfellowshipped members. The author envisages a situation where a disfellowshipped woman is in the Kingdom Hall car park with a flat tyre and suggests that human compassion demands that male members offer assistance. The article continues, 'Yet situations just like this have developed, perhaps in all good conscience, yet due to a lack of balance in viewpoint' (Watch Tower 1974a: 467). The comment indicates on the one hand the importance of kindness but on the other hand reveals that that some members have acted less than charitably in such situations. While stories circulate about disfellowshipped members being ordered out of their family homes, this is not a requirement, but it depends on the situation. A baptized minor would certainly not be sent away from the family home, and a disfellowshipped husband would continue normal familial relations with his wife (or vice versa), including sexual relationships; the husband still maintains authority over the wife, so long as she is not required to contravene biblical standards. However, if a family member were continuing to commit an offence that was offensive – for example, if a son or daughter continued to drink excessively after being disfellowshipped for drunkenness – then the father could insist that the offender should not be allowed to live under the same roof. If the penalties of disfellowshipping and shunning seem harsh, Jehovah's Witnesses perceive two important purposes: removing wayward members keeps the congregation pure, and it is hoped that offenders will see their error and be jolted into mending their ways (Watch Tower 1952: 131–48; 1955: 607). One of the Society's researchers at Warwick estimated that roughly one-third of disfellowshipped members are reinstated.

Working for Jehovah's kingdom is therefore no easy task, and the preparation leading up to baptism is designed to ensure that those who wish to belong have counted the costs of discipleship and will endeavour to keep the congregation pure.

4

Teachings

Official teaching and popular understanding

Writing about a religious community's teachings invariably presents a difficulty. Theological ideas are often complex, and expounding their content in detail can erroneously imply that adherents understand and believe everything that is officially taught. In the case of Jehovah's Witnesses, however, there tends to be closer proximity between official teaching and believers' understanding. Congregation meetings involve a considerable amount of instruction in the Society's doctrines, and members are expected to prepare substantially for the Watchtower Bible study. Notetaking is encouraged at conventions, ensuring that attendees keep themselves focused and have a tangible record of what they have learned. Not only are *The Watchtower* and *Awake!* magazines regularly available in hard copy and online, but the Society also regularly publishes books, many of which expound biblical themes, sometimes offering commentary on entire books of the Bible, and which are typically used as the basis for the Congregation Bible Study meeting. Additionally, the JW.org website and the JW Library App offer much by way of religious resources, including talks by members of the Governing Body, short audio-visual introductions to each book of the Bible and dramatized versions of biblical characters such as Esther, Josiah and Jonah. As mentioned in Chapter 3, a reasonable understanding of Watch Tower teachings is required before anyone can be baptized. Obviously, there are some teachings that the average member may be unable to explain: although most active members will have a little knowledge of biblical chronology, they may not be able to explain in detail the end-time calculations that lead to key dates such as 1914, and I doubt whether many practising witnesses would recall the dates at which the Society believes the various books of the Bible were written. What follows is therefore an account of the Society's official teachings; most members will know substantially less than this, while there may be a few who know more. Although what follows may seem detailed, most of this information is made available to all Jehovah's Witnesses in the Society's literature and online, and is in the public domain. It is best regarded as the bedrock of rank-and-file belief and practice, or a reservoir on which the Society's writers and congregational elders draw to disseminate its teachings.

The role of the Bible

The touchstone of Jehovah's Witnesses' teachings is the Bible. However, a number of Watch Tower articles suggest what is sometimes called 'natural theology' in mainstream Christian philosophy – in other words, there are basic truths about God which unaided human reason can recognize but which fall short of the complete set of Christian doctrines, for which scripture is needed. The Society continues to draw attention to various phenomena which suggest a form of the Argument from Design: for instance, the spider's ability to spin silk, the gecko's remarkable suction powers, the seagull's ability to stand on ice while retaining body heat, the monarch butterfly's navigational powers and many more examples have formed the basis of a series of *Awake!* articles, which concluded that such phenomena could not exist without a supernatural designer (Watch Tower 1996c; 2008a,b,d,e). The articles do not engage in the detailed critical discussion one would expect in a philosophy class, but they are offered as a basis for reflection for those outside the faith and serve to confirm the truth.

A further non-biblical source of knowledge comes from conscience. Writing about the Gentiles, who were not subject to Jewish law, Paul says that they 'demonstrate the matter of the law to be written in their hearts, while their conscience is bearing witness with them' (Romans 2.15). Paul is drawing attention to the fact that most of us have an innate sense of right and wrong, without having to rely on the instructions Moses received on Mount Sinai. Witnesses frequently speak of something being 'a matter of conscience' where there is no precise biblical instruction, yet decision is needed. For example, a window cleaner would not readily clean the windows of a church but might be concerned about whether to clean the windows of the local vicarage: the Bible instructs that one should not share in Babylon's sins (Revelation 18.4) – Babylon including apostate Christianity – but how far should one go in refusing to support mainstream churches? Jehovah's Witnesses may disagree on such matters, but the window cleaner would not be subject to any judicial action if some of the elders happened to disagree with his judgement.

The human mind alone, of course, cannot arrive at truths such as how sin entered the world, how Jesus Christ offered his life as a ransom sacrifice, the expectation of the imminent Battle of Armageddon and the everlasting paradise. All these and more are to be found in the Bible. Jehovah's Witnesses do not claim any special revelation. Leaders such as Charles Taze Russell and Joseph Franklin Rutherford were not prophets: they did not experience visions or special revelations but simply studied the Bible and arrived at interpretations that any reader of the Bible, in theory, should be able to find. Jehovah's Witnesses do not deny that God has directly spoken to people in the past: on the contrary, the Bible records that he spoke directly to Noah, Abraham, Moses and prophets such as Isaiah, Ezekiel, Amos and many others, but such direct revelations are now reckoned to have died out and became no longer necessary after the Bible was complete.

It is important to understand the precise position Jehovah's Witnesses take regarding the Bible. They have sometimes been labelled 'fundamentalists' and have been said to take the Bible 'literally'. Both these descriptions are wrong, for a number of reasons. First, they do not themselves accept the label 'fundamentalist' (Watch Tower 1974b: 629), noting that the term originated at the Niagara Conference of 1895, which was attended by a number of conservative Protestant leaders, who wished to rebut the emerging 'higher criticism' of the Bible and Darwinian theories of evolution. In response, they affirmed a number of 'fundamentals', from which the term 'fundamentalism' is derived. The inerrancy of scripture was one of these fundamentals, but only one of five. The others were Christ's deity, his Virgin Birth, his substitutionary atonement and his bodily resurrection and physical return. As will be explained, of these five principles, apart from scriptural inerrancy, Jehovah's Witnesses only accept the Virgin Birth and substitutionary atonement (although they prefer to speak of the 'ransom sacrifice' and do not accept that it was God who died on the cross). They do not accept Christ's deity; they hold that his resurrection was as a spirit, not bodily, and do not expect a physical 'rapture', as some present-day American fundamentalists do. It is also not accurate to claim that they take the Bible literally: they acknowledge the obvious point that the Bible contains symbols, metaphors, parables and recounting of visions. It is not mere pedantry to point this out: a substantial amount of their biblical exegesis involves unravelling what the Bible means by Daniel's beasts, Revelation's trumpets and seemingly mundane concepts like times, months and days.

It is much more accurate to state that Jehovah's Witnesses believe in the inerrancy of the Bible and that its authors were writing under the inspiration of God's holy spirit. However, the question arises: why rely on the Bible, rather than the many other spiritual books that the world's religious traditions have employed? An article in *Awake!* magazine itemizes five features of the Bible that should persuade the reader that it is the true authoritative religious text. The Bible, the author claims, is historically accurate, down to the last detail; it has candour and honesty; it has internal harmony; it is scientifically accurate; and, importantly, it contains prophecies that have been fulfilled (Watch Tower 2007c). Another publication adds a sixth feature, namely, practical wisdom (Watch Tower 2006a: 19). Each of these claims merits brief comment.

First, the Bible is held to accord with the findings of historians and archaeologists, and can be relied on for the dating of the events described in the history of Israel and Judah. This is particularly important for biblical chronology that relates to the end times. Jehovah's Witnesses also do not accept that the biblical narrative is myth rather than history: stories such as Adam and Eve, Noah and the flood, Job's tribulations and the accounts of Daniel in Babylon are not pieces of edifying fiction but accounts of events that genuinely happened and to which firm historical dates can usually be assigned. Second, the Bible's candour and honesty is held to be supportive evidence of the book's veracity. The Bible does not cover up the weaknesses of its characters: Moses loses his temper on a number of occasions; King David has an affair with Bathsheba, securing her husband's death; Peter is disloyal to Jesus; Paul and Barnabas quarrel – and there are many more instances where biblical characters are portrayed as less than perfect. Where historical material tells against its originators, this suggests reliability.

The third criterion is internal harmony. Jehovah's Witnesses believe that the Bible is entirely consistent, without contradictions. Where there are apparent inconsistencies, they believe that these can be resolved. For example, Matthew portrays Jesus as casting out money changers in the Jerusalem Temple towards the end of his ministry, whereas John places it at the beginning, as a kind of inauguration (Matthew 21.12-13; John 2.13-16). Watch Tower literature resolves the apparent contradiction by claiming that there were two such incidents and not merely one (Watch Tower 2018b: 428). Jehovah's Witnesses may appear to jump from one biblical passage to another at congregation meetings, where it is customary for speakers to ask the audience to look up biblical passages in various locations, rather than to expound one particular piece of narrative. This is justified by the belief that the Bible is a unity and that all of it originates from God, hence one passage can be used to shed light on another.

By scientific accuracy – the fourth feature – Jehovah's Witnesses acknowledge that the Bible is not a scientific textbook. As previously noted, it contains symbol and metaphor and when, for example, it mentions the 'corners of the earth', this is not to imply that the earth is flat, as some extreme American fundamentalists have affirmed. Indeed, Job and Isaiah talk about the 'circle of the earth' (Job 26.7; Isaiah 40.22), which Witnesses believe accurately portrays the way astronauts can see the earth from space (Watch Tower 1980b: 10–13). However, more important to Jehovah's Witnesses is the Bible's account of creation, which they believe fully accords with scientific findings while evolution theory does not. Witnesses do not hold that the universe was created in six 24-hour days: the word 'day' in the Bible need not always be understood literally; in the biblical account of creation it means an indeterminate and probably very long period of time. Jehovah's Witnesses are not 'young earth' creationists, but they hold that the Bible gives a reliable account of the order in which things were made, which, they believe, fully accords with the findings of geologists (see Furuli 2018).

The role of prophecy – the fifth feature – will be discussed in a separate chapter (Chapter 8), since it is of key importance. As has been noted, Jehovah's Witnesses do not proclaim new prophecies but seek to interpret biblical ones. Although they have a reputation for failed predictions, the Watch Tower Society has learned from the past errors of 1925 and 1975, and the only unfulfilled predictive biblical prophecies relate the coming battle of Armageddon and life beyond, for which the Society gives no definite dates but which are reckoned to be 'just around the corner'.

When Jehovah's Witnesses claim that the Bible offers practical wisdom, they are referring to its guidance for life. This involves basic moral teachings about honesty, respect for authority, sexual morality and so on, but it also refers to pragmatic qualities like astuteness. One of Jesus' parables refers to an 'unrighteous steward' (Luke 16.1-13). On first appearance, the story is a puzzling one: a steward (or business manager) is about to be dismissed, so he visits his master's debtors and illicitly reduces their bills. When the master discovers what the steward has done, instead of being angry, he commends him for his shrewdness. The import of the story is twofold: one should be worldly wise (the steward no doubt hoped that the debtors would help him when he was dismissed), but, more importantly, the spiritual message is that one should take appropriate steps now to secure one's everlasting future. Witnesses are encouraged to do both: as well as encouraging the spiritual life of their adherents, The Watchtower and Awake! magazines frequently publish articles about how to manage money and how to ensure one's physical safety, as well as the importance of virtues such as forgiveness and concern for others (Watch Tower 2014a: 179–88).

Jehovah's Witnesses hold that God seldom dictated the Bible directly to each of its authors. At times some of them used secondary sources; for example, when transcribing lengthy genealogies they would consult existing records, and the holy spirit's guidance ensured that these were conveyed accurately. Where the Gospel writers – particularly John – recorded lengthy sermons, Jehovah's Witnesses believe that the holy spirit's inspiration ensured that these were accurately remembered and transcribed. Jehovah's Witnesses acknowledge that scribes sometimes miscopied parts of manuscripts, and hence scholars must make judgements about the correct reading of certain texts. However, they do not accept 'higher criticism' of the Bible, which originated in the mid-nineteenth-century with the work of Karl Heinrich Graf and Julius Wellhausen, who claimed to detect multiple sources of the books attributed to Moses, and gave rise to a tradition of scholarship that suggested that certain books of the Bible were not a unity but were pieced together by editors and that some writings were not the work of the authors to whom they were attributed. For example, most mainstream scholars would contend that there are three distinct parts of Isaiah and that the letters to Timothy and Titus were not written by Paul but by a later author using Paul's name. Jehovah's Witnesses do not accept such conclusions.

Biblical authorship

Since prophets and visionaries are no longer around, God's word cannot be heard directly, but Jehovah's Witnesses hold that it is still possible to 'hear' God through the Bible, which records numerous direct revelations to patriarchs and prophets. The Bible states that God has communicated in a variety of ways (Hebrews 1.1): sometimes by direct dictation, for example, when Moses was given the Ten Commandments on Mount Sinai. At other times he allows biblical authors to use their own words to describe his message (Ezekiel 3.4). Other writers record dreams, angelic visitations and visions. Two of the four gospel writers – Matthew and John – are regarded as immediate disciples of Jesus and hence directly saw his actions and heard his teachings, while Mark and Luke, although not part of Jesus' inner circle of twelve disciples, nonetheless belonged to the early Church community and knew the earliest apostles. Luke, who wrote the book of Acts as well as his gospel, travelled with Paul and, Jehovah's Witnesses believe, was in a position to write accurately about their journeys. Where the Bible records that an intermediary was involved in transmitting God's word, for example an angel, the divine messenger speaks authoritatively in God's name. Paul writes to Timothy, 'All Scripture is inspired of God' (2 Timothy 3.16): the word translated as 'inspired' literally means 'breathed into', implying that the biblical authors were inspired by the holy spirit, and indeed spoke through the holy spirit's inspiration, thus guaranteeing that their words are authentically from God.

One consequence of the Watch Tower Society's belief in the close connection between biblical records and divinely inspired messengers is a tendency to suggest early dates rather than later ones for the compilation of the books of the Bible. For example, most mainstream biblical scholars claim that the books attributed to Moses (Genesis to Deuteronomy) were probably compiled in the fourth or fifth centuries BCE; by contrast, since Jehovah's Witnesses hold that they were written by Moses himself, they infer that they are much more ancient, reaching completion in 1473 BCE (the year in which he is believed to have died). Matthew is regarded as the primordial gospel, on which Mark and Luke draw for their material, and is dated at 41 CE. This contrasts with the view of most present-day biblical scholars, who regard Mark as the original canonical Gospel, copied in part by Matthew and Luke, and written some time between 69 and 70 CE. The Society holds that Matthew, being one of the original apostles and therefore an eyewitness, must have been writing shortly after the events he describes and must precede the others. Table 1 outlines the differences between Watch Tower and mainstream dating of biblical texts. It is also worth noting that the Society holds that Hebrews, which is only attributed to Paul editorially in older translations of the Bible, such as the King James Version, is authentically a Pauline piece of writing, even though the original Greek text makes no such attribution. Mainstream scholars regard Hebrews as an anonymous work; if that were correct, it would present obvious problems for Jehovah's Witnesses since, if the author were unknown, we could not know his or her relationship with God, Jesus or the early apostles.

TABLE 1 Watch Tower and mainstream datings compared.

	Watch Tower	Mainstream
Books of Moses	1473 BCE	Fifth/fourth century BCE
Matthew	41 CE	80–90 CE
Mark	60–65 CE	68–70 CE
Luke	56–58 CE	80–90 CE
John	98 CE	90–110 CE
Acts	61 CE	95–100 CE
Pauline writings	65 CE	55–70+ CE
Hebrews	61 CE	80–90 CE
Revelation	96 CE	68–96 CE

Jehovah God

God's inspiration of the biblical writers raises the question of who God is. Jehovah's Witnesses share a similar concept of God to that of other Christians: unlike the Church of Jesus Christ of Latter-day Saints, they believe that God is a spirit, not a physical being, that he is the creator of the universe and is omnipotent, omniscient and benevolent. God is not omnipresent, however: his dwelling is in heaven, but he is aware of everything through the holy spirit (Watch Tower 2011b: 27). Although Watch Tower literature sometimes portrays God as the stereotypical old man with a beard, sitting on a throne, Jehovah's Witnesses readily understand that such portrayals are symbolic. Nonetheless, they point to the importance of God's sovereignty: God demands obedience, but when Adam and Eve yielded to temptation in the Garden of Eden, they subjected themselves, and the rest of humankind, to Satan's rule.

God is the object of worship and a being with whom one can have a personal relationship. Hence, Jehovah's Witnesses attach supreme importance to his personal name, which they believe is Jehovah; other names such as 'God', 'the Lord' and 'the Most High' are regarded as generic. When addressing God, it is important to use this personal name, just as it is normal and courteous to address other human beings by name and not by their status, occupation or physical description. It is believed that the name 'Jehovah' is the name by which God revealed himself to Moses:

> This is what you are to say to the Israelites, 'Jehovah the God of your forefathers, the God of Abraham, the God of Isaac, and the God of Jacob, has sent me to you.' This is my name forever, and this is how I am to be remembered from generation to generation. (Exodus 3.15)

The word 'Jehovah' is not used in most modern mainstream translations of the Bible, and even in the King James Version it only appears four times. Since the Hebrew alphabet consists of consonants rather than vowels, the divine name appears as the tetragrammaton YHWH or JHVH. It is normally held that the missing vowels are 'a' and 'e', rendering the name as 'Yahweh', a name which the Jews came to regard as too sacred to pronounce. Consequently, when Jewish scholars introduced diacritics to indicate vowels, the vowels of the alternative name 'Adonai' were inserted, to prevent inadvertent pronunciation of the divine name. Misunderstanding this convention, Christians read the word as 'Jehovah', which gained momentum with the Protestant Reformation and found its way into mainstream Christian hymnody. Jehovah's Witnesses do not accept this explanation, however, deploring the Jewish reluctance to use God's personal name, arguing that, since the name was never pronounced in Jewish tradition, there is no reason to believe that it should be rendered as Yahweh. Further, they argue, there are men in the Bible whose names are derived from the divine name, for example Jehoash, Jehonadab and Jehoshaphat, thus providing confirmatory evidence that Jehovah is God's true name. In congregational gatherings, Jehovah is always addressed as one would a personal friend: the language used in prayer is colloquial and is always extempore. Just as one would not address a friend with a prepared speech, Jehovah's Witnesses talk to God naturally and informally.

Jehovah's Witnesses do not accept that God is a Trinity, and there are numerous Watch Tower publications that argue against the doctrine, including a booklet specifically targeting the belief, 'Should You Believe in the Trinity?', which appeared in 1989 (Watch Tower 1989c). Witnesses believe that the doctrine is confusing and incomprehensible, and even mainstream Christians who claim to espouse the teaching – including clergy – are unable to explain it coherently. The early disciples were ordinary simple people – we are told that four of them were fishermen – who would have had no rapport with such a complex theological idea. The Trinity doctrine makes God mysterious and has no relevance for daily living, whereas Jehovah is a knowable person with whom one can have a personal relationship, and who offers personal guidance. Importantly, Jehovah's Witnesses point out that the Trinity is not mentioned in the Bible. Although Jesus instructs his disciples to baptize 'in the name of the Father and of the Son and of the holy spirit' (Matthew 28.19), the threefold formula does not entail that the three are one, any more than the expression 'the God of Abraham, Isaac, and Jacob' implies that these three persons are one and the same. The doctrine of the Trinity gained momentum at the Council of Nicaea in 325 CE, although the Nicene Creed does not explicitly affirm God's triune nature; as Watch Tower literature points out, the first explicit affirmation of the Trinity is found in the Athanasian Creed, which was not written by Athanasius – the fourth-century bishop of Rome – but is a twelfth century document. If the Trinity doctrine is so important to the Christian Church, it is asked, why did it take so long for Christians to recognize it? Jehovah's Witnesses therefore firmly believe in the oneness of God, that Jesus Christ is a separate being and that the holy spirit is not a person but God's active force.

The person of Jesus Christ

For Jehovah's Witnesses, Jesus Christ is not God himself but the only begotten Son of God; he is not merely human but pre-existed in spirit form before entering the womb of the Virgin Mary. Jesus therefore did not have a natural father, unlike other human beings, who can be called 'sons of God' by dedicating themselves to Jehovah rather than by birth. Since Jesus Christ is not regarded as co-eternal with God the Father, Jehovah's Witnesses have sometimes been accused of Arianism – an ancient Christian heresy promoted by Arius (c. 250–c. 336), a presbyter of Alexandria who affirmed that Jesus was 'of similar substance' to God the Father, but not 'of the same substance', and that because he was the Son of God, there must have been a time when he did not exist, since sons are born after fathers. Although Jehovah's Witnesses' beliefs have some affinities with Arianism, they reject the label, mainly on the grounds of other aspects of Arius' teaching: Arius taught that God was eternally mysterious and unknowable, as well as triune, which of course Jehovah's Witnesses reject.

Jehovah's Witnesses therefore affirm Jesus' uniqueness but not his deity. Mainstream Christian critics frequently challenge them on their translation and interpretation of the first verse of John's gospel, which the Society's New World Translation renders as 'In the beginning was the Word [i.e. Christ], and the Word was with God, and the Word was a god' (John 1.1). The verse is inherently problematic, because John omits the definite article before *theos*, which one might expect to justify the more usual mainstream translation, 'the Word was God'. 'The Word was a god' is a possible translation of the Greek, but it raises the question of whether Jesus is regarded as only one god among several: this would be a strange assertion for Jehovah's Witnesses, who are strictly monotheistic. The Watch Tower Society explains the verse by claiming that the word *theos* in this context means an angelic being and that there are many angels whom God created, of whom Christ is the first and the chief.

This line of reasoning entails a further doctrine: according to Watch Tower teaching, Jesus is equated with the Archangel Michael. The Bible does not state explicitly that Jesus is Michael; however, the doctrine is not a Watch Tower invention but has its precedents elsewhere, notably within Adventism. Seventh-day Adventists, however, are at pains to point out that their position differs from that of Jehovah's Witnesses: contrary to Watch Tower teachings, they affirm Christ's full deity and indeed the triunity of God. In Jewish thought, as the book of Daniel affirms, Michael is the leader of the heavenly armies and is described as 'the great prince who is standing in behalf of your people' (Daniel 12.1). This description is mentioned in the context of a great battle, which the Witnesses associate with Armageddon and which will be the final battle between Christ and Satan; thus, there is believed to be a tacit identification here between Michael and Christ. The identification is further strengthened by noting that Michael is the only being whom the Bible describes as an 'archangel' (Jude 9). Although Gabriel, whom the Bible also mentions, is popularly described as an archangel, the Bible makes no such claim, and hence it is concluded that Michael alone occupies an archangelic position. The one other mention of an archangel in the Bible is in 1 Thessalonians, which describes Christ's return, 'at which the Lord himself will descend from heaven with a commanding call, with an archangel's voice and with God's trumpet' (1 Thessalonians 4.16).

Piecing together all this biblical evidence therefore suggests to Jehovah's Witnesses that Jesus Christ already had a special status before his birth as a human. However, they believe that Jesus was not born with his status as messiah but that God endowed him with this role at his baptism:

> At the moment when God's spirit, or active force, was poured out upon him that day, Jesus became the Messiah, or Christ, the one appointed to be Leader and King. (Watch Tower 2014d: 40)

Jehovah's Witnesses have been accused of Adoptionism, an early Christian heresy, whose exponents taught that that Jesus' human status as the Son of God was acquired, not at birth, but granted by God either at his baptism, his resurrection or his ascension. Although Jehovah's Witnesses' position is not an orthodox one, it is not quite the same as Adoptionism, which concerns divine sonship, not messianism. Witnesses do not teach a 'two sons' doctrine: Jesus was always the son of God, from the moment of his conception and at his birth:

> The apostle John reveals that at the appointed time, God's spirit Son 'became flesh and resided among us.' (John 1:14) In order to accomplish this change in Jesus' nature, God miraculously transferred Jesus' life from heaven into the womb of the Jewish virgin girl Mary. In that way Jesus remained God's Son, even though a human. Furthermore, since God, not any man, gave Jesus life, Jesus was born perfect, without sin. 'What is born will be called holy, God's Son,' said the angel Gabriel to Mary. – Luke 1:35; Hebrews 7:26. (Watch Tower 2006b: 13)

According to the biblical narrative, Jesus goes to the River Jordan where John the Baptist is preaching and baptizing; after presenting himself for baptism, he emerges from the water, whereupon the heavens open, and the holy spirit descends like a dove and a voice says, 'This is my Son, the beloved, whom I have approved' (Matthew 3.16-17). Jehovah's Witnesses do not construe the voice as declaring that Jesus became God's son at that moment – an Adoptionist view – but rather as Jehovah affirming that Jesus is, and always was, God's son. Although Jesus' baptism is held to be the point at which he becomes the messiah, this does not mean that Jesus changed in any way. One might compare it to a coronation, when it is a foregone conclusion that the inaugurated monarch is to be appointed, but is effectively no different after the ceremony: the rite is a formal affirmation of the candidate's new role. Similarly, there was no previous doubt that Jesus would come as the messiah, and his mission was already determined before he was conceived; his baptism was a public declaration of his messianic role.

Atonement: The ransom sacrifice

Jesus' messianic mission was not simply to teach but to redeem humankind, and the most important doctrine in Jehovah's Witnesses' theology is Christ's ransom sacrifice. The need for redemption from sin stems from Adam and Eve's disobedience to God in the Garden of Eden. God tells the couple that they may eat of any fruit in the garden, except the tree of knowledge: 'But as for the tree of the knowledge of good and bad, you must not eat from it, for in the day you eat from it you will certainly die' (Genesis 2.17). The Watch Tower Society, from its very inception, insisted that the punishment for sin is not eternal torment in hell, but death; as Paul reaffirms, 'For the wages sin pays is death' (Romans 6.23), but he adds, 'the gift God gives is everlasting life by Christ Jesus our Lord.' Adam and Eve's disobedience did not merely result in their own sinful nature and merited punishment but affected the whole of humankind with an indelible genetic imprint (Watch Tower 2006d: 29); hence, Christ's mission was to redeem the whole of the human race. Paul states, 'In Adam all are dying' (1 Corinthians 15.22). A homely analogy that I have heard several times at Bible talks in our local Kingdom Hall is of a baking tin: if it has a dent in it, every cake that is baked in it will come out with an imprint of the same corresponding dent. Similarly, Adam's disobedience has caused a sinful nature to be imprinted on all of his descendants – the entirety of humankind.

Jehovah is a loving God, but also a just one, and hence, if humanity is redeemed, there has to be a solution that is consistent with both his love and his justice. God gave his law to Moses, with its moral and ritual requirements, but no individual proved able to obey the law perfectly, and hence men and women could only pay the penalty for their own sins, by dying. The law and the system of animal sacrifices was therefore insufficient to atone for sin, but it foreshadowed the effective means of redemption: 'For since the Law has a shadow of the good things to come, but not the very substance of the things, it can never, by the same sacrifices that are continually offered year after year, make those who approach perfect' (Hebrews 10.1). Here Watch Tower theology draws on another idea that continues to be popular in Adventist circles, known as typology. Numerous events and entities mentioned in Hebrew scripture are held to foreshadow events in the Christian age – known respectively as 'types' and 'antitypes'. The Mosaic law and the animal sacrifices are types or shadows, which point forward to the true means of humanity's redemption. Jesus Christ was 'without sin' (Hebrews 4.15) and hence was the corresponding perfect keeper of the law and the perfect sacrifice to atone for human sin. Thus, Adam is a 'type' of Christ, who comes to pay the 'corresponding ransom' for humankind's sin: being sinless, Jesus had no need to atone for his own sin but could pay the debt owed for the sins of Adam and his descendants. Humanity has therefore been bought back in a way that simultaneously satisfies God's justice and God's love for humankind.

Much of the Jehovah's Witnesses' explanation of atonement is in line with mainstream Christian thought, but a few points of difference should be noted. First, ever since the time of Charles Taze Russell, the Bible Students and subsequent Jehovah's Witnesses have been firmly committed to the 'ransom theory' of atonement and firmly rejected rival explanations. By contrast, mainstream Christian theologians have supported a variety of atonement theories, the ransom theory being one of several, and the traditional Christian creeds do not explicitly refer to atonement theory. There are some differences between Watch Tower theology and mainstream Christian thought on the nature of original sin. Watch Tower literature tends to speak of 'the original sin' rather than 'original sin'. Christian theologians tend not to use the latter expression, differentiating between 'sin' (a human condition) and 'sins' (sets of actions). In mainstream theology, original sin is not to be equated with the first sin, which was Adam and Eve's act of disobedience by eating the forbidden fruit in the Garden of Eden. Watch Tower theology prefers to use the term 'Adamic sin' for the condition that is inherited before birth, even before a child commits any sinful act.

At this juncture it may be appropriate to note some other points relating to Adam's fall. What precisely was Adam and Eve's sin? What was so wrong about eating a piece of fruit (which Jehovah's Witnesses rightly note, contrary to popular imagination, was not an apple), and why should Jehovah be so concerned that one particular tree – the tree of 'knowledge of good and bad' – should be avoided? Although the word 'know' in older Bible translations often refers to sexual intercourse, Jehovah's Witnesses do not accept the view that Eve's sin was the sexual seduction of Adam, as has occasionally been held. God's prohibition is given when Adam is alone in the Garden of Eden, before Eve is created (Genesis 2.16-17, 20b-23), and Adam and Eve are described as husband and wife (Genesis 2.25). The tree cannot represent moral knowledge, for since Adam and Eve were created perfect, they would already know what was right and wrong. It is concluded that the explanation is in fact a simple one: the prohibition was made to demonstrate that it is God who defines the law, not humankind; it was a simple requirement with which Adam and Eve could easily have complied, but yet they chose to do otherwise (Watch Tower 1970: 645; 2006d: 28; 2018a: 676).

One further point about the story is worth noting. The first humans lived in a beautiful garden, not as primitive cave dwellers, and the Bible's depiction of the Garden of Eden is believed to tell against evolution theory. Men and women were not created as primitive beings whose descendants had to work their way up an evolutionary scale. Eden was a paradise, in which Adam and Eve forfeited their right to live, and the human race can only regain this paradise through divine action, which was accomplished by Jesus' ransom sacrifice (Watch Tower 1999b: 4–9).

Resurrection and ascension

Jesus' death involved giving up his physical body, since death was the punishment given to Adam for his sin. Without sin there would have been no death, and the earth would have been an everlasting paradise. Consequently, to restore the possibility of everlasting life, Jesus paid the price by offering his own sinless body. However, Jesus overcame death by his resurrection, although Jehovah's Witnesses believe that his resurrection body was a spiritual and not a physical one. Peter states, that Jesus 'was put to death in the flesh but made alive in the spirit' (1 Peter 3.18). There were previous examples of the dead being raised, as recorded in the Bible: Jairus' daughter (Mark 5.21-43), an unnamed youth in the town of Nain (Luke 7.11-17) and Lazarus (John 11.1-43), and in the Hebrew-Aramaic scriptures, Elijah and Elisha performed miracles of raising the dead (1 Kings 17.17-24; 2 Kings 4.8-37). All of these were physical resurrections and were not the same as that of Jesus, whose description as the 'firstborn of the dead' relates to the hope of the heavenly class of the 144,000 anointed ones, namely, spiritual life in Jehovah's heavenly kingdom, which cannot be entered by physical bodies. Paul writes, 'Flesh and blood cannot inherit God's Kingdom, nor does corruption inherit incorruption' (1 Corinthians 15.50), and, speaking of the type of body that is raised from the dead, says, 'It is sown a physical body; it is raised up a spiritual body' (1 Corinthians 15.44). The biblical accounts of Jesus' resurrection appearances have caused debate among mainstream scholars: his physical body was longer in the tomb, and some incidents suggest a physical resurrection, since he is able to eat breakfast on the seashore at Galilee, and Mary and Thomas seem able to touch him. However, he also passes through locked doors, and mysteriously disappears during the evening meal with disciples at Emmaus, which is uncharacteristic of a physical body (John 21.1-14; 20.17, 24-29; Luke 24.13-35). Jehovah's

Witnesses resolve such tensions by claiming that Jesus was able to materialize a physical body at will, in order to appear to his disciples, and subsequently dematerialize (Watch Tower 1966b: 26).

If the post-resurrection Jesus had a spiritual body, this does not imply that his physical body remained in the tomb: the Bible asserts that Mary Magdalene, Peter and John found his tomb to be empty, apart from Jesus' grave clothes (John 20.1-9). Paul, again, explains this by distinguishing between physical and spiritual bodies, claiming that at the resurrection the former will be transformed into the latter and that Jesus' resurrection sets the precedent for the forthcoming general resurrection. 'Look! I tell you a sacred secret: We will not all fall asleep in death, but we will all be changed, in a moment, in the blink of an eye, during the last trumpet. For the trumpet will sound, and the dead will be raised up incorruptible, and we will be changed' (1 Corinthians 15.51-52). Resurrection involves the transformation of the physical body into a spiritual one. Paul feels unable to specify exactly what a spiritual body is like, claiming that it is unreasonable to speculate, since God will determine its precise nature (1 Corinthians 15.35-36).

A spiritual body was needed for Christ to ascend back to heaven (Watch Tower 2018a: 186-8). Although the biblical account presents the ascension as an extraordinary miraculous occurrence, it is a private event, shared only with Jesus' disciples. The ascension has a number of functions, according to Watch Tower teaching. It is a fulfilment of biblical prophecy: the Psalmist writes about 'ascending on high and carrying away captives' (Psalm 68.18), which Paul relates to Christ when writing to the Ephesians (Ephesians 4.8-12): the captives, of course, are Adam's descendants who will now be able to follow Christ into Jehovah's heavenly kingdom. By returning to heaven to be with his Father, Jesus will prepare this kingdom for them (John 14.3), and he does this by presenting his sacrifice to the Father: as the writer to the Hebrews explains, he is the great high priest who presents the sacrifice on the Jewish Day of Atonement, but it is not an animal sacrifice, as in the Jerusalem Temple, but the sacrifice of his own life (Hebrews 5.1-10). Further, the ascension is a prelude to sending the holy spirit: Jesus explains to his disciples that 'I will ask the Father and he will give you another helper to be with you forever, the spirit of the truth' (John 14.16-17). This can only happen once Jesus has departed, and at the ascension Jesus specifically promises the sending of the holy spirit (Acts 1.8). Finally, the ascension is linked with the promise of Jesus' return; the two angels who suddenly appear tell the disciples that he will 'come in the same manner as you have seen him going into the sky' (Acts 1.11), thus implying that Christ's return will not be the dramatic event described elsewhere in the Bible, accompanied by the archangel blowing a trumpet (1 Thessalonians 4.16), but a more subdued happening, which Witnesses describe as the 'invisible presence', which began in 1914.

The holy spirit

The ascension anticipates the outpouring of the holy spirit, which occurred ten days afterwards. The term 'holy spirit' is always spelt with lower casing in Watch Tower literature, since it is not regarded as a person but rather as God's active force. Where the Bible seems to attribute personal attributes to the holy spirit, for example, portraying it as a helper, teacher, witness or guide, Watch Tower literature argues that this is personification, pointing out that the Bible personifies other inanimate concepts, such as wisdom in the book of Proverbs. The holy spirit is the means by which God creates the world (Genesis 1.2), and it is the inner power that gives spiritual life to believers (Acts 1.8).

The promised coming of the holy spirit was at Pentecost, which was the Jewish festival celebrating the first fruits of the wheat harvest. The Bible recounts that 120 disciples were in the upper room in which Jesus had celebrated his last evening meal – the first Memorial – with the twelve apostles. The disciples experience a loud noise from heaven and the sound of a strong wind, whereupon tongue-shaped flames appear and alight on each disciple's head, enabling them to acquire the ability to speak in other languages. While Christians in the Pentecostal and charismatic traditions associate the event with glossolalia – the ability to speak in a non-human spiritual language which is unintelligible to most – Jehovah's Witnesses believe that such a phenomenon is occultist practice, which has no place in true religion. The apostles' manner of speech led some of the audience to accuse the apostles of being drunk (Acts 2.13), which has suggested to some Christians, particularly in the Pentecostal tradition, that they were glossolaliating. However, Jehovah's Witnesses emphasize the earlier and plainer part of the account, which states that the assembled multicultural and multilingual gathering to whom Peter spoke each miraculously heard his sermon in their own language (Acts 2.6). The event reverses the effects of the Tower of Babel story, in which human beings were condemned to speak a multiplicity of languages, and to disperse throughout the earth, spreading many varieties of false religion (Genesis 11.1-8). The principal importance of Pentecost is that it marks the beginning of the Church, which Jehovah's Witnesses date as 33 CE: the disciples gained self-confidence, determined to preach the gospel, and the story recounts that 3,000 converts were made that day. The ability to speak miraculously in multiple languages, however, ended when the first generation of apostles died: as Paul predicted, 'If there are tongues, they will cease' (1 Corinthians 13.8).

Apostasy

After Pentecost, the Church was governed by the twelve apostles, together with a number of others such as Paul and Barnabas, who engaged in spreading abroad the teachings about sin, prophecy, the need for redemption, the coming of Jesus and his ransom sacrifice. Jehovah's Witnesses hold that it was during the age of the first generation of apostles that the books of the Bible were compiled and a decision made about which writings should be included as part of the canon of scripture. The apostle John is believed to have been the last of his generation to survive, having died in Ephesus around 100 CE. John's third letter is believed to be the final book to have been completed, dated at 98 CE, after which the canon was closed (Watch Tower 1990a: 260; 2019h). Later writings are considered to be non-inspired; some may be useful insofar as they help to explain the content of scripture, but they lack the same authority.

After the death of the first generation of apostles, Jehovah's Witnesses believe that the Church abandoned its original biblical practices and – in the words of the Watch Tower Society – became apostate. Instead of being a movement consisting of ordinary laypeople, a separate class of clergy arose, distinct from the laity, wearing elaborate robes and assuming pretentious titles such as Reverend, Bishop and Cardinal, and in some cases, for example, in monastic orders, separating themselves off from ordinary society completely. False teachings were introduced, some drawn from Greek philosophical ideas, causing clergy to preach doctrines such as the immortality of the soul. They formulated creeds containing non-biblical ideas, such as the Trinity, and introduced practices that lacked scriptural warrant, such as the veneration of saints and the Virgin Mary. They also formed alliances with civil authorities, instead of subjecting themselves to theocratic government. The Roman Catholic Church caused the Bible to be inaccessible to its members by having it read in Latin in churches and discouraging its availability to be read privately or in the vernacular.

In the course of history, some attempts were made to move the Church back towards its original nature. The Albigenses (also known as the Cathars) of twelfth-century France rejected the Trinity, eternal torment in hell and purgatory, and held that the elements of holy communion were not literally Christ's body and blood. Peter Waldo, the leader of the twelfth-century Waldensians, commissioned some scholars to translate parts of the Bible into the language of late-twelfth-century south France, and his followers rejected wealth as being an encumbrance to preaching the gospel and objected to the notion that spiritual practices such as pilgrimage and venerating relics could confer merit. However, neither of these movements totally reflected first-century Christian practice, and both were suppressed by the Roman Catholic Church. John Wycliffe (c. 1330–1384) in England and Jan Hus (c. 1369–1415) in Bohemia championed the Bible's importance, urging that it should be read by the laity, and Wycliffe is renowned for commissioning the translation of the Bible from the Latin Vulgate. The Protestant Reformation, of which these leaders were precursors, initiated changes in Christendom that Jehovah's Witnesses welcome. Martin Luther (1483–1546) regarded the Bible as the supreme source of authority; Ulrich Zwingli (1484–1531) opposed the celibacy of the clergy and 'mariolatry', while John Calvin (1509–1564) introduced important changes in church government.

However, the Watch Tower Society contends that these Reformers did not go far enough: they still retained a class of clergy, they practised infant baptism, they continued to believe in the Trinity and John Calvin in particular is renowned for his predestinarian ideas to which Charles Taze Russell took exception. At the more radical edge of the Protestant Reformation, the Anabaptist movement insisted on believers' baptism – which the Watch Tower Society welcomes – rather than infant baptism, but its surviving communities, principally the Hutterites and the Mennonites, in the wake of persecution withdrew into their own closed groups, instead of expanding outwards to preach the gospel to all nations. Although the Reformers brought about numerous welcome changes, none of them succeeded in restoring the Christian faith to its original apostolic character.

It took a further three centuries before true Christianity was restored, according to Watch Tower teaching. Russell's Bible Student movement was a lay organization, based on biblical teachings, uncontaminated with pagan philosophies and extra-biblical creeds, and without a hierarchy of clergy with prestigious degrees, titles and clerical garb. His movement practised baptism and the celebration of the Memorial, in accordance with what they regarded as authentic first-century Christian practice, and, importantly, Russell and his Bible Student movement made a point of restoring God's original name, Jehovah.

5

Congregational life

The Kingdom Hall

The Kingdom Hall is the central focus for congregational life. It is not necessary to complete the Bible study sequence for seekers to attend; any member of the public can walk into a congregation meeting or to a larger convention and be welcomed. Formerly most congregations had their own Kingdom Hall, but since Kingdom Halls tend to lie empty when they are not used for spiritual purposes, it makes sense to stagger meeting times between two or more congregations, if possible, in order to use accommodation efficiently. Jehovah's Witnesses, unlike most mainstream Christian congregations, do not let their premises out for secular purposes and do not organize fundraising events or interest groups: there are no coffee mornings, guardian and toddler groups, 'knit and natter' gatherings or any non-spiritual activities. This is not because Kingdom Halls are especially sacred; when the building of a Kingdom Hall is completed, it is not consecrated, but dedicated. In mainstream Christianity, a consecration is a special rite that fundamentally transforms a place or a person, accompanied by ritual acts and performed by a specially authorized individual, such as a bishop. Nothing like this happens when a Kingdom Hall is opened; instead, there might be a dedication service, at which thanks are given to God, and prayers – always extempore – are offered that it may further Jehovah's kingdom. Nothing that is done in a Kingdom Hall cannot be done elsewhere: Jehovah's Witnesses are happy to meet in a school hall or part of a hotel, if necessary, since Jehovah can be accessed anywhere. However, Kingdom Halls are used exclusively for religious purposes, principally their twice-weekly meetings, but also weddings and funerals, occasional talks by visiting overseers, meetings prior to field ministry, occasionally for congregational singing practice, and sometimes for training courses for pioneers or elders.

Jehovah's Witnesses prefer the term Kingdom Hall to 'church', partly because the Bible uses the word 'church' to refer to the entire body of Christians rather than to buildings and partly to remind people of Jehovah's coming kingdom. A Kingdom Hall is an unpretentious building – a hall, in fact – rather more like a secular lecture theatre, usually without any pictures and certainly not a central cross or altar: worship comes from the heart, not from external images. More often than not, Kingdom Halls are purpose-built, although some are adapted from disused mainstream church buildings or secular premises. They consist of seating and a dais at the front with a lectern and microphone, and a screen behind. There is often a small anteroom for mothers with young children who might become a distraction during meetings: it is often separated off from the main meeting area by a glass panel, with speakers connected to the auditorium's microphones, so that they need not miss any of the content. Outside meeting time, this room can usually be screened off for elders' meetings. The only religious artefact is a yeartext: this is a short verse or part of a verse defined by the Governing Body as a theme, which changes each year. In 2020 the yeartext was 'Go, therefore, and make disciples ..., baptizing them' (Matthew 28.19). Until recently the text was displayed on a large plaque, in a prominent position at the front or side of the hall, and congregations had discretion regarding its precise design. In the wake of the electronics revolution, where the technology is available, the yeartext is now often projected on to the screen before a meeting commences. The text is intended to inspire, and speakers are encouraged, although not obliged, to refer to it where appropriate.

The simplicity of Kingdom Halls enables quick construction, and between the early 1970s and around 2016, many were erected in two weekends, or even two single days – a practice often called a 'quick build'. Nine different templates were made available by the Society's headquarters for the congregation to choose. The labour was largely provided, free of charge, by members of the congregation, many of whom engage in trades and have the necessary skills; to speed up the construction, neighbouring congregations would assist. In order to commence the work, a congregation had to demonstrate that the project was financially viable and to have the branch office's approval. The building was financed by donations and, if necessary, loans from other nearby congregations or from the Society Kingdom Hall Fund. During the construction, members would begin with prayer and readings, to encourage them in their work. Although such quick construction was a remarkable feat, its swiftness was sometimes at the expense of high quality, and members would sometimes talk about snagging – identifying and fixing minor defects. Around 2016 the practice was modified, and the building of new premises is now organized at branch level rather than by individual congregations, but still with volunteer labour. The seating capacity of a Kingdom Hall is typically around 200, the usual congregation size being between 100 and 200. When a congregation risks being too large for its premises, it is split, or local congregations are redefined to ensure an optimum size for each. Witnesses are discouraged from deciding which venue to attend: individuals are assigned to a congregation, which is normally in close proximity to their homes.

In the past, there were five Kingdom Hall meetings each week, each of around one hour's duration: a public meeting at the weekend, normally – but not necessarily – on a Sunday, followed by a *Watchtower* study, and a further meeting on Tuesday (the Congregation Book Study, later known as the Congregation Bible Study), often held in someone's home. Thursdays were taken up with two further meetings: Theocratic Ministry School and the Service Meeting. The former gave instruction for public speaking while the latter provided guidance for house-to-house ministry. Additionally, there were regional, national and even international conventions, some of which were up to eight days in duration. The pressures of modern living are not so conducive to such demanding time commitments, people's attention spans are arguably shorter and children in particular found it difficult to sit through meetings that consisted primarily of discourses; hence, meeting times have been adjusted. At the time of writing there are meetings on two separate days: the weekend meeting (usually Sunday) consists of a thirty-minute Bible discourse, followed by the 'Watchtower Study', which lasts for an hour. The weekday meeting is entitled 'Our Christian Life and Ministry' and is divided into three parts: Treasures from God's Word; Apply Yourselves to the Field Ministry; and Living as Christians. Meetings consist of singing, prayer and instruction. Attendees are expected to conform to a dress code. In the United States, Europe and Australasia, men should wear suits and ties, and women dresses – not trousers – that cover the knees. In other countries, smart attire conforming to national custom is the norm, and foreign visitors may adopt the conventions of their home country. Attention to one's appearance shows respect for Jehovah. Only men are allowed to address the congregation; women do not hold office and are not permitted to have a teaching role; they should 'learn in silence with full submissiveness' (1 Timothy 2.11-12). All meetings begin promptly and follow a close outline given by the Society, with precise timings, to ensure that everything runs according to schedule.

The first part of the weekend meeting is a talk, usually given by one of the elders, on a biblical theme and how it applies to everyday life. Although this talk is about the Bible, Kingdom Hall meetings do not formally read Bible passages as lessons, as they do in mainstream churches. The focus of the meeting is on Watch Tower literature, and the congregation is directed to various biblical verses as they become relevant to the talk. The second part consists of singing and an extended study of the designated *Watchtower* article for that week. This is found in the Study Edition of the magazine, which is not normally offered at the literature carts but is readily available online.

An elder, known as the study conductor, presides over the gathering, while another elder or ministerial servant reads the article, one paragraph at a time. Each paragraph is followed by a key question, which the conductor reads out and which attendees are invited to answer by raising a hand. The conductor will call on several members sequentially, and a brother will go around the hall with a roving microphone, so that everyone can clearly hear the answer. (In less technologically advanced congregations, attendees are simply encouraged to speak clearly.) The questions are generally aimed at ensuring comprehension: for example, the theme for 20 April 2020 was 'Pursue Peace by Fighting Envy' (Watch Tower 2020b), and, after an opening song, the congregation was directed to the story of Joseph and the coat that his brothers envied. The audience was asked, 'What were Joseph's brothers able to do, and why?' Other questions focused on applicability, for example, 'How can we help others to fight envy?': the paragraph gives some answers, which a member may echo, but it is also acceptable for members to add their own personal experiences. However, the meeting is not a discussion but for building one's spiritual life, and it would certainly be inappropriate to criticize the article. Answers should be concise, and the recommended length is less than half a minute: members are usually well trained in this regard and know not to ramble on or introduce irrelevancies.

The mid-week meeting, Our Christian Life and Ministry, is normally held in the evening and is a weekly event, except in Memorial and convention weeks. It has an assigned theme, defined in the Life and Ministry Meeting Workbook, which is made available in advance (it can be found online), and is used by the elders and ministerial servants who will be leading. The first part – Treasures from God's Word – begins with a song and prayer, and a brief introduction, followed by a ten-minute talk by a designated elder or a qualified ministerial servant, which introduces two or three themes from the workbook. This is followed by 'Digging for Spiritual Gems', which is a ten-minute question-and-answer session based on the weekly Bible passage. It is followed by a Bible reading, which is assigned to a brother: this is a student assignment, where the member is given formal feedback on his ability to read accurately and fluently. The meeting then flows uninterrupted into Apply Yourselves to Field Ministry: this is training for field ministry, where designated members of the congregation come on stage, having prepared their material, to give sample demonstrations of witnessing, simulating activities such as house calls, informal witnessing or part of a Bible study. Sometimes a video may be used in place of a live demonstration. The conductor provides feedback, praising good practice and indicating aspects that need to be developed.

A song is then sung, acting as a bridge between Apply Yourselves to Field Ministry and Living as Christians. This last part of the meeting involves a thirty-minute congregational Bible study from an approved elder, followed by a summing up by the conductor. There may be brief announcements, and the meeting concludes with another song. If the Circuit Overseer is visiting, he will normally give the Bible study talk, and he is permitted to conclude the meeting with a song of his choice – songs for meetings are usually specified in the *Watchtower* Study Edition and in the meeting workbooks for Our Christian Life and Ministry.

Congregational singing

Singing is an important part of congregational worship, and every Kingdom Hall meeting and convention involves 'singing the truth' as well as teaching it. Jehovah's Witnesses prefer to speak of 'songs' rather than hymns, since the word 'hymn' can be associated with pagan worship. The Watch Tower Society has produced numerous song books throughout its history, and the early ones made use of mainstream Christian favourites like 'All people that on earth do dwell' and 'Nearer my God to thee'. As time passed, however, the Society progressively distanced itself from mainstream Christian worship and removed items that were sung in churches. Its current song book, *'Sing Out Joyfully' to Jehovah*, introduced in 2016, has no overlap whatsoever with mainstream Christian hymnody. In 2007, when the Governing Body invited experienced composers to contribute items, their brief was to avoid 'music that sounded like hymns' (Watch Tower 2011a: 18). By exclusively singing the Society's selection of songs, the congregation demonstrates vocally that it has 'come out of Babylon'.

Singing is entirely congregational. There are no soloists or choirs, although the Society has a small orchestra and group of singers, who do not perform to audiences but meet twice a year to record items for the JW.org website or for audio tracks to be used at congregational gatherings. Songs at Kingdom Hall meetings are now generally introduced and accompanied by audio tracks of pre-recorded instrumental music. Traditional song books are giving way to the projection of lyrics on to a screen, which encourages the congregation to sing out rather than to bury themselves in their books. The songs that are used are always biblical, and the song book (available in electronic format) invariably provides a key text on which the lyrics are based. The words are almost invariably addressed to Jehovah, very occasionally to Jesus, but never to the holy spirit, in contrast with mainstream hymnals. The language is always up to date, avoiding archaic words like 'thee', 'thou' and 'unto', and care is taken to ensure biblical accuracy and alignment with the most recent version of the New World Translation. For example, one song's refrain is 'Keep on seeking first the Kingdom', underlining the continuous imperative of Jesus' words.

Although the material is initially published in English, efforts are made to ensure that the songs can be sung in other languages. Since it is impossible to produce an exact translation of a song that also fits the music, a translator is commissioned to write a literal translation of the words, after which an indigenous speaker creates lyrics that capture the song's essence.

Elders and ministerial servants

The congregation's elders are the senior members who are appointed to direct the congregation, presiding over its worship and giving pastoral support to its members. Jehovah's Witnesses are a lay organization, and leaders do not require intensive seminary training or assume titles such as 'Father' or 'Reverend', which are held to be departures from first-century Christian practice. The Bible does not mention a separate clergy class but speaks of two offices: *presbyteros* and *diakonos* in Greek. The word *presbyteros* literally means 'older man', and *diakonos* is often rendered as 'deacon' in mainstream translations. Jehovah's Witnesses prefer to use the terms 'elder' and 'ministerial servant' to correspond to these two roles.

Elders are men who are appointed to oversee the congregation's spiritual life. This involves teaching, spiritual counselling, the oversight of field ministry and, where necessary, serving on judicial committees. There is no prescribed number of elders for a congregation, since some congregations may have more suitably qualified candidates than others, and if there are relatively few elders, some of their work may be done by eligible ministerial servants, or else elders may be assigned multiple functions. The body of elders discuss periodically which members might be suitable additions to their number: their names are sent to the branch office, to ensure that there are no disqualifications from office; the Circuit Overseer will then decide on their suitability when he visits the congregation – an event that happens twice yearly. Newly baptized individuals cannot be appointed, and, although it is not an official requirement, it is normal practice for a new elder to have previously been a ministerial servant. Sometimes an individual may be thought to show potential for office but does not sufficiently display all the prescribed qualities; for example, if he is sometimes tactless, this weakness would be mentioned to him, and he would be advised to work on this aspect of his personality and reconsidered for office at a later date. Those who are recommended will subsequently be informed verbally, after which the appointment will be announced at the end of the weekday meeting, without any ceremony of ordination or accompanying celebrations.

Spiritual maturity is reckoned to be more important than theological qualifications, and elders are expected to have the various qualities that Paul outlines to Timothy and Titus (1 Timothy 3.1-7; Titus 1.6-9).

> The overseer should therefore be irreprehensible, a husband of one wife, moderate in habits, sound in mind, orderly, hospitable, qualified to teach, not a drunkard, not violent, but reasonable, not quarrelsome, not a lover of money, a man presiding over his own household in a fine manner, having his children in subjection with all seriousness (for if any man does not know how to preside over his own household, how will he care for the congregation of God?), not a newly converted man, for fear that he might get puffed up with pride and fall into the judgment passed on the Devil. (1 Timothy 3.4-6)

Most of these qualities are self-explanatory, but one or two deserve comment. Being 'irreprehensible' does not, of course, mean sinless, but a brother cannot be appointed as an elder if accusations have been upheld against him. A candidate for eldership is asked in advance whether there have been incidents or practices in his life which might disqualify him. A reputation for handling money poorly would be an impediment, for, as Paul goes on to state, 'he should also have a fine testimony from outsiders' (1 Timothy 3.7), which would include any creditors. His marital status should be appropriate: there is no objection to an elder being unmarried or even having an unbelieving wife, but if he marries after taking office, his spouse should also be a believer (2 Corinthians 6.14). His children should also behave well; a family member who had been disfellowshipped, for example, raises the question, as Paul does, of whether someone who cannot manage his own family members can effectively manage people within a congregation.

There are several roles that need to be fulfilled by the body of elders: the congregation secretary, service overseer, Watch Tower study conductor, and Life and Ministry Meeting overseer. If there are insufficient elders, an elder may be assigned more than one role. One of these elders will act as the coordinator of the body of elders, who chairs elders' meetings. The service overseer, as the title implies, directs the congregation's field service work and makes a point of visiting each field service group in turn, assisting them with their work.

These field service groups (each typically consisting of between fifteen and twenty Witnesses) follow Jesus' practice of sending seventy disciples in pairs, after giving them appropriate encouragement (Luke 10.1-11). Sometimes one or two groups will meet together immediately before their field service: the important consideration is gaining inspiration and working efficiently; hence, these meetings are kept short. If they occur directly after a congregation meeting, the group should already have received appropriate spiritual nourishment for their work. This meeting is prepared for; it is more than simply a short prayer for guidance, and the meeting might include watching a short video, some guidance on how to approach householders, how to deal with someone who speaks a different language or advice about health and safety. These meetings are conducted by a group overseer, who is ideally an elder, but alternatively a ministerial servant or a capable baptized brother may preside.

The group overseer is responsible for collecting field service reports, which are then passed on to the secretary. The congregation service committee consists of the coordinator, the secretary and the service overseer (all elders): its functions include authorizing the use of the Kingdom Hall for weddings and funerals, assigning groups for field service and processing applications for special appointments, such as pioneering or Bethel service (Watch Tower 2020a). Elders may also be assigned tasks such as serving on patient visitation groups, a Hospital Liaison Committee and Convention committees, or they may be asked to be involved in building a Kingdom Hall.

Ministerial servants are responsible primarily for the congregation's material affairs. The qualifications for office are much the same as for elders, but they are likely to be younger and not quite as experienced. Paul says that they 'should be tested as to fitness first; then let them serve as ministers' (1 Timothy 3.10). They should be reliable, efficient and enthusiastic, leading an appropriate and irreproachable lifestyle, with sound family life; they should dress well and be careful and discreet about what they say. Each ministerial servant is assigned a particular role. One might be assigned to be a 'literature servant', whose task is to ensure that adequate quantities of literature are available and appropriately displayed for congregational use and for field service. Another might be designated as the 'accounts servant', who keeps records of the congregation's financial matters, while another may keep the territory records for their field service. The 'sound and audio servant' operates the sound equipment and organizes a rota of people to go around the congregation with roving microphones when comments are elicited from the audience. Others may have responsibilities for greeting visitors on arrival at Kingdom Hall meetings ('attendant servants') or be designated the task of coordinating the cleaning of the premises. The tasks assigned to ministerial servants are known as 'privileges', for it is considered a privilege to serve Jehovah, rather than a chore, or a role to be coveted or to boast about. The assignment of specific tasks by Jehovah has biblical precedent going back to the world's beginning: Adam was allotted the task of tilling the ground in the Garden of Eden; angels were given the role of guarding the Garden, following Adam and Eve's expulsion; Noah was assigned the task of ark building; and

Judas Iscariot was designated as the disciples' treasurer (Genesis 3.24; 6.14-16; John 12.6). If there are insufficient elders in a congregation, a ministerial servant might be delegated certain tasks that are normally an elder's prerogative: for example, they could be asked to review doctrinal questions with a baptismal candidate, act as a group overseer for field ministry or even conduct a Congregation Bible Study.

The role of women

Congregations are invariably male-led, and women are ineligible for office. Paul writes, 'Let a woman learn in silence with full submissiveness. I do not permit a woman to teach or to exercise authority over a man, but she is to remain silent' (1 Timothy 2.11-12). In exceptional circumstances, a woman may lead an all-female congregation, for example, if it is small and newly formed, with no men being present. However, she should cover her head, as Paul instructed (1 Corinthians 11.3-16), and she should remain seated, facing the congregation. She should not give a discourse but should read from the Society's publications. If there are insufficient ministerial servants to carry out duties at a particular location, an 'exemplary sister' may be permitted to stand in, but they cannot be appointed as ministerial servants (Watch Tower 2019a: 55). If no man is present at a field service group meeting, or if a male member is ineligible because of disability or withdrawal of privileges, a sister may preside. However, she must cover her head and avoid the appearance of giving instruction; if another sister is invited to say the prayer, she must also wear a head covering. If the only male is a young baptized brother, perhaps not yet in his teens, it is acceptable for the meeting to be conducted by the women, although the male adolescent may be invited to say the prayer, if he is considered capable (Watch Tower 2015b). Women may offer comments from the floor at the Watchtower study, may be given roles in demonstrations and of course spread the truth by public witnessing; but, with the exceptions mentioned above, they may not address the congregation directly from the platform.

Jehovah's Witnesses do not claim that women are inferior, or that they are cursed by God. According to the book of Genesis, Eve is assigned the role of Adam's 'helper', which they regard as a complementary rather than a subordinate role. Although they are excluded from conducting worship and from governance, they have other important roles. Women undertake much of the congregation's publishing work, both in house-to-house evangelism and on literature carts, and the majority of the follow-up Bible studies tend to be undertaken by women. They are eligible for Bethel service and for pioneering work, and many of the researchers at branch offices and at the Warwick headquarters are women. Although women often undertake catering tasks when construction work is underway, women frequently assume traditionally male roles: I have come across women doing plastering and erecting scaffolding, and there are more women than men who operate forklift trucks on construction sites. Importantly, women, as well as men, are reckoned to be part of the 144,000 anointed class.

Conventions

Belonging to a local congregation involves being part of a much larger and wider organization. In addition to Kingdom Hall meetings, Jehovah's Witnesses attend annual regional assemblies, which are larger gatherings of brothers and sisters who belong to a circuit or a region. Conventions are larger events, now held twice a year: the book of Deuteronomy instructs the Israelites to assemble three times annually, for the Festival of Unleavened Bread, the Festival of Weeks and the Festival of Booths (Deuteronomy 16.16). The Festival of Unleavened Bread is, of course, the Passover, which Jesus transformed into the annual Memorial (see Chapter 7); however, since the Memorial marks Jesus' final meal with his disciples, rather than the Exodus from Egypt, it is not celebrated as a convention. Consequently, the three conventions consist of two one-day circuit assemblies and one three-day regional convention. (A circuit is a group of around twenty congregations.) It is usual, additionally, to hold an international convention: this is a large gathering, but obviously time and cost prevent most members from attending. Circuit conventions typically take place in an Assembly Hall, which is a substantially larger building than a Kingdom Hall, with a seating capacity of between 1,500 and 2,000. In the UK, a number of old cinemas were modernized by their volunteer workers for this purpose, with slight adaptations to accommodate features such as a stage and a baptismal pool. These buildings continue to be of interest to cinema enthusiasts, who not infrequently ask to view the interior. Larger conventions, where audiences can reach around 10,000, require larger accommodation, and it is common practice for Jehovah's Witnesses to hire a stadium or a convention centre for this purpose. In Africa a satellite channel broadcasts meetings, conventions and special events in sixteen languages.

Assemblies and conventions typically have a varied programme, built around an overarching theme. The programme includes singing, various talks by elders from the area, dramatized presentations and sometimes a new film that the Society has produced. With the advent of the World Wide Web it is now customary to feature a member of the Governing Body, who gives a pre-recorded talk, and, if there is some new publication, a convention affords an opportunity to release it. In 2019 the theme was 'Love Never Fails!', and talks took the form of symposia: for example, the first block consisted of brief talks by elders on the ways in which other things could fail, such as wealth, status, human wisdom, strength and beauty. This led on to further clusters of talks on the themes of barriers to love, God's love for creation, loving one's congregation, love in the ministry and so on. A three-day convention usually allows at least one slot in which the audience hears reports about the Society's work in some other part of the world, so on this occasion attendees heard how their members were showing love in each continent.

Conventions are open to the public, but delegates – their word for their own attendees – wear a badge. Many travel together, often by coach, partly to save costs, but also to enjoy the community atmosphere that such events involve. They are expected to dress appropriately, as they would for a Kingdom Hall meeting, and, as with congregation meetings, there is no separate programme for children, who are encouraged to take notes, just as many adults do. As well as being the setting in which baptisms take place, regional conventions provide an opportunity for people to enquire about further work within the organization. They may be invited to special meetings about serving in a Bethel or applying for the School for Kingdom Evangelizers. (This school provides training for those in full-time service.)

In addition to these large conventions, an Annual Meeting is held in New York, where members of the Governing Body present reports on the Society's work over the previous year. In 2019 over 20,000 Witnesses attended, including those linked in by video. Topics include reports on both the material and spiritual aspects of the Society, developments that have taken place in property acquisition, technological developments and means of promoting the Society's teachings. This meeting is also used to announce any doctrinal clarifications. In the past, conventions included passing resolutions, but this has rarely occurred in the post-war years. The last resolution to be passed was at the 2004 convention 'Give God Glory Not Man', where a ten-point resolution focused on various ways in which members might give glory to Jehovah. The resolution was not voted on but was put to the assembled gathering, who unanimously responded 'Aye!' Such meetings are not for making policy or for petitioning politicians: Jehovah's Witnesses are apolitical, and their government is not democratic, but theocratic; hence, decisions are entrusted to the Governing Body.

Organizational structure

The greater part of the meetings described above is carried out by elders. To understand their role, they must be seen as part of a much wider highly structured organization. The ultimate source of authority is the Governing Body, which is located at the headquarters in Warwick and Patterson, New York. They oversee the work done by six committees: a Personnel Committee, a Publishing Committee, a Service Committee, a Teaching Committee, a Writing Committee and a Coordinators' Committee. The Writing Committee is responsible for the production of *The Watchtower* and *Awake!* magazines, the various books and booklets, and most recently the extensive written material that appears online. The Teaching Committee oversees conventions and Audio-Visual Service. The Governing Body is described as the 'faithful and discreet slave'. In this context 'discreet' means wise, and the expression alludes to a saying of Jesus:

> Who really is the faithful and discreet slave whom his master appointed over his domestics, to give them their food at the proper time? Happy is that slave if his master on coming finds him doing so! Truly I say to you, he will appoint him over all his belongings. (Matthew 24.45-47)

Jesus is talking here about the end times and goes on to speak of a master of a household who goes off on a journey, leaving a slave (or servant) in charge of his affairs. The competent servant will ensure that the household is fed and that everything will be ready for the master's return. We are to understand, of course, that Jesus Christ is the master, having ascended to heaven and whose return can be expected at any moment; his followers must be ready, and it is important that they receive the appropriate 'spiritual food', which is provided under the direction of the Governing Body.

Subject to the central authority of the Governing Body and its committees are the various branches. Every country is served by a branch office, of which there were eighty-seven worldwide in 2019, and almost every land in which Jehovah's Witnesses have a presence is overseen by a branch office. The first of these was set up in England in 1900, with a second in Germany in 1903, and most Western countries have their own exclusive branch office. Some branch offices cover a cluster of countries: for example, the Central America Branch now encompasses Costa Rica, El Salvador, Guatemala, Honduras, Nicaragua and Panama (Watch Tower 2013b: 11–14). In 2012 some consolidation took place: cyber-technology made communication less dependent on physical proximity, and, while some staff were relocated to the consolidated offices, it was felt that the remaining staff members could be better employed in preaching work.

The branch office is overseen by the Governing Body, and representatives from the international headquarters make regular visits. It is responsible for the overall operation of affairs within its country or cluster. This involves making decisions about establishing and organizing congregations, building premises, appointing elders, ministerial servants and pioneers, and much more. It also deals with disciplinary matters, keeping records of decisions of judicial committees within congregations and offering guidance when serious matters arise. The branch office is usually a complex of buildings, containing a Bethel, which is residential accommodation for those who undertake work there – typically the production and distribution of Watch Tower literature.

In addition to the Bethels there are Remote Translation Offices (RTOs), of which there are currently over 300 worldwide, with 6,000 translators and support staff. Some of these are attached to a Bethel, while others exist in their own right. The RTOs are responsible for translation work, which the Society believes should be carried out in the regions in which a language is spoken, rather than centrally at its international headquarters. The intention is to ensure that the translation of Watch Tower material is presented in proper idiomatic language and that translators keep abreast of linguistic changes that occur through time. It is common practice for a translator to read a translated article out loud within a small team of RTO workers; if the reader stops or stumbles over an expression, it is revisited, to determine whether it can be better expressed.

Bethel service

Some baptized members wish to do more for the Society than attending congregation meetings and undertaking publishing work. One such form of service is working at a Bethel. In order to do so, one must first have the support of the local elders and then submit an application, which the branch office will consider. Bethelites should be young (normally between 19 and 35 years of age), with good mental and physical health, and having no other commitments that might interfere with their position at the Bethel.

Becoming a Bethelite involves a commitment of at least one year of community living, with a small monthly allowance, and the hours are fairly demanding: the working week is around 40 hours, and additionally Bethelites are assigned to a congregation, where they are expected to attend meetings and undertake publishing activities at weekends. They are also eligible to be ministerial servants and elders in their assigned congregation. If they have to prepare a talk, which the Bethel or the congregation may require, they need to find additional time in the course of a busy day to do so. Bethelites are allowed a minimum of twelve days of vacation, progressively increasing with length of service. Accommodation is modest: unless Bethelites are married, they can expect to share a room with at least one other member. If a member decides to marry, continued work at that Bethel is not automatic: the couple must reapply to the Branch Committee, whether or not both partners already reside at the Bethel. Children may not reside in a Bethel, and if a woman becomes pregnant, the couple must revert to normal congregational service work. Bethels do not accommodate children.

The day begins with breakfast at 7.00 am, and members sit at their appointed places, where a chairman – an experienced elder – sits at the head of the table and begins the day by inviting discussion on the day's text before food is served. (A text for each day of the year is given in a short booklet *Examining the Scriptures Daily*, which can be also found on the JW.org website.) Each Bethelite is given a specific work assignment within the Bethel, such as printing and binding, writing, preparing food, doing laundry or cleaning. Outside the working day the Bethel has its own devotional activities, including a Monday evening *Watchtower* study: it is particularly important that new members should deepen their understanding of the faith with appropriate study, and in the course of one's first year, a Bethelite will read the Bible in its entirety. The Bethel community is a closed one, and outsiders are not invited to its devotional meetings, unless they are overnight guests, who may be invited to stay on a limited number of occasions. However, depending on the work that is needed at any particular time, the Bethel community can be augmented by temporary Bethelites (who may be appointed for only a month or for much longer), 'commuter Bethelites', who live at home but come to the Bethel to assist with its work, remote volunteers and 'Bethel consultants'. A consultant is someone who is co-opted for a specific task, such as the legal transfer of property.

Full-time Bethelites receive a modest stipend. All are paid the same amount: there is no system of increments or salary bands. This includes the Governing Body, whose members receive slightly less than US$160 per month. Additionally they are entitled to a small amount of expenses, which, I am told, start at a monthly US$30, with slight increases according to seniority. It is true that additionally they receive accommodation (an unpretentious suite of rooms), meals, healthcare and some other benefits, but when one considers that they are in effect the directors of a multinational organization, the remuneration is very modest indeed, compared with multinational company executives, some of whom command annual salaries that run into millions of dollars.

Visiting a Bethel by those outside the community is particularly encouraged. Although its main purpose is to prepare and distribute the Society's publications, conducted Bethel tours are offered. These enable visitors, by prior arrangement, to see the organization's work in progress, and there are normally displays showing artefacts and events relating to the Society's history. Visitors are expected to observe the usual smart dress code, as if they were attending a congregation meeting.

Jehovah's Witnesses do not undertake pilgrimages as such, but the closest they come to undertaking such spiritual journeys is to visit the places which assist their understanding of the Bible. Of particular interest is the Society's new headquarters at Warwick, which were completed in 2017. Visitors, who must make prior arrangement, but without charge, can view three self-guided exhibitions: one is 'The Bible and the Divine Name', which includes all editions of the Bible, highlighting the divine name Jehovah; 'A People for Jehovah's Name' sets out the historical background to Jehovah's Witnesses, showing how Jehovah has guided his people in the past; 'World Headquarters – Faith in Action' is an interactive exhibition demonstrating how the organization's various committees function and make their publications available to members worldwide.

In recent times a few tour companies have been set up by Jehovah's Witnesses. These are privately run but are used by some congregations for spiritually edifying outings. Naturally, the Holy Land is of particular interest to members, although normally constraints of time and money prevent them from undertaking expensive tours. However, Betheltours is a small company run by brothers, which enables members to visit the Bible lands and to be guided by local brothers. There are less expensive, localized tours. In Britain, in addition to visiting the British Bethel, weekend tours also include the British Museum, where specially approved guides explain the role of artefacts in biblical history and prophecy. These tours have themes such as 'This Is History Written in Advance' and 'The Stones Are Crying Out'. Also popular are London tours: one is a coach tour, the theme of which is 'The Rise of the Seventh World Power', and a guided walking tour beginning at the Houses of Parliament is entitled 'United in A Disunited World'. The Royal Observatory at Greenwich is also a venue for a specialized tour. A weekend package is available, incorporating all these venues, and affords time for study of the Bible and Watch Tower literature. These tours would not be regarded as pilgrimages in any sense, but those who take part evidently find them beneficial and inspiring. One participant has described the experience as 'a spiritual multivitamin' (Betheltours 2021).

There is much involved in belonging to a congregation of Jehovah's Witnesses, and the expected commitment exceeds that of most mainstream denominations. It is important that one's spiritual progress is made through Jehovah's theocratic organization. Informal study groups are discouraged: unlike mainstream churches, where groups of the laity get together, particularly in seasons such as Lent, to study the Bible together, Jehovah's Witnesses wish to ensure that false teachings do not contaminate the truth through inexperienced or self-appointed teachers. The Governing Body alone delivers spiritual food in due season.

6

Lifestyle

World renouncing or world affirming?

Sociologist Roy Wallis claimed to identify three broad categories of religion: world-affirming, world-renouncing and world-accommodating. In his study of Jehovah's Witnesses, Andrew Holden places them in the world-renouncing category, and it is tempting to portray them in a negative light as people who have separated off from the world and rejected worldly standards. However, Wallis's categories do not neatly fit Jehovah's Witnesses. On the one hand, they teach that the world is ruled by Satan and reject worldly standards such as wealth and fame; they do not support any earthly political regime, rejecting nationalism and patriotism, refusing to salute national flags or take part in military service; and they describe themselves as being 'in the truth' in contrast to all other forms of spirituality, which they reject as 'false religion'. On the other hand, they do not live in seclusion from the rest of the world: they have no monastic communities or even a priestly class but emphasize the value of marriage and family life, and – with the exception of their Bethel workers and full-time pioneers – pursue ordinary secular employment. Even their theology cannot adequately be described as world-renouncing: although they acknowledge that there is much wrong with human society and the state of the physical earth, they hold that historical events have been part of Jehovah's plan of salvation and that the earth will be renewed after Armageddon, becoming an earthly paradise to be enjoyed to the full by Jehovah's people. Zoe Knox encapsulates their position by pointing out that they regard themselves as being in the world but, in Jesus' words, 'are no part of the world' (John 15.19). They live in the world pursuing family life and employment, while looking for the world's renewal, when Satan is finally conquered and Jehovah and Christ establish their rule.

Family life

The popular conception of Jehovah's Witnesses tends to be negative, and the public at large are aware of little more than the fact that Witnesses reject blood transfusion and that they do not celebrate popular festivals such as Christmas and birthdays. By twenty-first-century Western standards, Jehovah's Witnesses' attitudes and lifestyle may seem old-fashioned, but Jehovah's Witnesses perceive present-day permissiveness as a mark of declining moral standards.

Marriage and family life are highly prized. Although most Jehovah's Witnesses marry, there is certainly a place for single men and women, as well as childless couples, who may even be in a better position to serve Jehovah, being unencumbered by family commitments. However, sexual relationships may only take place within marriage: trial marriages and premarital sex are not permitted within the organization and are seen as contravening Jehovah's law. Such practices, as well as adultery and homosexuality, can lead to judicial proceedings. Even being alone with someone of the opposite sex could be construed – at least in some circumstances – as 'brazen conduct'.

Jehovah's Witnesses tend to stick together as family units; they come to congregation meetings as families, have meals together as a family and study the Bible together in a Family Worship Evening, which they are encouraged to hold during the week. They believe that the Bible promotes family life as the ideal: God tells Adam and Eve, 'Be fruitful and become many' (Genesis 1.28). The father is regarded as the head of the household, in accordance with Paul's teaching: 'Let wives be in subjection to their husbands as to the Lord, because a husband is head of his wife just as the Christ is head of the congregation' (Ephesians 5.22-23), although the relationship should be a loving rather than a domineering one (Ephesians 5.28). Husbands and wives tend to have traditional role demarcations: the husband is normally the breadwinner, while the wife engages in domestic tasks like keeping the home and doing the shopping. The book of Proverbs enumerates the qualities of the ideal wife (Proverbs 31), which suggest that she should offer words of encouragement to her husband, seek to live modestly, enable him to have time for congregational activities and not to ask him to divulge confidential congregational matters (Watch Tower 2016b: 2). The traditional role demarcation is not inviolable, however; I know at least one Witness family where the wife successfully runs her own aromatherapy business. The book of Proverbs states that the wife also 'sees that her trading is profitable' (Proverbs 31.18), implying that the woman's place is not necessarily confined to the home.

Many Watch Tower publications address issues relating to childbearing and childbirth. Having children tends to be the norm, although, unlike some

American fundamentalist groups, 'become many' is not taken to mean that they should have as large a family as possible. On the contrary, Witnesses are encouraged to plan their families and to consider the cost of having children (Watch Tower 1996b: 12–14). Contraception is acceptable, but not abortion, since the Bible considers abortion to be murder. The intrauterine device (IUD) might appear to be a borderline case in this regard, but the Society regards the couple's decision to use such devices as a matter of conscience. The organization has been somewhat cautious about sterilization, mainly because it is irreversible, and counsels couples to discuss such issues with qualified medical practitioners (Watch Tower 1996b:12-14).

Being an 'old new' religion, many Jehovah's Witnesses are children, who have been brought into the organization by birth, rather than by the Society's publishing work. Parents are therefore faced with the challenge of faith maintenance by the second and third generation of members; given that roughly two-thirds of those who are born into the faith decide to withdraw their allegiance, this is no easy task. There are three principal environments in which learning occurs: home, congregation and school, and it is therefore important to ensure that all three environments are conducive to keeping children 'in the truth'. Many Watch Tower articles give advice on parenting, and Jehovah's Witnesses emphasize qualities like obedience, discipline and respect for one's parents and for older members of one's family and the congregation. Discipline should be firm, but loving, encouraging and never humiliating. Corporal punishment is not particularly favoured, although the Bible states, 'The one holding back his rod is hating his son' (Proverbs 13.24). However, where state law forbids it, parents will refrain from spanking their children. The family should be the place where children are introduced to the Bible's teachings, and in addition to the Family Worship Evening, children should be encouraged to say prayers at bedtime and have a Bible story told to them when they are younger. Witnesses are allowed to include Bible studies with non-baptized children as part of their field ministry report, up to two hours per week; while it is anticipated that more time will be spent on studying the Bible, that would be regarded as normal parenting.

At congregation meetings and conventions, there are no concessions made to children, who are expected to sit and be attentive, just like their parents. There are no special activities for children: no Sunday schools, crèches, kindergartens, special children's songs, youth camps or even a Children's Corner in *The Watchtower* or *Awake!* As they are able, they prepare for congregation meetings by reading the relevant *Watchtower* article for study and attempting to answer the questions. Their contributions may be invited from the platform, and I have even heard a three-year-old boy, with some prompting by his parents, contribute a comment. At Our Christian Life and Ministry meetings, older boys are given instruction in reading the Bible publicly and in preparing short talks. Since women are not required to perform such tasks, girls can learn how to participate in on-stage 'demonstrations' (role-plays). In 1979 the children's book *My Book of Bible Stories* was released – the first Watch Tower publication specially targeted at children. Ten years later, the Society released *Questions Young People Ask – Answers That Work*, which provides adolescents with advice on a range of aspects of growing up, spanning family life, education, sex and dating, leisure, drugs and alcohol. The book was subsequently expanded into two volumes, to take aboard issues relating to new electronic media, such as cell phones, the internet and electronic games.

The other environment in which Jehovah's Witness children meet others is, of course, school, which raises issues which parents and children have to address. Parents will usually inform children's teachers that they cannot participate in birthday celebrations, Christmas and Easter preparations, Valentine's Day, Halloween, Mother's Day and Father's Day, and normally they will be provided with alternative activities, so that they do not participate in practices that can be regarded as nationalistic or involving false religion. Attending morning assemblies is acceptable, except where it involves religious acts of worship, and Jehovah's Witnesses do not object to their children being taught about religion, so long as this is done in an objective and not a confessional way. Sex education is best provided in the home, although Witnesses are willing for their children to be taught its biological aspects at school; however, they disapprove of modern trends to teach homosexuality and families with same-sex couples as 'parents'. Many Jehovah's Witnesses who have subsequently left the society have reported feeling the odd one out and even being subjected to bullying. Jehovah's Witnesses do not have their own religious schools, where their requirements could be accommodated, and some Jehovah's Witness parents have therefore decided that it is better to provide a home education for their children.

While children are encouraged to work hard at school, only a minority go on to university or college; according to a 2016 Pew Research Center survey, 63 per cent of Jehovah's Witnesses in the United States have no more than a high school diploma and do not proceed to higher education. This compares with 37 per cent of mainstream Protestants (Lipka 2016). Their main concerns about university life are 'bad associations': Paul writes, 'Bad associations spoil useful habits' (1 Corinthians 15.33) – a verse frequently quoted in Watch Tower literature. Paul is referring to harmful human contacts that could damage one's spiritual life, and many Jehovah's Witnesses fear that going to college or university could encourage sexual promiscuity, drugs and excess alcohol drinking; hours spent studying or socializing can also erode time that could be spent on studying the Bible or on field ministry. Further, a Witness should not be seeking qualifications that lead to a high salary or status, and numerous professions, such as law, medicine and dentistry, will not be needed in the coming new world which Jehovah's Witnesses expect after Armageddon. Jehovah's Witnesses tend to pursue trades rather than professions, the former being more immediately useful to the Society: plumbers, carpenters, painters and electricians are immensely useful for construction work. Self-employment is particularly conducive to flexible work, which is no doubt why one popular occupation is window cleaning.

Employment

Young people should give careful thought to choosing a career. In a world ruled by Satan, those who are trying to find an occupation for the first time can be easily tempted into worldly forms of employment that appear to offer promotion, prestige and material wealth. It is important, however, to have a job that is compatible with pursuing 'kingdom interests', allowing the worker to display integrity and to have sufficient time for field service. Unlike some other minority religious organizations, Jehovah's Witnesses have never made a point of publicizing members who have achieved fame and fortune, such as Michael Jackson, Prince, Serena Williams and others. Michael Jackson only receives one mention in Watch Tower literature, and that is in connection with his video *Thriller*, which he later came to regret (Watch Tower 1984a: 18–20; Chryssides 2019: 141). When the pop artist Margaret Keane wrote a brief autobiography that appeared in *Awake!* magazine, her name was left out, in line with the Society's anonymity policy (Watch Tower 1975b: 12–16).

Witnesses are concerned that fame is accompanied by worldly wealth, 'bad associations' and time commitment that detracts from evangelizing. Men and women who pursue sporting careers are often obliged to engage in acts of patriotism, such as singing the national anthem or honouring a national flag. However, Jehovah's Witnesses have no particular objection to watching sport on television or listening to some popular music, but they are vigilant about the values that aspects of popular culture often convey. Those embarking on a career are advised to consult the Bible first: Moses, for example, gave up life in the Pharaoh's royal palace in order to serve God and his people; in a less well-known story, Baruch, Jeremiah's scribe, complains that he is tired of transcribing Jehovah's words, and Jeremiah rebukes him, saying, 'But you are seeking great things for yourself. Stop seeking such things' (Jeremiah 45.5). Working tirelessly for Jehovah must come before personal ambition. Jehovah's Witnesses must not be employed in any sector that involves violating Jehovah's laws, for example, pursuing a military career, or working in a gambling casino or abortion clinic. It is sometimes believed that Jehovah's Witnesses may not join a police force. This is not strictly true: whether or not a Witness could become a police officer depends on the country and whether the job requires them to be armed; if it does, then they should look elsewhere for employment, otherwise there is no objection to upholding the laws of the land, which Jehovah's Witnesses believe should be kept.

Inevitably, there are grey areas. It would be unacceptable for a barber to work inside an army barracks; however, what if the barber's shop was just around the corner, and many of the customers were military personnel? What if a Jehovah's Witness was employed by a supermarket and asked to work at the newspaper counter, where they would be expected to sell cigarettes to customers? What is the situation for a male driving instructor, who might find himself alone with a female pupil? Where the Society does not provide explicit guidance on a situation, it is a matter of conscience for the individual to decide. An important consideration would be how close the action came to the biblical prohibition. The barber might consider what proportion of the customers came from the barracks, or the supermarket assistant the proportion of sales that involved tobacco. The driving instructor, like every citizen, should obey the law, so he cannot refuse to instruct women; however, perhaps he could suggest that the woman is accompanied or ensure that they do not practice in areas where there is little traffic. Other considerations might involve the availability of other jobs, or the extent to which the worker needed the money. The elders' advice can also be sought, and the Society provides guidance about situations, which may change over time. Until recently, nurses could exercise their conscience about whether to give a blood transfusion, if asked by a doctor (although, of course, receiving a transfusion is a serious transgression); however, in 2018 the Governing Body sent a letter to Hospital Liaison Committees stating that administering a blood transfusion contravened Jehovah's law (Furuli 2020: 10–11).

Although some Jehovah's Witnesses are employed in healthcare and social work, they recognize that these are not ultimate solutions for the human condition. Similarly, charitable work has limits. Jehovah's Witnesses are often criticized for not establishing relief organizations or supporting charities. The Watch Tower organization is critical of major charities on the grounds that much of the monies they collect are absorbed in administrative and distribution costs, or sometimes high directors' salaries, and political regimes can often prevent aid from reaching its appropriate destination. Jesus' final instruction was to make disciples of all nations, since spiritual help is preferable to physical assistance, and Jehovah's Witnesses look to a world in which there will be no disease, famine, poverty and other ills that afflict society. It is sometimes said that Jehovah's Witnesses only help their own members: when there is an earthquake or flood, they are quick not only to make funds available to them but also to offer practical help in rebuilding Kingdom Halls or individual dwellings. While acknowledging the importance of helping the needy, one

Watchtower article quotes Paul's advice to 'work what is good toward all, but especially toward those related to us in the faith' (Galatians 6.10; Watch Tower 2005b: 16). Jehovah's Witnesses do give to charities from time to time, but giving should be on a personal basis, with due caution and discretion. It is regarded as a private matter, since Jesus said, 'When you go making gifts of mercy, do not blow a trumpet ahead of you, just as the hypocrites do in the synagogues and in the streets, that they may be glorified by men' (Matthew 6.2; Watch Tower 1990b: 16). For this reason, if a street collector offers a Jehovah's Witness a lapel sticker in acknowledgement of a contribution, most will not wear it in public.

Recreation

Despite fears about drinking being a part of university life, many Jehovah's Witnesses drink alcohol in moderation. Paul advises Timothy, 'Do not drink water any longer, but take a little wine for the sake of your stomach and your frequent cases of sickness' (1 Timothy 5.23). The use of alcoholic wine in ancient times was widespread, and it would be difficult for grapes not to ferment in a warm climate. The first Lord's Evening Meal would be celebrated with alcoholic wine, and Jehovah's Witnesses follow this practice at the annual Memorial. When Jesus was present at the wedding feast in Cana, he miraculously changed six outsize jars of water into wine, reckoned to contain somewhere between 260 and 390 litres. (One *Watchtower* article suggests that it was not all consumed at the event, but that a proportion was stored for subsequent use; Watch Tower 1984b: 31; 2000: 21). However, the Bible counsels against heavy drinking: 'Wine is a ridiculer, alcohol is unruly; Whoever goes astray by them is not wise' (Proverbs 20.1). Occasionally biblical characters become drunk, with harmful consequences. After surviving the great flood, Noah plants a vineyard and very soon begins to drink to excess, leading to his curse on Canaan (Genesis 9.20-27); Lot's two daughters get him drunk and persuade him to commit incest (Genesis 19.30-38); and Paul reproves some of the early Christians for excess drinking at the Lord's Evening Meal, making them unfit to partake, as well as highlighting problems of inequality among the congregation, many of whom could ill afford food and drink. The book of Leviticus (10.8-11) reminds the priests that they should not drink alcohol before performing their religious duties, and hence Jehovah's Witnesses avoid drinking before congregation meetings and certainly would always be in a state of sobriety when undertaking field ministry.

While alcohol is permitted, smoking is not. Early editions of *Zion's Watch Tower* contained readers' letters that deplored the use of tobacco on the grounds that it was harmful to health, addictive and a waste of money

(Watch Tower 1895: 1849). In 1946 *Consolation* magazine published an article exposing fraudulent cigarette advertising, and, somewhat later, *Awake!* magazine pointed to the health hazards, including cancer, heart disease and the dangers to pregnant women and those who inhaled secondary smoke: this was some time before the public at large were made aware of the hazards of smoking. Some Witnesses, however, continued to smoke, until 1973, when the Governing Body announced that, in order to be regarded as 'an acceptable member of a congregation', they must quit the practice. When preparing for baptism, one of the tests of good Christian practice is whether the candidate smokes: if so, that person is not yet ready to be baptized.

Gambling has seldom been a problem for Jehovah's Witnesses, although there is no specific scriptural prohibition of the practice. The Bible mentions casting lots: the Roman soldiers who attended Jesus' death cast lots to determine who should keep his garments, but the incident is seen as a fulfilment of biblical prophecy (Psalm 22.18) rather than a practice for condemnation. In ancient times, lots could be used to settle controversies on which it was impossible to reach a conclusion, thus placing the decision in God's hands: 'Into the lap the lot is cast down, but every decision by it is from Jehovah' (Proverbs 16.33). 'The lot puts even contentions to rest, and it separates even the mighty from one another (Proverbs 18.18). When the early disciples looked for a successor to Judas Iscariot, they prayed before casting lots, thus calling on God for the appropriate decision (Acts 1.21-26).

However, Watch Tower articles construe recreational gambling as covetous and greedy; it is done at the expense of others, since winning a jackpot is only possible if many others lose. Witnesses also point out that gambling can be addictive and draw attention to the very substantial losses that gamblers have been known to incur. Isaiah mentions 'those setting a table for the god of Good Luck, And those filling up cups of mixed wine for the god of Destiny' (Isaiah 65.11-12), which suggests to Jehovah's Witnesses that luck is construed as some kind of mystic force, relating to false religion. Witnesses avoid expressions such as 'Good luck!', which they regard as pagan invocations. They heed the Bible's teaching that 'the love of money is a root of all sorts of injurious things, and by reaching out for this love some have been led astray from the faith and have stabbed themselves all over with many pains' (1 Timothy 6.9). While some money is needed in order to live, desire for excessive wealth can be morally corrosive, and one's income should be acquired by work, not by chance. Even small-scale gambling should be avoided: Jehovah's Witnesses will not enter tombolas or buy lottery tickets, since they feel that this could put them on a slippery slope towards more substantial gambling. However, they have no objection to games of chance, such as card games, provided that players use tokens or scorecards rather than real money.

It has sometimes been suggested that Jehovah's Witnesses are not allowed to play chess, since it is based on war strategy (Witness 007 2012). This misunderstanding is based on an old 1973 *Awake!* article, which gave a skeletal account of the game's origins and rules (Watch Tower 1973b: 12–14). The author concluded by saying that chess was a 'fascinating game', but 'there are questions regarding it that are good for each one who plays chess to consider'. This simply meant that chess players should exercise their consciences on such matters, taking into account its background and its adversarial nature, and, since attaining proficiency demands considerable time investment, whether studying and playing the game is an appropriate use of one's time. Subsequent Watch Tower articles involving chess mentioned chess computers and artificial intelligence, leading to theological issues about whether human technology could ever rival the human brain, which is God's creation. Other articles about board games emphasize the importance of honest play, and being a good loser, and also recommend the involvement of the entire family in order to reinforce family life. Perhaps predictably, some articles recommended quiz games involving biblical knowledge, and there are at least two online stores run by Jehovah's Witnesses that market such items.

Since Witnesses draw friends substantially from their own community, friendship with outsiders tends to be discouraged. A recent *Watchtower* article advised, 'When we choose to live according to Bible truth, our ties with friends and relatives may change,' citing Jesus' prayer for his disciples, 'Sanctify them by means of the truth; your word is truth' (John 17.17; Watch Tower 2018e: 6). To sanctify, as the article explains, means to set apart, and those who are in the truth are set apart from the rest of the world. The Bible teaches that there is a 'time to weep and a time to laugh' (Ecclesiastes 3.4), so Jehovah's Witnesses have no problem about enjoying themselves. Like most people, they watch television – although in moderation – and occasionally visit the cinema or theatre. However, they find most of the cinema releases unsuitable, owing to the amount of sex, violence and occultism that they contain.

One important consideration in making moral decisions is the concept of 'stumbling' – a term frequently used by Jehovah's Witnesses. It relates to the saying of Paul: 'If food makes my brother stumble, I will never again eat meat at all, so that I will not make my brother stumble' (1 Corinthians 8.13). Elsewhere, Paul compares the Christian life to a race (1 Corinthians 9.24); if I trip someone else up, I may make it to the finish line, but I have prevented someone else from achieving the goal. In other words, Witnesses should consider the impact of their actions on others. Paul is here discussing 'food offered to idols' – a practice still carried out today in some eastern religions, where food is presented to images of deities before being eaten by the congregation. The practice does not seem to have worried Paul unduly, but he considers the possibility that others might copy his action and find their conscience troubled. If they previously belonged to the pagan temple, they might feel that they were betraying their new-found faith, or they may even be lured back into 'idol worship'. Another situation is where one person can control a type of action, but others cannot: for example, if I am able to drink alcohol moderately, drinking wine or beer might be acceptable for me, but if I am in the company of someone who is prone to excess drinking, I might lead that person into alcoholism. In Jehovah's Witnesses' parlance, the word 'stumble' is used as a transitive verb as well as an intransitive one: one may talk about 'stumbling a person' rather than 'making a person stumble' (Watch Tower 2013a: 3–7).

The word 'stumble' can also be used where the behaviour in question is regarded as inherently reprehensible. Jehovah's Witnesses believe that this occurs within the mainstream churches, whose clergy are held to preach false doctrines and tolerate immoral behaviour:

> Who will be collected out from the Kingdom, and how do they cause stumbling and do lawlessness? (Matt. 13:41) The weedlike clergy of Christendom have misled millions for centuries. They have done this by means of God-dishonoring teachings, 'things that cause stumbling', such as the doctrine of eternal punishment in hellfire and the confusing and mysterious Trinity. Many religious leaders have set a bad example for their flocks by their adulterous friendship with this world and in some cases by their flagrant immoral conduct. ... How happy the sons of the Kingdom are to be separated from such weedlike influences and corrupt teachings that cause stumbling! (Watch Tower 2010b:19–23)

Health matters

Jehovah's Witnesses are best known for their refusal of blood transfusion, but this is only one aspect of their attitudes to health and medical treatment. Many Watch Tower articles encourage fitness among their members, promoting healthful activities such as walking, cycling and gardening, while others feature advice on diet, dental care, weight control and much more. The Bible teaches that one's body is God-given; Paul instructed the Christian community at Rome, 'Present your bodies as a living sacrifice, holy and acceptable to God' (Romans 12.1). There have been some popular misunderstandings about their attitudes to health, possibly due to some of the health fads of the 1930s, when Witnesses were opposed to vaccination, were slow to accept germ theory, which had only recently been discovered at the time, and urged the avoidance of aluminium cooking utensils. All that has changed, however, as scientific advances became accepted, and Jehovah's Witnesses accept most forms of conventional medical treatment.

Witnesses are amenable to forms of alternative medicine, and Watch Tower literature suggests that they are even mentioned in the Bible, which refers to oil, balsam and wine as ways of treating maladies, and Isaiah recommends King Hezekiah to apply a poultice when he is ill (2 Kings 20.7; Watch Tower 2000b). Some Witnesses therefore make use of acupuncture, aromatherapy, chiropractic, homeopathy, herbal remedies and massage. However, one should exercise discrimination: as at least one *Awake!* article highlights, many practitioners of alternative medicine lack qualifications and may not be capable of diagnosing ailments reliably. This is particularly the case in countries where the practice of medicine is unregulated, hence Witnesses are strongly advised to consider the therapist's qualifications. Some forms of therapy are judged to be unacceptable: as well as abstaining from blood, Jehovah's Witnesses should not undergo hypnotherapy, since this is judged to be an occult practice, in which the patients lose control of their minds and bodies. Yoga is also undesirable, on account of its associations with pagan religions. Certain forms of sex therapy are unacceptable, for example, if the therapist's treatment involves masturbation.

Jehovah's Witnesses do not practise faith healing. They acknowledge that Jesus and the early disciples, as well as the ancient Hebrew prophets Elijah and Elisha, performed healing miracles, and that Jesus' final instructions to his disciples included a command that they should heal the sick (John 14.12). However, they believe that such practices died out after the first generation of apostles. This view, which is known as cessationism, is not confined to Jehovah's Witnesses but can be traced back to Protestant reformers such as Martin Luther and John Calvin, and was supported by some famous Protestant preachers such as Jonathan Edwards and C. H. Spurgeon. The doctrine is based on Paul's famous passage about Christian love, when he writes, 'But if there are gifts of prophecy, they will be done away with; if there are tongues, they will cease; if there is knowledge, it will be done away with' (1 Corinthians 13.8). Paul, it is argued, is referring to special 'signs and wonders', while acknowledging that the non-miraculous gifts of the spirit will remain; he lists 'love, joy, peace, patience, kindness, goodness, faith, mildness, self-control' (Galatians 5.22-23). Therefore, Jehovah's Witnesses do not hold healing meetings or recommend visits to shrines that purport to offer miraculous cures. They do not have 'deliverance ministries' – the favoured Protestant term for exorcisms – although they acknowledge the existence of demons and believe that demonic powers can exacerbate illnesses. Practising exorcism, they believe, is a form of occultism, to be avoided. Even using prayer to bring about healing is not encouraged. One might legitimately pray for help with one's spiritual life or with witnessing. One might pray for opportunities to spread the truth, to be able to attend a congregation meeting despite difficulties or for endurance in the face of hardship, including the strength to endure pain and suffering; however, using prayer to effect healing would imply the continuation of miraculous curative powers.

Blood

No discussion of Witnesses' lifestyle would be complete without explanation of their blood doctrine. The issue almost inevitably arises when one mentions Jehovah's Witnesses to those who know little about the organization, and it can readily assume undue prominence in discussion. Most Witnesses will never need a blood transfusion at any point in their lifetime, and hence the Society's stance will have little effect on them. Many Witnesses carry a 'No Blood' card on their person, with a signed leaflet giving instructions to medical staff, in event of their being unable to do so personally. There is also a 'No Blood' app available for mobile phones.

Blood was first able to be stored during the First World War, but blood transfusion did not become widely available until the end of the Second World War. There was therefore little reference in Watch Tower literature to medical use of blood before 1945. Zoe Knox cites a news item in a 1940 edition of *Consolation*, which recounts with apparent approval how a woman accidentally shot herself in the heart but was saved by being given a litre of blood (Knox 2018: 157; Watch Tower 1940b: 19). It was not until 1945 that the prohibition on blood was first introduced. After the Great Flood, God gives Noah permission to eat any animal, bird or fish, but with the restriction, 'Only flesh with its life – its blood – you must not eat' (Genesis 9.4). Blood was regarded as the life force: 'You must not eat the blood of any sort of flesh because the life of every sort of flesh is its blood. Anyone eating it will be cut off' (Leviticus 7.14). It should be noticed that Moses here prescribes the penalty for consuming blood: being 'cut off' means banishment from the community – disfellowshipping, in Jehovah's Witnesses' vocabulary. Despite the fact that this instruction belongs to the old covenant, it is reinforced in the new, at the First Council of Jerusalem, which the Book of Acts recounts. This meeting of the early apostles was convened because of a dispute about attitudes to the Mosaic law and the extent to which it applies to Gentile converts. The agreement that was reached, suggested by the apostle James, was that the rite of circumcision was no longer required but that the Christian community should 'abstain from things polluted by idols, from sexual immorality, from what is strangled, and from blood' (Acts 15.20).

It should therefore be noted that, for Jehovah's Witnesses, blood doctrine is a dietary law as well as a medical one. Jehovah's Witnesses will not eat black pudding (aka blood sausage), since it is substantially an animal's blood. They may eat game, but only if the animal's blood has been drained (Watch Tower 1954: 286–7). This is not the same as Jewish dietary law, for two reasons: first, kosher food laws are not themselves biblical but come from later rabbinical interpretation of Hebrew scripture; second, Jehovah's Witnesses do not discriminate between clean and unclean animals, since such laws belong to the Old Covenant and are not reinforced in the New. When the apostle Peter, an upholder of traditional Jewish practice, is about to meet a Roman centurion, he falls into a trance and receives a vision in which all kinds of animal descend from heaven in a net, and he is instructed to eat, irrespective of whether they are defined as clean or unclean (Acts 10.1-23). Jehovah's Witnesses do not have a problem about eating rare steaks, for example, since the blood has been substantially removed from the meat.

The Society's position on blood was first defined in two editions of *The Watchtower* in 1944 and 1945 (Watch Tower 1944b: 355–64; 1945: 195–204). The earlier article is about 'the stranger' in Israel and points out that the law given to Noah concerning the sanctity of blood applies beyond the Jewish people, and that 'the stranger was forbidden to eat or drink blood, whether by transfusion or by the mouth' (Watch Tower 1944b: 362). The 1945 article is about the application of God's command to Noah to present-day believers, and states, 'It cannot be said that such regulation applies to the blood of animals lower than man but not to human blood' (Watch Tower 1945: 200). A subsequent 1948 notice in *Awake!*, entitled 'Dangers of Blood Transfusion', explicitly reaffirmed that blood transfusions were contrary to God's law, adding that they also presented health hazards such as hepatitis (Watch Tower 1948: 12). It was not until 1961, in response to a reader's question, that the Society affirmed plainly that receiving blood transfusion was a judicial matter, meriting disfellowshipping (Watch Tower 1961: 63–4). In 2000 it was announced that anyone voluntarily receiving blood would not even have to appear in front of a judicial committee: the act itself would automatically result in disfellowshipping, being an indication of disassociation.

Some points of clarification should be mentioned. The Jehovah's Witnesses' policy on blood does not disallow organ transplantation. Inevitably, the Bible does not mention transplantation, and it was initially held to be a matter of individual conscience; in 1967, however, it was declared that accepting a part of another person's body was tantamount to cannibalism. In 1980, the Society's stance had changed, acknowledging that there was an important difference between blood and tissue and bone. Bone marrow transplantation is a borderline case, since it is not clear whether it constitutes flesh, and any decision to undergo this procedure is therefore a matter of individual conscience. The use of dialysis machines is acceptable, since dialysis is a process of purifying and circulating one's own blood, rather than receiving new blood from another person. However, storing one's own blood for possible future transfusion is deemed unacceptable, since this involves introducing blood from outside one's body, even though it is one's own. The use of blood derivatives – red cells, white cells, platelets and plasma – has been a source of uncertainty, and the Society's position has changed over the years. At the time of writing, the acceptance of blood derivatives in medical procedures is a matter of conscience.

Although Jehovah's Witnesses will sometimes point to health hazards associated with blood transfusion, such as AIDS and hepatitis, these possible consequences are merely regarded as confirmatory evidence of the wisdom of Jehovah's laws; however, the principal reason for refusing blood is God's law itself, as understood in scripture. Witnesses acknowledge that there have been situations in which members have died through refusing blood. A 1994 edition of *Awake!* carried an article entitled 'Youths Who Have "Power Beyond What Is Normal" ', which featured five young people – between the ages of 12 and 17 – who declined blood transfusions and three of whom died. The article commended their determination and courage, although it was highlighted by the Society's critics. Of course, death is not the inevitable alternative to refusing blood: Jehovah's Witnesses claim to have been particularly proactive in encouraging the medical profession to develop alternatives, such as blood volume expanders. The Society has set up Hospital Liaison Committees (HLCs) in various countries throughout the world for the purpose of alerting the medical profession to its members' wishes and has produced materials itemizing acceptable alternatives. The elders in each congregation have a list of their nearest HLC members, who can be contacted in the event of emergencies. HLC members visit local hospitals to disseminate relevant information and to ensure that they possess relevant forms for patients or their representatives to sign, which clearly set out which forms of treatment are acceptable and which are not. HLC members can be called upon to advise patients when they are admitted to hospital.

Politics

All the issues discussed above arise on account of an imperfect world that is ruled by Satan. In the coming paradise, by contrast, there will be theocratic rule, in which men and women are governed by Jehovah, Jesus Christ and the 144,000 anointed ones who will reign from heaven. The 144,000 are specially chosen by God and not democratically elected. While they await this coming kingdom, the present 'system of things' – the period of time that precedes Armageddon – is governed by Satan, who was cast out of heaven in 1914. It is only through this cosmic battle that Satan and his governments will be defeated. While changes in government, social and economic aid, relief work and social services may improve matters, they are not the ultimate solution to humankind's problems. Jehovah's Witnesses therefore do not support any human government but seek to advance theocratic rule by their evangelizing work. Nationalism and patriotism have no place in their way of life. They therefore steer clear of politics: no Jehovah's Witness would ever stand in a political election, join a political party or attempt to influence government policy through campaigning or protesting, since they are 'no part of the world' (John 15.19).

Because of their conviction that only theocratic government can solve humankind's problems, it is popularly believed that Jehovah's Witnesses do not vote. Many Witnesses avoid voting, but the Society's position is that going to polling booths is a matter of individual conscience. If voting is required by law, then Witnesses will normally obey the law of the land, since Paul instructs the Roman Christians to obey civil authorities (Romans 13.1). The Society offers a number of principles that should be considered regarding voting (Watch Tower 2014e: 212–15). Christians should take care not to compromise their neutrality, remembering that they are 'no part of the world' but part of Christ's kingdom; they should also bear in mind that supporters of successful candidates must share in the responsibility for what the government does. Just as one should not interfere with the affairs of a foreign country in which they live, a similar principle applies to the physical land in which Jehovah's Witnesses reside, since their true country is God's kingdom. They should bear in mind biblical precedents: Nimrod, they believe, acted in opposition to God by setting up his kingdom in Babylon, and the Israelites acted against God by setting up a monarchy in place of the previous theocratic rule under which they had lived (Genesis 10.8-11; 1 Samuel 8.7). Where voting is required by law, they would therefore avoid voting for specific candidates or political parties. Witnesses have been known to spoil their ballot paper, perhaps leaving it blank, or sometimes writing 'I vote for Jehovah'. Children are discouraged from taking part in school elections, for example, for a class captain, since school politics somewhat resembles adult political life (Watch Tower 1983a: 16). However, voting is acceptable in non-political contexts, for example, if one is on a company board. Although voting for congregational office bearers was abolished in 1938, congregations occasionally take votes on minor matters, such as the timing of meetings. All this does not mean that Jehovah's Witnesses are uninterested in world events. 'Watching the World' has been a regular feature in *Awake!* magazine, in which topical issues are mentioned but without expression of any political opinions.

They therefore endeavour to pay their taxes honestly and to fulfil their civic responsibilities. If summoned, they will undertake jury service, and they do not object to taking oaths in a court of law, since the Bible records that the taking of oaths was an ancient Hebrew practice when attempting to settle certain disputes (Exodus 22.10-11; Numbers 5.21-22). Jesus himself was also placed under oath by the High Priest (Matthew 26.63), and when he said, 'Do not swear at all,' he added, 'Just let your word "Yes" mean yes, your "No," no, for what goes beyond these is from the wicked one' (Matthew 5.34, 37). Jehovah's Witnesses conclude that Jesus was forbidding the casual use of swearing, for example, when someone says, 'I swear to God that I didn't do that.' Invoking God or any other guarantor should be unnecessary, since it should be assumed that Jehovah's Witnesses will speak the truth.

War

However, the dictates of civil authorities are not absolute, and if they contravene Jehovah's law, then the Christian should obey Jehovah. When Peter and some of the other apostles continued to preach despite the Sanhedrin's strict orders, they replied, 'We must obey God as ruler rather than men' (Acts 5.29).

Anyone reading the Bible for the first time might be somewhat confused about its stance on war. On the one hand, Jesus is described as the Prince of Peace, and he makes claims like 'If my Kingdom were part of this world, my attendants would have fought' (Isaiah 9.6; John 18.36). On the other hand, he allows the disciples to take two swords into the Garden of Gethsemane (Luke 22.38), and the Hebrew-Aramaic Scriptures are full of accounts of military combat, and even genocide, undertaken in obedience to God's instructions (1 Samuel 15.3). When the Israelites invade Jericho, this is no act of self-defence: God's people have a history of territorial expansion, until they are finally defeated by Nebuchadnezzar's armies. And the present system of things will end in the cosmic battle of Armageddon.

Jehovah's Witnesses navigate their way through these scriptural complexities by claiming, first, that the battles described in the Hebrew-Aramaic Scriptures were undertaken at God's command and for the purpose of his kingdom, and that, if God called upon his people to fight, then they would be obliged to do so. However, present-day wars are not undertaken for any divine purpose but are for the furtherance of material ends and for ideological reasons. The Battle of Armageddon will be a spiritual, not a physical, conflict, and hence only the 144,000, not the great crowd, will engage in that war. Jehovah's Witnesses, therefore, do not describe themselves as pacifist but prefer to use the term 'conscientious objectors' when called upon to undertake military service.

Jehovah's Witnesses have been consistent in refusing to accept conscription. They do not actively protest against wars, but they will seek to use the mechanisms of the state in order to gain exemption from military service, where that is possible. Since 1996, Jehovah's Witnesses have been amenable to accepting alternative service in times of peace, provided it is not under military control, and have worked in hospitals as kitchen staff or nursing auxiliaries. Not all countries, however, make provision for alternative service, and some require the period of alternative service to be substantially longer than that of military service. Where there is no provision for alternatives, Jehovah's Witnesses have been willing to be subjected to fines and to go to prison for their beliefs. Their aims are not to secure either political or legal reforms, although there have been some landmark legal cases which have benefited not only the Watch Tower Society but also other religious and secular organizations; their main aim is service to Jehovah, which takes precedence over obligations to the state, and they are strictly neutral with regard to political systems. As they often point out, their actions in refusing military service do not weaken a country's military strength, since Jehovah's Witnesses in opposing countries are taking a similar stance.

In sum, the description of being in the world but not of the world sums up Jehovah's Witnesses' lifestyle. They are not a closed community, but engage in everyday worldly activities. They obey the law of the land, unless doing so would transgress Jehovah's law, for they regard themselves as being part of Jehovah's kingdom and must always accept Jehovah's theocratic rule above all else.

7

Festivals and rites of passage

Attitudes to conventional celebrations

Critics often portray Jehovah's Witnesses in a negative light, emphasizing what they appear to miss out on rather than what they actively do. It is easy to focus on their non-celebration of Christmas, Easter, birthdays and other festivals, while ignoring the fact that they find other ways of gaining pleasure and other causes for celebration.

Saints' days and Easter have never been celebrated, from the very inception of the Bible Students' organization. Saints' days, together with the veneration of the Virgin Mary, have never been popular in Protestant circles, and Jehovah's Witnesses have maintained this tradition. Saints, they believe, are the creation of an apostate Church and never featured in the earliest Christian communities. They avoid the celebration of Easter on the grounds that it is a pagan festival, and its non-celebration predated the Society's origins. The problem about Easter stems from the Adventist tradition, which links Jesus' death and resurrection to the Jewish calendar rather than to the days of the week (Friday through to Sunday), the latter being the custom of other mainstream churches.

Jehovah's Witnesses have no problem in affirming Jesus' death and resurrection. The early Bible Students were happy to celebrate the resurrection, and indeed the first edition of their song book includes two traditional Easter hymns – 'Jesus Christ is risen today' and 'The Lord is risen indeed' (Watch Tower 1890). Although it is acknowledged that Jesus died on a Friday, and rose on a Sunday morning, Adventists did not link this part of their liturgical calendar to the days of the week but in accordance with Jewish practice. Seventh-day Adventism, where worship takes place on Saturday, being the Jewish sabbath, precludes a celebration of the festival at a regular weekly service. In Second Adventism, while Sunday remained the day of worship, the dating of Good Friday and Easter was related to Jewish months, although there appears to have been some disagreement on the precise dating. The communities with whom Russell associated favoured 14 Nisan for the date of Christ's death, which did not necessarily fall on a Friday; thus, 16 Nisan – the date for the resurrection – would fall on a weekday more often than not. In early copies of Zion's Watch Tower we find invitations to the Memorial (the celebration of the Lord's Evening Meal) on the date corresponding to 14 Nisan, with a further invitation to celebrate Christ's resurrection two days later. There is only a one in seven chance that this would fall on a Sunday.

Watch Tower thinking came to associate Easter with pagan religion, and it was noted that the name derived from Eostre, or Ostara, the Anglo-Saxon goddess of spring and the dawn. Easter eggs and bunnies are associated with fertility, and thus, as one Watch Tower publication puts it, 'Easter, therefore, is really a fertility rite thinly disguised as a celebration of Christ's resurrection' (Watch Tower 2014e: 144–59). The author continues, 'Would Jehovah condone the use of a filthy fertility rite to commemorate his Son's resurrection? Never! (2 Corinthians 6:17, 18)'. The Bible contains no instruction to celebrate Easter, and in any case Jehovah's Witnesses lay emphasis on Christ's death being the ransom sacrifice that restores humanity from their sinful state.

Christmas

The early Bible Students celebrated Christmas, in line with most other denominations. Although it was recognized that 25 December was probably not the authentic date of Jesus' birth, it was nonetheless considered appropriate to mark the event, and it was customary at the Brooklyn Bethel to erect a Christmas tree. Instead of his usual morning greeting 'Good morning', Russell would wish everyone a happy Christmas, and there would be a celebratory meal later in the day (Watch Tower 1975a: 147). This was to change under Rutherford's presidency, when the festival's pagan roots were identified, and the year 1926 marked the Society's last celebration at Brooklyn, as well as at the branch offices in Britain and the rest of Europe.

Jehovah's Witnesses hold that there is no biblical injunction to celebrate Christmas and no evidence that it was early Christian practice. The date of Christmas was not defined until the fourth century, when Christianity became the Roman Empire's official religion, and Christmas came to replace the Roman Saturnalia, which took place at the winter solstice. Jehovah's Witnesses believe that it was unlikely that Jesus was born at this time of the year, since the Bible states that there were shepherds keeping flocks in their fields when Jesus was born, and the December weather would make this a most unlikely practice.

The Society's views on Christmas appear to be associated with a book titled *The Two Babylons* by Alexander Hislop (1807–1865), a Free Church of Scotland minister, which was first published in 1858. The book obviously appealed to Rutherford. This work was never mentioned in Watch Tower literature in the Russell era. Superficially the book looks erudite, going into detail about the origins of festivals such as Easter and Christmas, but Hislop's analysis is largely based on dubious etymology, which most scholars would reject. According to Hislop, all false religion derives from Nimrod, the first Bible character to be named as a king and whose subjects were dispersed throughout the earth when the Tower of Babel collapsed (Genesis 11.8-9). The volume has not been cited in Watch Tower literature since 1989, however, and appears to have fallen out of favour. Hislop claims that Nimrod's birthday was 25 December and that Nimrod became defined as the sun god who was slain by his enemies. The Yule log represents his 'cutting down' (i.e. his death), but he came back to life, his return (or regrowth) being symbolized by the Christmas tree. All this associates Christmas with false religion and explains why Witnesses avoid the festival. Watch Tower literature asserts that it is more likely that Jesus was born around October, 2 BCE.

A further consideration about Christmas relates to the giving of presents. Jehovah's Witnesses believe that Christmas has become unduly commercialized and associated with selfish desires for extravagant items: giving presents is also associated with the visit of the Magi, who brought Jesus gold, frankincense and myrrh, and Jehovah's Witnesses have a different interpretation of the story from the more conventional one. The Bible does not specify that there were three wise men – this is a popular assumption because three types of gifts are mentioned – and the Magi are not given names, which later tradition has added. The Bible does not say that they were kings, or that the star was sent by God, and they do not visit the manger, as they are so frequently depicted on Christmas cards. They arrive at a house, when Jesus appears to be a young child rather than a baby (Matthew 2.9,11), and they gave gifts to Jesus, not to each other. Coming from the East, the Magi were probably Zoroastrians and thus adherents of false religion, and their searching for signs in the stars indicates that they were astrologers and hence practitioners of the occult. They are therefore not the commendable characters that Christian piety and popular culture supposes. Additionally, Witnesses believe that they aided King Herod and that by visiting him they put Jesus' life in jeopardy; however, God thwarted their plan to return to Jerusalem to inform Herod of Jesus' whereabouts, causing them to return by another route (Watch Tower 1979: 30).

New Year celebrations, which come hard on the heels of Christmas, likewise receive disapprobation, even though they are not connected with misunderstandings about Jesus' birth. They are also associated with false religion, being traceable back to ancient Babylon in the third millennium BCE, where the god Marduk purportedly decided the nation's fortunes for the coming year. One Watch Tower article mentions the association of 1 January with the Roman God Janus (Watch Tower 2005c: 4–7) and points out that it can involve heavy drinking, leading to road accidents and domestic violence (Watch Tower 2002a: 20–1). Even for those who can celebrate moderately, New Year festivities are associated with superstitions; the same article refers to a South American belief that good luck will result from bringing in the New Year standing on one's right foot, and a Slovak tradition in which putting money or fish scales under one's tablecloth is reckoned to offer prosperity and guard against ill fortune.

Similar criticisms apply to non-Christian celebrations, for example, the Chinese New Year in February. Not only is it associated with good luck but also with ancestor veneration. In East Asian countries it is popularly believed that one's ancestors are present on New Year's Eve, and banquets are spread, leaving places for deceased family members (Watch Tower 2009b: 20–3). Although the Bible teaches respect for parents, belief that they remain present after death is contrary to scripture, since the Bible states that 'the dead know nothing at all' (Ecclesiastes 9.5), meaning that the dead are not conscious. Jehovah's Witnesses believe that the dead – with the exception of the 144,000 – are asleep until they are resurrected after Armageddon. Any spirits that may be present at such gatherings, therefore, cannot be spirits of the dead but must be evil spirits masquerading as one's ancestors, trying to bring the living under evil control. Christian should therefore avoid participating in occultist practices such as these.

Birthdays

The avoidance of birthday celebrations may appear to be linked with the abandonment of Christmas festivities. However, the celebration of birthdays appears to have continued for some considerable time after the last Christmas party in 1926. In the Society's early years, marking birthdays was positively encouraged. In 1905 a short devotional booklet was published, entitled *Daily Heavenly Manna for the Household of Faith*, commonly referred to as 'Daily Manna', and reissued in 1907 with the subtitle 'Daily Heavenly Manna and Birthday Record'. The booklet contained devotional material on the left-hand page for each day of the year, leaving the right page blank for its owner to invite friends to enter their names against the date of their birthday, and sometimes a photograph; the owner might then send their friends a card and birthday greetings. In 1909 at a convention in Jacksonville, Russell was ushered on to the stage to receive a surprise birthday present of a box of oranges, grapefruit and pineapples (Watch Tower 1998: 30–1).

It is not altogether clear precisely when birthday celebrations ceased. A brief paragraph in *The Golden Age* in 1936 reads,

> There are but two such celebrations mentioned in the Scriptures, one of the heathen king Pharaoh of Egypt, in the days of Joseph, and the other of that Herod the celebration of whose birthday cost John the Baptist his life. In the Bible there is no instance of celebrations of birthdays by any of God's people, either His typical people or His actual people. (Watch Tower 1936: 499) [Text as original]

This does not amount to a prohibition, however, and it seems that some Witnesses continued to celebrate birthdays. One *Watchtower* reader wrote the following in 1940:

> I just can't help letting you know how much I appreciate the phonograph which came to me on the morning after the 8th, which was my 80th birthday. It was indeed a birthday gift from Jehovah, to be used in proclaiming his name. (Watch Tower 1940a: 16)

It appears that the celebrations were abandoned by 1951, when the Society's new book *What Has Religion Done for Mankind?* discusses birthdays mentioned in the Bible, and a reader's letter in *The Watchtower* elicits the advice that such events should be avoided (Watch Tower 1951a: 234; 1951b: 607). Jehovah's Witnesses regard the birth of a child as an occasion for rejoicing; when John the Baptist is born, neighbours and relatives visit his mother Elizabeth and share her joy (Luke 1.57), and therefore some members will send cards to celebrate the birth of a child, although not for subsequent birthdays. While there is no explicit prohibition on celebrating birthdays in scripture, Ecclesiastes somewhat gloomily states that 'the day of death is better than the day of birth' (Ecclesiastes 7.1), and Witnesses will note that only two birthdays are mentioned in the Bible: both were celebrated by pagans – the Egyptian Pharaoh and the Roman governor King Herod (Genesis 40.20-22; Matthew 14.6-11) – and on both occasions there was an unpleasant outcome. On his birthday Pharaoh condemns his chief baker to be hanged, and when Herodias' daughter pleases Herod with her dancing, he undertakes to grant her any request, whereupon she asks for the head of John the Baptist to be delivered on a salver, and so John is executed.

The biblical authors record the years of birth and death of the patriarchs and the kings but not the exact dates. Witnesses hold that reliance on birth dates is connected with astrology, since astrologers use such information to predict one's fortune. Practices associated with birthdays include birthday cakes, which, they point out, originated with the ancient Greeks, celebrating the birth of Artemis. Lighting and blowing out candles, accompanied by making a wish, are superstitious magical practices. The Bible never mentions candles, only lamps. There are two biblical passages which might seem to mention birthday celebrations without condemnation, and on which Watch Tower literature comments. One is in the book of Job, who is portrayed as having seven sons and three daughters, and it is stated that 'each of his sons would hold a banquet at his house on his own set day' (Job 1.4). However, the Hebrew word translated as 'day' here is not the same as the word 'birthday' in Genesis 40.20 and thus need not imply that Job's sons held birthday celebrations. The Society reckons that it is more likely that the family held a week-long celebration of some kind, in which each son would act as host on successive days (Watch Tower 2006c: 13). The second reference is to 'the day of our king' (Hosea 7.5): Watch Tower literature points out that the reference is to an apostate king and that it is not clear whether it is his birthday that is being celebrated or the anniversary of his accession. At any rate, the party does not seem to have been a resounding success: Hosea continues, 'Princes have become sick – They are enraged because of wine.'

More generally, Jehovah's Witnesses believe that birthdays focus unduly on the individual, whose day is being celebrated, and are materialistic, encouraging children – and indeed adults – to covet material possessions, which do not promote spiritual development or ultimately lead to happiness. If Jehovah's Witnesses want to give someone a present, they can do so at any time of the year. Some families adopt the practice of holding 'presents days', where family members exchange gifts, but not on birthdays or traditional festival days. Other families will simply give someone a present when they feel it is needed; as one Jehovah's Witness once said to me, 'If my son wants a skateboard, and I think he should have one, then I can do it at any time – he doesn't have to wait until his birthday.'

Baptism

Jehovah's Witnesses observe two rites that they regard as biblical: baptism and the Memorial. Baptism is important, being the public acknowledgement that an individual has become one of Jehovah's Witnesses. It is not undertaken lightly but involves extensive preparation, and it can only be done in the context of Jehovah's true organization. Although mainstream Christian denominations largely accept each other's baptism as valid, believing that there is one Church that transcends denominational barriers, Jehovah's Witnesses do not take this view. Exemption from baptism cannot be gained by invoking a past rite undergone within some other Christian denomination, since mainstream Christian churches are believed to have abandoned the original apostles' teachings and organization. Baptism should be carried out in accordance with first-century Christian practice, which was by total immersion in water and as an expression of commitment as an adult. Jehovah's Witnesses do not accept child baptism, or baptism that is carried out by sprinkling or pouring water over the candidate's head. When Jesus was baptized, he presented himself to John the Baptist at the River Jordan, and the Bible clearly states that he 'came up from the water' at the completion of the rite (Matthew 3.16). In Western countries and in Australasia it is customary to administer baptism in an Assembly Hall or in a large stadium, where it is publicly visible. Assembly Halls typically have a section of floor that can be lifted to access a small reservoir, and where baptisms take place in properties not owned by the Society, such as a stadium, a portable pool is installed. With modern technology, it is now usual for baptisms to take place outside the auditorium and to be viewed on closed-circuit television. However, baptism need not necessarily be public: the Bible does not state whether there was anyone present at Jesus' baptism apart from Jesus and John. In countries where the Society is under threat, baptisms have often been secret, and during the Covid epidemic, when it was not possible to hold public baptisms, some Witnesses were baptized at home in bath tubs or in garden pools. The baptism could be disseminated online with facilities such as Zoom, which gave it a public dimension.

Although Jehovah's Witnesses reject child baptism, there is no stipulated minimum age of eligibility. I have personally known a thirteen-year-old youth being accepted for baptism, and one ex-member reports having been baptized at the age of eleven – in the late 1950s, where the requirements were not so stringent. (Zieman 2016: 55–8). Today the baptismal candidate must undergo extensive instruction and must be able to respond appropriately to a range of questions on which he or she must satisfy the elders. Such instruction is typically done individually, although small groups of two or three may be brought together for this purpose. There are now some sixty questions in all, and they are itemized in a way that is somewhat reminiscent of a mainstream Christian catechism which was used in previous generations. The precise nature and wording of these questions has undergone modification over the years. The current 2019 publication *Organized to Do Jehovah's Will* divides them into two categories: Christian belief and Christian living. The first part addresses the basic teachings of the Watch Tower Society, and candidates should be able to explain Jehovah's nature, why it is important to use his personal name and how one can address him in prayer. They should, above all, be familiar with the nature of Jesus Christ and particularly his ransom sacrifice. The questions move on to cover the role of the Governing Body, the holy spirit, the nature of Satan, what happens when one dies and the coming kingdom of which one might expect to be part. Part Two aims to ensure that candidates know how to behave appropriately as members of Jehovah's organization. The topics that are covered include marriage and family life, sexual morality, respect for life, attitudes to popular celebrations and recreational activities, and awareness of the Society's stance on blood.

At the baptism, the following questions are publicly put to the candidates, who must answer in the affirmative:

1. Have you repented of your sins, dedicated yourself to Jehovah and accepted his way of salvation through Jesus Christ?

2. Do you understand that your baptism identifies you as one of Jehovah's Witnesses in association with Jehovah's organization? (Watch Tower 2019a: 206).

The elders who immerse the candidates in the water do not recite the formula, 'I baptize you in the name of the Father, the Son, and the Holy Spirit' (Matthew 28.19), which is considered an essential part of mainstream baptismal liturgy. It is held that their practice is effectively a baptism in the threefold name, without it having to be explicitly stated. It is customary for the congregation to applaud candidates as they emerge from the baptismal pool, since it is a joyous occasion. Some Witnesses send greetings cards to candidates to mark the event, particularly in the United States; this practice is not so common elsewhere.

Baptism is a once-in-a-lifetime rite and is not normally repeated. However, there can be occasional circumstances in which it is readministered, for example, if someone had undergone baptism but was ineligible at the time – perhaps because they had been living with a partner to whom they were not married. However, baptism cannot be readministered if one fails to live up to one's commitment. Even if someone has been disfellowshipped, repentance is the way back into the community, not re-baptism. One might compare the situation with marriage: if one partner is unfaithful to the other, the remedy is reconciliation and mending one's ways, not undergoing another marriage ceremony. I have known one Jehovah's Witness who underwent a second baptism since she had arrived late for the elder's baptismal talk; she later felt that she should undergo baptism again and was allowed to do so. This is extremely rare, however, particularly in view of the preparation and prior explanation that is given.

The Memorial

The other rite in which Jehovah's Witnesses take part is the annual Memorial of Christ's Death. Unlike Easter, the celebration of Jesus' death is explicitly instructed in the Bible. Jesus says, 'Keep doing this in remembrance of me' (1 Corinthians 11.24). Mainstream Christian liturgies typically use the expression 'Do this in remembrance of me'; however, the instruction in the original Greek uses the present rather than the aorist imperative, thus indicating it was not a one-off directive to the disciples but that the rite was to be celebrated in perpetuity.

The Memorial is not an elaborate ceremony. While some mainstream churches employ extravagant ritual for celebrating the Eucharist – priests in ornate robes, a complex liturgy, perhaps choral singing, incense, recitation of the Nicene Creed, meticulous acts of consecration and proper disposal of unconsumed bread and wine – Jehovah's Witnesses note that the original final meal between Jesus and his disciples was held in a simple upper room. The Bible does not mention all the details, except that it needed preparation, and Witnesses will prepare, not only by ensuring that the premises are attractive but often by leafleting the neighbourhood, inviting the public to attend. Originally, only Bible Students (Jehovah's Witnesses after 1931) were invited, and until 1938 only the anointed class attended; but after that date members of the great crowd were also permitted to be present, and today all are invited, irrespective of any religious affiliation.

Mainstream scholars continue to debate whether Jesus' final meal was a Passover celebration or indeed whether it was a genuine historical event. However, Jehovah's Witnesses are confident that this was a Passover, and they follow the Jewish practice of waiting until after sunset before commencing the Memorial. The bread and wine are referred to as 'emblems', rather than 'elements', the latter being the mainstream Christian term: this is to highlight the belief that no miracle takes place, such as transubstantiation, which is the Roman Catholic doctrine that in some real sense the bread and wine miraculously become Christ's body and blood. Jesus' words of institution, as found in the New World Translation, are 'This means my body'. The Watch Tower Society acknowledges that this is not a literal translation of the Greek, which reads, 'This is my body', but argue that this rendering is for clarification; Jesus could not have meant that the bread and wine were literally his body and blood, since his body was there, beside the disciples, and his body and blood had not yet been broken and shared, since the event anticipated his death.

The bread is unleavened, made according to a simple recipe, instructions for which can be found online. Flour is simply made into a dough, without yeast or any other additives, and baked for about ten minutes on an oiled tray. Jewish matzoth can be used, provided they do not contain salt or eggs.

The wine should be red and unfortified; while some Christian denominations whose members disapprove of alcohol substitute grape juice for wine, this is not acceptable for Jehovah's Witnesses, whose literature points out that the Passover season was long after the grape harvest, and it would be impossible to prevent fermentation for that length of time.

The service begins with a song that is relevant to the event, after which an elder says an extempore prayer. The main part, which is a Bible talk, follows; the speaker uses an outline provided by the Society, which typically has a fourfold pattern. It begins with an explanation of how sin entered the world through Adam and Eve's transgression; the second part recounts how Christ's ransom sacrifice provides redemption. Third, the speaker reminds the congregation of the distinction between the 144,000 and the great crowd, explaining that only the former should partake of the emblems. This restriction lies in the fact that Jesus was addressing his immediate disciples and says that he would not eat or drink with them again until the kingdom of God comes (Luke 22.14-18), thus implying that eating with his disciples would only resume in heaven. At this point in the talk the speaker pauses, and another elder is invited on to the platform to give an extempore prayer before the distribution of the unleavened bread. Elders then come forward to receive the plates containing the bread, which are then passed around the congregation. Because few of the 144,000 remain on earth, it is unusual for anyone to consume the bread and wine, and more often than not, the emblems are respectfully passed unconsumed, from one attendee to another. After the elders return with the plates of bread, another elder offers a prayer, and the wine is then passed around in a similar manner. Finally, the speaker ends his talk by reminding the congregation that they should show gratitude for Christ's sacrifice and recommends that they continue to attend congregation meetings and persevere with their field ministry. The Bible records that Jesus' last meal ended with singing, hence the meeting ends with another song.

Marriage

Marriage is not an expectation: neither Jesus nor Paul were married, but Jesus' approval of marriage is indicated by his presence at the wedding at Cana at the beginning of his ministry (John 2.1-11). Jehovah's Witnesses are not obliged to have a religious ceremony, but most will want to do so, and the Kingdom Hall is the obvious venue. In order to be eligible for a Kingdom Hall wedding, both partners must be baptized members, or at least be progressing towards baptism. Jehovah's Witnesses are strongly encouraged not to marry outside the organization; Paul wrote, 'Do not become unevenly yoked with unbelievers' (2 Corinthians 6.14), and a marriage ceremony would not be permitted in a Kingdom Hall if one partner was a non-believer.

Finding an appropriate marriage partner in a relatively small congregation can be a problem, since there will probably be only a small number of members of the opposite sex of similar age in a community of between one and two hundred, and conventions can therefore provide an opportunity to widen one's options and initiate relationships. Online dating is not encouraged, although there are one or two dating sites that purport to offer relationships with other members. Because of the Society's views on extramarital sex, it is expected that the man and woman will not show undue intimacy. In order to give appropriate guidance to young people, the Governing Body endorsed the two-volume publication *Questions Young People Ask – Answers That Work* (see Chapter 6), which includes advice for developing relationships with the opposite sex. A young person should not invite someone out on a date unless they consider marriage to be a possibility; casual dating is discouraged. (Interestingly, the Society has no problem with the woman taking the initiative.) If teenagers want more transitory company of members of the opposite sex, they are encouraged to find it in groups, rather than in a one-to-one situation. Watch Tower literature identifies three types of inappropriate behaviour that the Bible condemns: fornication, uncleanness and loose (or 'brazen') conduct. Young people are reminded of the potential consequences of yielding to the temptation to have sexual relationships before marriage: they might acquire sexually transmitted diseases, the woman risks unwanted pregnancy and, importantly, the couple incur God's disfavour. Paul writes,

> For this is the will of God, that you should be holy and abstain from sexual immorality. Each one of you should know how to control his own body in holiness and honor, not with greedy, uncontrolled sexual passion like the nations have that do not know God. No one should go beyond proper limits and take advantage of his brother in this matter, because Jehovah exacts punishment for all these things, just as we told you previously and also strongly warned you. (1 Thessalonians 4.3-6)

'Uncleanness' is a quality that is not exclusively confined to sexual morality but encompasses 'physical, moral, and spiritual uncleanness' (Watch Tower 2018a: 481). In the context of dating, examples of uncleanness would be heavy petting, conversation that provoked sexual arousal, or 'sexting', the last of which has increasingly become a concern to some Jehovah's Witnesses.

'Brazen conduct' is the widest category of transgressions and need not refer exclusively to acts of sexual immorality. The Society defines it as 'acts that are serious violations of God's laws and that reflect a brazen or boldly contemptuous attitude; a spirit that betrays disrespect or even contempt for authority, laws, and standards' (Watch Tower 2020a: 12:15(1)). In the film *To Verdener* (2008, English title 'Worlds Apart'), the protagonist Sara, who is a seventeen-year-old Jehovah's Witness, strikes up a relationship with Teis, who is an atheist, and goes to visit his home. After missing the last train, she returns to Teis's apartment, where she spends the night in a separate room. Although no sexual impropriety was involved, her action constituted brazen conduct on several grounds. She should not have been dating a non-believer; the visit was undertaken without her parents' knowledge; and their spending the night in the same residence laid them open to obvious temptation. Predictably, Sara, being impenitent, is disfellowshipped when her conduct is discovered.

In sum, the Society's advice about romantic attachments is to ensure that partners should either be baptized or moving towards baptism and that their activities are conducted in an open manner, never clandestinely. If they are young, parents should be involved and their advice sought and heeded. Although it is not a requirement, the presence of a chaperone is recommended, since having a third party present ensures that a couple do not get carried away by physical desire. The consequence of chaperoning, however, is that the first time the couple are alone together may be on their wedding night.

Once married, sexual relationships are of course permitted. At one point the Society was prescriptive about sexual practices, and forbade oral and anal intercourse, and sex when the woman was menstruating. The Society now takes a less prescriptive attitude to such matters and no longer wishes to intrude on what happens in the bedroom, allowing such issues to be matters of conscience. The same applies to contraception: Jehovah's Witnesses believe that sex can be enjoyed and not necessarily practised solely for procreation; hence, they are amenable to methods of contraception, which are also matters of conscience for the couple.

If a couple are already married in a legally recognized way, they may repeat the ceremony in a Kingdom Hall if they wish to reaffirm their vows before Jehovah (Watch Tower 2006e: 18–22; 2006f: 28–31). However, unlike baptism, Jehovah's Witnesses do not exclusively recognize marriages conducted within the organization; a legally valid marriage involves the same commitments whether it is entered into by a civil ceremony, in a mainstream Christian church or in a temple or mosque.

Marriage is normally preceded by counselling, in which elders will recommend relevant Watch Tower literature about marriage and its responsibilities. The elders need to be satisfied about the couple's eligibility to marry, which goes beyond the bare legal requirements: the couple must have 'scriptural freedom' to marry. For example, if one partner is divorced, the elders will need to assure themselves that the divorce was on the grounds of adultery and for no other reason. Most of the invited guests will probably be baptized members and their children, but it is acceptable to invite family and friends who are not Jehovah's Witnesses, provided that they have not been disfellowshipped from the organization and that their lifestyle does not grossly conflict with Jehovah's standards.

Weddings are relatively simple, and extravagance is avoided. The bride may have a wedding dress, often made by sisters or friends of the congregation; it should be modest, not low-cut. The Kingdom Hall may be decorated, for example, with flowers, subject to the elders' approval. Only music from the Society's own song book may be used; the couple may not request popular music from CDs, as increasingly happens in mainstream Christian weddings. An elder presides over the ceremony, and the couple may choose another elder to give the wedding talk. The talk reminds the bride and groom, using biblical quotations, of how God joined the first human couple in marriage and intended it to be a permanent union with love and happiness. They are reminded that the husband is the head of the household, but not a tyrant, and that the wife's complementary role is supportive, not servile or inferior. The couple should set aside time to talk, pray, study the Bible and worship together. As in mainstream marriage services, the couple make their vows and are pronounced husband and wife. The presiding elder may then introduce the couple to the congregation with words like 'It is my pleasure to introduce to this marriage gathering Brother and Sister [surname]'.

The ceremony may or may not involve the couple exchanging rings. In the past there was some uncertainty about whether the use of rings was a pagan practice, but it is noted that the Bible mentions rings with apparent approval. King Ahasuerus gives Haman's ring to Mordecai as a symbol of authority, and when the prodigal son returns home his father orders his servants to place a ring on his finger (Esther 8.2; Luke 15.22). At a practical level, a ring makes it clear that a couple are married and not simply living together, and that each partner is not available for dating. Popular customs such as throwing rice or confetti should be avoided, since these are regarded as superstitious pagan practices; greetings cards are welcome but should not wish the couple 'good luck' or include good luck symbols such as horseshoes.

The wedding is usually followed by a reception. Jehovah's Witnesses tend not to have extravagant gatherings. It is quite common in the UK for them to hire a community or school hall and for meals to be prepared by friends or ordered from a takeaway. They may hire a band or make their own entertainment, but the music should not be so loud as to prevent conversation; dancing is acceptable, so long as it is reasonably restrained; alcoholic beverages are permitted, but not drinking to excess. The wedding should not be organized in a way that troubles anyone's conscience, or causes 'stumbling'.

Marriage is for life. The wedding vows taken by the bridegroom are as follows:

I – [name] – take you – [name] – to be my wedded wife, to love and to cherish in accordance with the divine law as set forth in the Holy Scriptures for Christian husbands, for as long as we both shall live together on earth according to God's marital arrangement. (Watch Tower 2007d)

The bride's vows reverse 'wife' and 'husband' but insert 'and deeply to respect' after 'cherish': Paul recommends that 'the wife should have deep respect for her husband' (Ephesians 5.33).

Two points should be noted about the couple's promises. First, the phrase 'as long as we both shall live together on earth' indicates that marriage is dissolved in death. Marriage is not eternal, as it is for members of the Church of Jesus Christ of Latter-day Saints. (What can be expected in the everlasting paradise will be discussed in the next chapter.) Because death terminates the marriage relationship, a widow or widower is free to remarry, as if they were single (Watch Tower 2018f: 10–14). Second, because the wedding couple are entering into a lifelong relationship, divorce does not end the marriage, except on the biblical ground of 'sexual immorality' (Matthew 5.31).

It is not uncommon for someone who is already married to undergo baptism as a Jehovah's Witness, while the other partner remains outside the organization; more often than not it is the woman who joins without her partner. Inevitably, such a situation may require negotiation. Jehovah's Witnesses believe that, notwithstanding the husband's unwillingness to accept the truth, the biblical injunction for wives to obey their husbands still stands; hence, a wife should be obedient and supportive, so long as this does not involve contravening Jehovah's law. There have been occasions where a believing wife has come under pressure from the rest of the family to celebrate traditional festivals; if the wife is asked to cook a Christmas turkey, her conscience must decide whether obedience to her husband takes priority over avoiding pagan festivals.

Mention should be made about polygamy. Numerous biblical characters had multiple wives, but Jehovah's Witnesses contend that God instituted only monogamy as the proper marital institution and that he only tolerated polygamy as a temporary measure. The Bible does not record any early Christian convert as being polygamous, and the teachings of Jesus and Paul emphasize monogamy as God's requirement (Matthew 19.4-5; 1 Timothy 3.2). While Jehovah's Witness would not seek a second husband or wife, the question of polygamy arises when evangelizing in countries where polygamy is permitted. What is the situation of a polygamous husband (not so usually a polygamous wife) who has already committed himself to multiple marriage partners? This is a problem that has exercised mainstream Christian missionaries, not always with an agreed solution, but it is an issue on which Jehovah's Witnesses are uncompromising. In a 1947 edition of The Watchtower, it was made clear that, irrespective of local practice, no allowance could be made for polygamy (Watch Tower 1947: 22–3), and a letter was sent to congregations who had accepted polygamous members, giving them six months to regularize their marital affairs. Effectively, this meant a husband putting away all wives except his first, since only a first marriage is regarded as consistent with God's law. In his visit to Africa that year, president Knorr reinforced this message. This did not mean that a polygamous husband should not continue to care for his subsequent wives, but in order to be eligible for baptism a candidate must have one marriage partner only.

Old age and death

There comes a time when health and mobility deteriorate. For most, this comes later in life, but younger people can also be unfortunate victims of disability or terminal illness. Witnesses hold that they should continue with their ministry service as far as they are able, and it is not uncommon to see a wheelchair user at a literature cart, or even engaged in house-to-house visiting. However, there often comes a point at which a Witness cannot be independent and needs special care. If a Witness has to go into a care home, there are still opportunities to spread the truth is to other residents. The Watch Tower Society does not organize its own care facilities, but a number of Witnesses have set up their own private care homes with facilities for the elderly. In Britain in 1985, Ida Eccles, a former pioneer who was then 79 became in need of care. One of the local brothers had come to own a guest house, which he used as a large family home, and he decided to offer Sister Eccles appropriate care there. This was a small beginning to a number of care homes in the UK, and at the time of writing there are four, with a fifth being developed. They have adopted the name 'Jah Jireh': the Hebrew word 'Jah' is a contraction of 'Jehovah' and appears in the Hebrew-Aramaic scriptures in numerous places. Jah Jireh (or Jehovah-jireh) means 'Jehovah will provide' and is an allusion to the story of Abraham and Isaac (Genesis 22.1-18). After being called upon to sacrifice his only son Isaac, Isaac notes that they have forgotten to bring a lamb to Mount Moriah, whereupon Abraham tells him that Jehovah will provide the sacrificial animal. Once Abraham has shown his willingness to sacrifice his son, an angel commands him to desist, and he finds a ram to substitute. He then names the place Jehovah-jireh, since Jehovah provided for Abraham and Isaac.

These homes are not the Society's property but are privately owned and managed. They offer the obvious advantage of enabling the residents to enjoy the ethos of a Jehovah's Witness community, free from any worldly or harmful associations, since all the residents and most of the staff are Jehovah's Witnesses. Residents' spiritual as well as physical needs are catered for, since they can be taken out to attend congregation meetings and conventions if they are able. Elders will come to celebrate the annual Memorial at these homes, so that all have the opportunity to attend this important gathering.

Death

A Kingdom Hall funeral is granted to baptized members or their children; however, non-Witness friends and family are likely to attend, and indeed Jehovah's Witnesses' funerals are open to the public. Family are recommended to keep the event simple and brief: as one *Watchtower* article states, it should be 'dignified, modest, and pleasing to God' (Watch Tower 2002b: 29–32). The coffin, for example, is usually relatively inexpensive, in order to use money wisely. There should not be excessive displays of grief, since Jehovah's Witnesses confidently expect the resurrection, so there are no wakes and no celebrations of death anniversaries. Watch Tower literature reminds readers of how, when Jairus' daughter died, Jesus commanded the hired mourners, who were wailing excessively, to cease (Luke 8.52). Watch Tower literature suggests that Witnesses should give an advance written directive expressing such preferences, and most funeral directors in English-speaking and European countries have access to advice from the Society about how the ceremony is conducted.

The funeral service is conducted by an elder of the family's choice and consists of a song, extempore prayer and a brief talk. The talk covers four points: why people die, the condition of the dead, the hope for the dead and how the congregation can benefit from being there. The first point recounts Adam's sin and the penalty imposed by God; the second reminds the congregation that for most Witnesses death involves unconscious sleep until the resurrection; and the third part of the talk mentions the hope to which believers are entitled owing to Christ's ransom sacrifice. This third section will typically acknowledge the distinction between the 144,000 anointed class and the great crowd, and the deceased's resurrection hope. The presiding elder may make some brief reference to the deceased's life, particularly if they had undertaken commendable service, but care is taken not to eulogize the person. In the final section the congregation might be reminded of life's brevity and how death's certainty should make them reflect on how they are using their lives. After the Kingdom Hall service, the funeral party will proceed either to a cemetery or crematorium: there is no preference about whether a Jehovah's Witness should be buried or cremated.

Although the funeral does not include a eulogy, some Jehovah's Witnesses are given a memorial service (not to be confused with the annual Memorial) some time afterwards. As with the funeral, friends as well as Witnesses are invited. The memorial includes a couple of songs, prayer and a more extended discourse by an elder, who might outline the member's life, focusing particularly on their active service to the Society. As well as looking to the past, the service is used to remind the congregation of the future hope of being reunited after the resurrection. The service can be followed by refreshments – something that does not normally happen at the end of congregation meetings – making the event a social as well as a religious gathering. Sympathy cards for relatives are welcome, as it is natural to have fond memories. One Jehovah's Witness who runs a small aromatherapy firm has named one of the scents after her late mother.

A Jehovah's Witness elder might be asked to conduct the funeral of a non-believing family member or someone who has been disfellowshipped. This is a matter of conscience, but it cannot be conducted in a Kingdom Hall; the ceremony would be conducted on other premises, such as a crematorium chapel. The situation can also arise where a Jehovah's Witness may be invited to the funeral of a non-believer at a location such as a mainstream church. Although worshipping in a mainstream congregation is normally disallowed, and even a potential ground for disfellowshipping, death provides exceptional circumstances, and whether or not a Jehovah's Witness should attend is a matter of conscience. However, anyone attending a funeral in a mainstream congregation, or in some other religious community, should take care to avoid active participation in unacceptable practices. This might include singing hymns that proclaimed doctrines contrary to the Society's teachings or actions such as making the sign of the cross, lighting candles or receiving the sacrament at a requiem Mass.

8

Expectations

End-time expectations

'They keep changing the dates' and 'What's their latest date for the end of the world?' are comments that are typically made about Jehovah's Witnesses. Such remarks betray a serious lack of knowledge about the Witnesses' belief system. While there have undoubtedly been some changes in expectations over the years, and some disappointments, it is not true that they make continual changes to the end-time calculations, or that Witnesses spend their time arithmetically calculating dates.

Some clarifications must be made about their views on end-time prophecy. First, the expression 'end of the world' is misleading: Jehovah's Witnesses do not expect the world to end, since they believe that they will live in an everlasting paradise on the earth. What they do expect is an end to the present 'system of things', by which they mean forms of government which are incapable of solving the world's problems and which are ultimately ruled by Satan. This system will be replaced by theocratic rule over the world, once Satan is defeated at the Battle of Armageddon, an event which Jehovah's Witnesses believe is 'just around the corner'.

Clarification is also needed about what Watch Tower publications mean by prophecy. Jehovah's Witnesses do not claim to be prophets in the sense of special divine messengers with a new revelation. Charles Taze Russell and Joseph Franklin Rutherford did not claim to have received some new revelation, unlike Joseph Smith, who founded the Church of Jesus Christ of Latter-day Saints, or Sun Myung Moon, who established the Unification Church, both of whom introduced extra-biblical teachings. By contrast, the Watch Tower Society offers no new extra-biblical revelation but seeks to interpret the revelation that has already been given by God to his messengers in ancient times. According to Watch Tower teaching, prophecy came to an end with the first generation of apostles, as Paul predicted (1 Corinthians 13.8). Critics have sometimes pointed out that the Society has applied the term 'prophet' to itself, but such self-descriptions are rarely found in its literature. One such example is the following:

> This 'prophet' was not one man, but was a body of men and women. It was the small group of footstep followers of Jesus Christ, known at that time as International Bible Students. Today they are known as Jehovah's Christian witnesses. They are still proclaiming a warning, and have been joined and assisted in their commissioned work by hundreds of thousands of persons who have listened to their message with belief. (Watch Tower 1972: 197)

The quotation marks around the word 'prophet' are original and indicate the figurative use of the word. No Jehovah's Witness can claim any new revelation: the biblical writers received divine dictation, angelic visitation, dreams and visions, but all these phenomena came to an end. God's messages to them through such media have been recorded in the Bible, whose interpretation God has entrusted to his 'faithful and discreet slave', and the rest of his people who constitute Jehovah's Witnesses (Watch Tower 2018a: 1203). The Society's role is therefore to interpret and publicize God's word, not to add new revelation to it. Watch Tower Literature therefore purports to be interpretation and clarification of scripture. Being God's faithful messenger does not mean, however, that the Society is infallible; from time to time it announces changes in its understanding, sometimes quoting the text, 'But the path of the righteous is like the bright morning light / That grows brighter and brighter until full daylight' (Proverbs 4.18).

Prophecy is not to be confused with clairvoyance or prediction. The Society's literature defines prophecy as follows:

> An inspired message; a revelation of divine will and purpose or the proclamation thereof. Prophecy may be an inspired moral teaching, an expression of a divine command or judgment, or a declaration of something to come. Prediction, or foretelling, is not the basic thought conveyed by the root verbs in the original languages (Heb., nava'; Gr., propheteuo); yet it forms an outstanding feature of Bible prophecy. (Watch Tower 2018b: 690–1)

Critics who associate the Society's prophetic role with failed prophecy therefore seriously misunderstand its teachings on the subject, although it must certainly be acknowledged that there have been some failed expectations.

End-time prophecy

Jehovah's Witnesses are particularly associated with biblical end-time prophecy. The popular belief that they have suggested various dates that have failed to materialize is partially true. What many critics fail to realize, however, is that there is no single end-time event but a timetable of events which are expected to occur at different intervals. These events are not brought together in any single place in scripture but are scattered throughout various apocalyptic passages. Protestant fundamentalists have included the following in their interpretation of biblical prophecy: Armageddon; the great tribulation; Christ's second coming; the resurrection(s); casting down Satan from heaven; cleansing of the sanctuary; the last judgement; the binding and loosing of Satan; the thousand-year reign of Christ (the Millennium); the new heaven and new earth; the faithful meeting Christ in the air (frequently referred to by the non-biblical expression 'the Rapture'); appearance of the Antichrist; the wild beast; the mark of the beast; the number of the beast (666); the dragon; the two witnesses; the false prophet; the burning of the earth; and the marriage of the Lamb. The majority of these references occur in the book of Daniel, the latter parts of the synoptic gospels, some passages in Paul's writings and the book of Revelation. For believers in biblical inerrancy, the problem lies in fitting these phenomena together, deciding whether some of them may be identical, and the order in which to place them in end-time chronology. Given the multiplicity of these end-time phenomena, the question arises as to which, if any, can be assigned specific dates and how this might be done.

Jehovah's Witnesses note that the Bible does not speak of the Antichrist as a specific being and, despite their Protestant ancestry, do not identify it with the papacy. The word is mentioned five times in John's letters, once in the plural and elsewhere designating anyone who denies God and Christ. (It never occurs in Revelation.) The word embraces all false messiahs and false prophets, and anyone who is opposed to the truth, particularly apostates. Although false messiahs and prophets are associated with the last days, the Antichrist is not a malevolent spiritual being who is expected in the end times and therefore does not feature in the Society's end-time chronology.

Watch Tower literature defines a calendar of events, rather than predicts a single one; hence, different dates can designate different happenings. For example, 1918 is not a substitute for a failed 1914 date: 1918 (or early 1919) is the time at which Christ began to gather the 144,000 in heaven. Jesus promised his disciples that he would prepare a place for them, and preparation takes time, which Jehovah's Witnesses reckoned to be three and a half years (paralleling the length of Jesus' earthly ministry) – hence the additional 1918 date. Also, in the past Jehovah's Witnesses have sometimes expected a single date to involve more than one occurrence. Thus, it was expected that 1914 might see the commencement of Armageddon, but it also designated the end of the Gentile Times, as well as the casting out of Satan. The fact that the present system of things did not end in 1914, therefore, did not lead to an abandonment of that date, and 1914 remains crucially important to members. Although Armageddon did not happen, it could still be claimed that the Gentile Times ended and that Satan was cast down.

Calculating end-time chronology is complex, and the Society's views have developed over time, with some changes to dating and some adjustments to their chronological schemes. It is therefore not surprising that few Jehovah's Witness can fully explain the complexities involved. The books of Daniel and Revelation, which feature largely in the organization's eschatology, are difficult to understand, although those who have been in the organization for a reasonable period will be familiar with publications such as *Revelation – Its Grand Climax At Hand!* (1988, reissued in 2006) and *Pay Attention to Daniel's Prophecy* (1999a). Those who wish to explore such complexities can be referred to discussions elsewhere (Chryssides 2010, 2016; Crompton 1996). Both Daniel and Revelation contain vivid, but often cryptic, imagery, which has exercised the minds and the imagination of biblical interpreters ever since they were written. The meaning of the book of Daniel is reckoned to have been hidden for most of the ages: Daniel is told to seal the book that he is given and that it will only be opened near the time of the end (Daniel 12.4), which was taken to imply that its meaning would become apparent in the last days. By contrast, the book of Revelation recounts that the Lamb opens the seals of the scroll he is holding (Revelation 5–12; Russell 1886: 168).

The book of Daniel is set in Babylon during the period in which the Jews were exiled there, from 618 to 536 BCE, according to Watch Tower publications (Watch Tower 1999a: 13). Mainstream scholars regard the book as a relatively late piece of writing, compiled between 167 and 164 BCE, using the Babylonian setting as an imaginative device to encourage the Jews who were undergoing persecution by Antiochus IV Epiphanes at that time. Watch Tower literature does not support this view, regarding it as the product of higher criticism, which they firmly reject. Jehovah's Witnesses (in common with mainstream Protestant fundamentalists) hold that the stories of Daniel and his companions, recounted in the first half of the book, are genuine historical happenings and that the prophetic second half foretells events that are to come.

The book of Daniel recounts that King Nebuchadnezzar of Babylon has a troublesome dream (Daniel 2.1-49). He calls upon his astrologers and magicians, and gives them the challenge not only to interpret the dream but clairvoyantly also to declare what the dream was. When they reply that the task is too difficult for them, the King orders them all to be executed, together with Daniel and his companions. Daniel requests an audience with the King and proves able to reveal both the dream and its interpretation. The dream was of an enormous, dazzling bright statue, with a gold head, silver chest and arms, a copper abdomen, legs of iron and feet which were part iron and part clay. A rock was carved out by an invisible force, and smashed the statue, causing the crumbled ruin to blow away like chaff in the wind. The rock, however, stands firm and becomes an enormous mountain that fills the whole earth (Daniel 2.31-35). Daniel explains that the five components of the statue represent five kingdoms: the gold head is Babylon, which will fall and be followed by three inferior kingdoms (silver, bronze and iron) and finally a divided kingdom, signified by its dual components – iron and clay. The rock represents a kingdom that God himself will set up and which will be everlasting and indestructible, bringing all other worldly kingdoms to an end (Daniel 2.44-45).

Later in the narrative, Daniel has a dream in which four beasts emerge from the sea (Daniel 7.1-28). One is a lion with eagles' wings; the second looks like a bear; the third is like a leopard, with four heads; and the fourth beast is particularly terrifying, having large iron teeth with which it crushes and devours its victims, trampling any survivors under its feet. This fourth beast has ten horns, but Daniel observes an eleventh small horn that grows up and devours three; the small horn has human eyes and a mouth 'speaking arrogantly' (Daniel 7.8). This is followed by thrones being set out and the 'Ancient of Days' takes his seat in front of the heavenly court where there is a river of fire. The first three beasts are allowed to live for a limited period, but the fourth beast is thrown into a furnace. The vision ends with 'someone like a son of man' approaching the Ancient of Days and being given authority over peoples of all nations and languages, and everlasting dominion over them.

The Society's publications interpret these visions as relating to successive world powers that grew up after Babylonian domination. Babylon is represented by the gold head, whose dominion (according to Watch Tower chronology) lasts from 607 to 539 BCE, Medo-Persia the silver (539–331 BCE), Greece the bronze (331–30 BCE) and Rome the iron (30 BCE–1763 CE). Thereafter humanity is dominated by the Anglo-American World Power, the two allied powers being represented by the iron-clay amalgam, leading to a politically divided world in the end times (Watch Tower 1999a: 56). The book of Revelation elaborates on this model: the angel shows John a seven-headed scarlet wild beast, explaining that each head represents a king, or an empire: 'And there are seven kings: five have fallen, one is, the other has not yet arrived, but when he does arrive he must remain a short while' (Revelation 17.9-10). Since John was writing at the time of Roman persecution, the Roman Empire must be the one that 'is', and in order to make the number of the preceding kingdoms up to five, the Society's interpretation adds Egypt and Assyria as precursors to Babylon, thus arriving at the list: Egypt, Assyria, Babylon, Medo-Persia, Greece, and Rome, to be followed by the Anglo-American alliance. However, the angel adds an eighth king: 'And the wild beast that was but is not, it is also itself an eighth king, but springs from the seven, and it goes off into destruction' (Revelation 17.11). This eighth king who emanates from the seven is the League of Nations, which emerged from powers previously mentioned in the book, such as Greece, Persia (now Iran) and Rome (part of Italy), and although the United States never joined the League, the Anglo-American power was in the ascendant at the time of its inception, and the United States gave impetus to the organization and subsequent support. The United States took the lead in setting up its successor, the United Nations. The Watch Tower Society believes that the United Nations is referred to as a king on account of the fact that it appears to be a world government, with its own armies and negotiating powers, but it is no more than an image of the wild beast mentioned earlier in the book, to which the other nations have given life (Revelation 13.14-15; Watch Tower 1988: 254). The United Nations will end in destruction, just like the League; 'the wild beast was, but is not, and yet will be present' (Revelation 17.8) alludes to the inception and demise of the League and its continued presence as the United Nations.

If Daniel and John were foretelling the future, it is unlikely that any of their readers would have grasped the meaning of these words in such detail. Like much prophecy, its import is only recognizable with hindsight. Its function, therefore, lies not so much in its predictive power but in assuring those of subsequent generations that God has had a firm plan for humanity and that they can be assured that it is being fulfilled. These two visions, however, regardless of their predictive qualities, gave no indication of the chronological periods involved, and these timescales were deduced by considering other parts of the book. Particularly within the Adventist tradition, there was a keen interest in working out an end-time chronology based on the books of Daniel and Revelation, using numbers and time periods mentioned in both. The *Daniel's Prophecy!* book affirms that 'Jehovah is the Great Timekeeper' (Watch Tower 1999a: 181) and, in line with the Adventist tradition, Jehovah's Witnesses believe that an exact chronology of key events in God's purpose for humanity can be ascertained. There is a problem, however, in working out a timescale from the times and numbers that Daniel mentions. When we read the book, we encounter references to 'seven sevens', '62 sevens' (Daniel 9.25), 'a time, times and half a time' (Daniel 12.7), 1290 days and 1335 days (Daniel 12.11-12). The New World Translation translates 'sevens' as 'weeks', and 'an appointed time, appointed times, and half a time' for the 'times' prophecy. This probably does not particularly help the uninitiated reader, who is still left with problems: if these are time periods, when do they begin and end, and what is meant by some of the stranger concepts that Daniel mentions? The

1290-day period, evidently, runs 'from the time that the constant feature has been removed and the disgusting thing that causes desolation has been put in place' and the 62-week period ends when 'Messiah will be cut off, with nothing for himself'. And who are we to understand by the King of the North and the King of the South (Daniel 11.5-6)?

Before Daniel is asked to seal up the book, the angel Gabriel tells him,

There are 70 weeks that have been determined for your people and your holy city, in order to terminate the transgression, to finish off sin, to make atonement for error, to bring in everlasting righteousness, to seal up the vision and the prophecy, and to anoint the Holy of Holies. You should know and understand that from the issuing of the word to restore and to rebuild Jerusalem until Messiah the Leader, there will be 7 weeks, also 62 weeks. She will be restored and rebuilt, with a public square and moat, but in times of distress.

And after the 62 weeks, Messiah will be cut off, with nothing for himself.

And the people of a leader who is coming will destroy the city and the holy place. And its end will be by the flood. And until the end there will be war; what is decided upon is desolations.

And he will keep the covenant in force for the many for one week; and at the half of the week, he will cause sacrifice and gift offering to cease. (Daniel 9.24-27)

The book of Revelation portrays God sitting on his throne with the Lamb on his right hand, with a scroll that is closed with seven seals. When the Lamb opens the final – seventh – seal of the scroll, there is a dramatic moment in which there is a long silence in heaven, followed by seven angels successively sounding seven trumpets, after which a pregnant woman appears, 'arrayed with the sun', with the moon beneath her feet and a twelve-starred crown. An enormous red dragon is then seen in front of the woman, waiting to devour the newborn child, but just as her son is born, he is snatched up to God's heavenly throne. This son 'is to shepherd all the nations with an iron rod' (Revelation 12.5), and the woman flees to the desert, where God looks after her for 1,260 days. The archangel Michael then arrives; war breaks out in heaven, and the dragon is cast down to earth.

How are we to interpret these enigmatic Bible passages without recourse to any new divine revelation? The Protestant tradition acknowledges that not all parts of scripture are equally clear, and hence one important exegetical principle is to search for other clearer passages. If one wants to interpret biblical numbers and time periods, therefore, we must look in the Bible to ascertain how this should be done. Accordingly, the Protestant Reformers found guidance in the book of Ezekiel, where the prophet says, 'A day for a year, a day for a year, is what I have given you' (Ezekiel 4.6). This principle, known as the Year-for-a-Day (or Year-Day) Rule, became particularly prevalent within the Adventist tradition and has found its way into Watch Tower exegesis. The principle involves construing certain references to days as signifying years, noting that there are 360 days in the Jewish year. Clearly, 'year' should not be invariably substituted for 'day' when reading the Bible, particularly where common sense dictates otherwise. When John says that Jesus waited for two days before visiting Lazarus (John 11.6), it is clear that he did not wait two years before setting out! However, when Daniel speaks enigmatically of 1,290 and 1,335 days (Daniel 12.11-12), the Year-Day principle unlocks the meaning of the text.

The key events that are relevant to Daniel's prophecy are the Babylonian exile, the decree of King Cyrus of Persia which enabled the Jews to return to their home country and the rebuilding of Jerusalem. Watch Tower dating of these events diverges from that of the majority of scholars of ancient history, but in order to understand its teaching it is sufficient to note that the Society dates the exile at 607 BCE, Cyrus' decree at 455 BCE and the rebuilding of Jerusalem's city walls at 406 BCE. Daniel's 'seven weeks' therefore stretch from 455 to 406 BCE, and 62 'weeks' become 434 years, terminating with the appearance of the Messiah, which is dated at 29 CE, being the date on which Jesus' ministry commenced with his baptism at the River Jordan.

The period of '70 weeks' is reckoned to run from Nehemiah's return to Jerusalem, after the Babylonian Exile, reckoned to be 455 BCE, which works out as 490 years. A period of 49 years occurs between the decree and Nehemiah's rebuilding, and a further 434 years between the rebuilt Jerusalem and the Messiah's appearance. (It should be remembered that, according to Jehovah's Witnesses, Jesus becomes the Messiah at his baptism, not at his birth.) This line of reasoning leaves a further seven years, which takes us to 36 CE. This year is regarded as significant since it is the year in which Peter visits Cornelius, who is a Roman centurion and therefore a Gentile (Acts 10.28). Cornelius has received a vision, in which a man in shining clothes instructs him to seek out Peter. Meanwhile, Peter, who has previously held that Christians should obey the Jewish law, receives his own vision in which God instructs him to make concessions for the Gentiles. Cornelius comes to accept the Christian faith, and thus the year 36 CE marks the availability of the Christian message to Gentiles as well as Jews. The halfway point between 29 CE and 36 CE is 33 CE, which marks the date of Jesus' death – the 'cutting off' of the Messiah.

Failed prophetic dates

The years 1914, 1918, 1925 and 1975 are frequently identified by critics as failed prophetic dates. It was anticipated that the year 1914 might mark the translation of the saints into heaven and the setting up of Christ's kingdom. When an expected event fails to materialize, however, believers in the prophecy have two options: they can recalculate or they can 'spiritualize' the event. The Bible Students came to regard the 1914 date as marking Christ's entering the heavenly sanctuary and casting Satan down to earth. This would be followed by a 'harvesting period' in which the saints would be translated into heaven. However, the year 1914 had another function: as Russell declared on the morning of 2 October that year, 'The Gentile Times have ended.' According to Watch Tower teaching, the Jewish Age ran from the establishment of the nation of Israel, which started at the patriarch Jacob's death, reckoned to be 1711 BCE, and stretched to 607 BCE, the date the Society gives for Nebuchadnezzar's invasion of Jerusalem, when the Babylonian exile began. The Gentile Times are held to be of equal length to the Jewish Age; here the arithmetical calculations are somewhat complex, but it is sufficient to say that the Society deduced that 1914 marked the end of the Gentile Times and the return of the Jews to God's favour. When the Balfour Declaration was signed in 1917, and Jews began to return to Palestine, this was thought to be confirmatory evidence. Since the Jewish New Year begins in October rather than January, and the Declaration was signed on 2 November, it could be claimed that a 1918 date might be attributed to it.

The year 1925, however, was an unequivocal prophetic failure. The date is found in Rutherford's *Millions Now Living Will Never Die!*, first published in 1920, and it was reckoned to mark the end of seventy 'Jubilees' of fifty years each. In ancient Israel, Jubilee year was a special year of celebration, in which slaves were freed, debts cancelled, and the ground lay fallow. To calculate Jubilee years, Rutherford started from the time at which the Israelites began to own land, since leaving land fallow presupposes cultivation, which was impossible during the Israelites' nomadic existence in the Sinai Desert. The period of the Jubilees therefore began when Joshua captured Jericho, the date of which, according to Rutherford's chronology, was 1575 BCE. There was some uncertainty as to whether one should count the years in which the Jews were exiled in Babylon and hence were no longer landowners, but at any rate Rutherford correctly calculated that 3,500 years on from that date was 1925. The ancient Hebrew Jubilees were the 'type', and hence an antitype should follow (see Chapter 4) – 'the beginning of the restoration of all things'– which he believed would start with the dead being brought back to life, commencing with Abraham, Isaac and Jacob and 'other faithful ones of old' (Rutherford 1920a: 88). These 'faithful ones of old' could not be part of the 144,000, since they lived before Christ's ransom sacrifice and hence should expect a life of paradise on earth instead. As the Letter to the Hebrews explains after enumerating names of key figures in ancient Jewish history, 'yet all of these, although they received a favorable witness because of their faith, did not obtain the fulfillment of the promise, because God had foreseen something better for us, so that they might not be made perfect apart from us' (Hebrews 11.39-40).

The prediction was too specific to explain away, leaving Rutherford no option but to admit that the expectation was false. At a convention in Basle the following year, this exchange occurred:

> Question: Have the ancient worthies returned? Answer: Certainly they have not returned. No one has seen them, and it would be foolish to make such an announcement. It was stated in the 'Millions' book that we might reasonably expect them to return shortly after 1925, but this was merely an expressed opinion. (Watch Tower 1980a: 63)

Despite this admission of failure, however, Rutherford continued to expect the ancient worthies to return, and in 1929 he commissioned a house to be built on the outskirts of San Diego for this event. The house was called Beth Sarim, meaning House of the Princes, and in the absence of their return, Rutherford himself moved in in 1930. The house, which is still standing, was sold to a private purchaser shortly after Rutherford's death in 1942.

Expectations in 1975

The year 1975 is frequently cited as a subsequent date for Watch Tower failed prophecy. There is actually relatively little by way of written sources that aroused the expectation that Armageddon would come in that year, but speeches given at conventions gave rise to considerable anticipation. The year appeared to be significant, being the end of the sixth millennium. The 1975 expectation was not based on Daniel's prophecies but on much simpler considerations. The Society's literature had explained that the creation of the world was completed in 4026 BCE, and hence six millennia would have elapsed since that date. The interpretation of the word 'day' as a thousand-year period, rather than a single year, draws on Psalm 90.3: 'For a thousand years are in your eyes just as yesterday when it is past.' The year 1975 would therefore mark the beginning of Jehovah's seventh, sabbatical, 'day', the number seven having particular significance, marking the beginning of God's heavenly rule.

Watch Tower publications did not state explicitly that the present system of things would end in 1975, but a *Watchtower* article appeared in 1968, entitled 'Why Are You Looking Forward to 1975?', and stated,

Are we to assume from this study that the battle of Armageddon will be all over by the autumn of 1975, and the long-looked-for thousand-year reign of Christ will begin by then? Possibly, but we wait to see how closely the seventh thousand-year period of man's existence coincides with the sabbathlike thousand-year reign of Christ ... Our chronology, however, which is reasonably accurate (but admittedly not infallible), at the best only points to the autumn of 1975 as the end of 6,000 years of man's existence on earth. It does not necessarily mean that 1975 marks the end of the first 6,000 years of Jehovah's seventh creative 'day'. (Watch Tower 1968: 494)

The Society's book *Life Everlasting in Freedom of the Sons of God*, published in 1966, and subsequently withdrawn by the organization, was more explicit:

According to this trustworthy Bible chronology six thousand years from man's creation will end in 1975, and the seventh period of a thousand years of human history will begin in the fall of 1975 C.E.

So six thousand years of man's existence on earth will soon be up, yes, within this generation. (Watch Tower 1966a: 29)

On 10 February 1975, Frederick Franz, then the Society's vice president, addressed an audience of over 20,000 at a convention in the Los Angeles Sports Arena, with a radio link to thousands more. His talk was entitled 'Time in Which We Are Now Interested', in which he stated categorically that the 6,000-year period would end on 5 September 1975 'according to the lunar calendar' (Gruss [2001] 2007: 295). Franz explained that one could soon expect the great tribulation, the destruction of Babylon the Great, the demise of all political systems and the binding of Satan and his demons to be followed immediately by Christ's millennial rule. However, he added, 'Well now, we're not saying that by the end of this year 1975 all these things cannot take place ... But, in view of what the Scriptures inform us, we are warranted in expecting so much to occur by September 5, 1975' (quoted in Gruss [2001] 2007: 295).

However, Franz introduced a small note of caution. The year 4026 BCE marked the creation of Adam, not necessarily the end of the first creative day, since an unspecified period of time elapsed between Adam's creation and that of Eve (Genesis 2.20-22). Nonetheless, this period must be short; hence, if the present system did not end on 5 September, one might expect it to happen in October or November, and certainly before the year 1975 had elapsed.

These imminent expectations released a sense of urgency among many Jehovah's Witnesses and caused them to intensify their preaching work. A number of them sold their houses and cashed in life insurance policies, in order to finance their increased publishing activity. Some gave up high-earning jobs in favour of more casual physical labour in order to free up time to devote to the Society, and some moved to locations where the need was believed to be greater. Some Witnesses postponed medical and dental treatment, believing that they would be restored to perfect physical well-being after Armageddon. The book *God's Kingdom of a Thousand Years Has Approached* (1973a) was particularly promoted, since it urged readers about the urgency of living in the last days and expecting God's kingdom.

Having put so much effort into preparing for the end of the present system, Witnesses were understandably disillusioned with Armageddon's failure to arrive. Many were prepared to wait until 1976, accepting the possibility of some delay in its coming, but by 1977 it became apparent that this was a false expectation. A substantial number left the Society, amounting to 3 per cent each year in the United States and 2 per cent in Britain between 1977 and 1978. While these percentages may not seem high, they should be set against 15 per cent and 10 per cent increases in membership in the United States and Britain, respectively, in 1974, and numerically the drop in peak publishers between 1976 and 1978 amounted to just over 66,000 worldwide.

Since the Society had little written evidence that they encouraged these expectations, there seemed no need to refer explicitly to the disappointment. A 1976 *Watchtower* article made a veiled reference, placing the responsibility on its members rather than on the Governing Body. It bore the somewhat upbeat title 'A Solid Basis for Confidence' and stated,

> If anyone has been disappointed ..., he should now concentrate on adjusting his viewpoint, seeing that it was not the word of God that failed or deceived him and brought disappointment, but that his own understanding was based on wrong premises. (Watch Tower 1976: 441)

The article added,

> However, say that you are one who counted heavily on a date, and, commendably, set your attention more strictly on the urgency of the times and the need of the people to hear. And say you now, temporarily, feel somewhat disappointed; are you really the loser? Are you really hurt? We believe you can say that you have gained and profited by taking this conscientious course. Also, you have been enabled to get a really mature, more reasonable viewpoint. – Eph[esians]. 5:1-17.

> The Scriptures repeatedly tell us that the end will come as a complete surprise upon the world. (Watch Tower 1976: 441)

Franz, however, referred explicitly to the disappointment in a speech at Georgetown, Canada, in 1976, and reportedly said, 'Do you know why nothing happened in 1975? It was because *you* expected something to happen!' Whether or not those who remained in the organization were persuaded to take the blame for the false expectation, they continued in their evangelizing work, and numbers returned to their previous level by the end of 1979.

The 'generation' doctrine

Although Jehovah's Witnesses were careful not to set further precise dates for the commencement of Armageddon, Jesus had said, 'Truly I say to you that this generation will by no means pass away until all these things happen' (Matthew 24.34). The Society had taught that this applied to the generation that was alive in 1914, but with the passage of time fewer members who were born in 1914 remained alive, thus raising the question of whether this prophecy might also fail. The question therefore arose as to how we should understand the word 'generation'. Demographically it can denote a period of between 15 and 20 years (as when referring to Generations X, Y and Z); biologically, the average age for a woman to bear her first child is 30 years. However, if one looks to the Bible, it states that 'the span of our life is 70 years, Or 80 if one is especially strong' (Psalm 90.10). If a generation is a biblical lifespan, then the year 1984 seemed an appropriate time to revisit the organization's eschatological expectations, 1984 being seventy years on from 1914. Outside the Society, some believed that 1984 was another date set for Armageddon (Anon 1984: 66–7; Botting and Botting 1984), but this is not mentioned in Watch Tower literature. An oft-cited article '1914 – The Generation Will Not Pass Away' appeared in the 15 May edition of *The Watchtower* in that year and continued to affirm the imminence of Armageddon. However, the article does not mention date calculations but briefly discusses the concept of generation, citing Walter Bauer's (1958) *A Greek-English Lexicon of the New Testament*, in which he defines 'generation', as used in the Bible, as 'the sum total of those born at the same time, expanded to include all those living at a given time generation, contemporaries'. Thus, the end of the present system can be expected within the lifespans of those born in 1914 or alive at the time. Generations are defined by frames of reference, and, as the author mentions, the First World War, which began in 1914, marked a watershed in human history. As the article pointed out, there were still many of that generation who were still alive. However, rather than hinting at any precise date, the author cites Paul's words: 'You yourselves know quite well that Jehovah's day is coming exactly as a thief in the night. Whenever it is that they are saying: "Peace and security!"

then sudden destruction is to be instantly upon them' (1 Thessalonians 5.2-3; NWT 1984). Armageddon can be expected at a time of complacency: the author suggests that religious leaders, politicians or the United Nations might inspire confidence that we are living in times of peace, leading to a false sense of complacency. The article confidently affirmed, 'Just as Jesus' prophecies regarding Jerusalem were fulfilled within the life span of the generation of the year 33 C.E., so his prophecies regarding "the time of the end" will be fulfilled within the life span of the generation of 1914.'

With the passage of time and Armageddon's non-arrival, such confidence appeared to be misplaced, causing the Society to look again at biblical prophecy and reconsider. In 1995 another *Watchtower* article appeared, promoting a different view. While reiterating the Bible's teaching that we cannot know the day or the hour, it quotes from Robert Wohl's book *The Generation of 1914*, which had previously been cited to support the 1984 interpretation. Wohl writes, 'A historical generation is not defined by its chronological limits ... it is not a zone of dates' (1979: 210). The *Watchtower* article revisits biblical uses of the term 'generation' and notes that Jesus uses it to refer to groups of people, often with negative connotations, for example, 'a wicked and adulterous generation' who keep seeking a sign (Matthew 16.4) and Jesus' statement that 'the Son of man ... must undergo many sufferings and be rejected by this generation' (Luke 17.24). Paul also talks about 'a crooked and twisted generation, among whom you are shining as illuminators in the world' (Philippians 2.15). Jehovah's people keep themselves pure from this 'generation' but are expected to remain until the end. The article therefore suggests that 'in the final fulfillment of Jesus' prophecy today, "this generation" apparently refers to the peoples of earth who see the sign of Christ's presence but fail to mend their ways' (Watch Tower 1995a: 20). Being 'illuminators' does not merely mean setting an example by impeccable Christian behaviour, but lighting the path of this 'generation' by fulfilling Jesus' commission: 'This good news of the kingdom will be preached in all the inhabited earth for a witness to all the nations; and then the end will come' (Matthew 24.14). Meanwhile, this article affirms, Christ has gathered the anointed 'generation' in heaven, after his accession to God's throne. This new interpretation of the 'generation' prophecy does not suggest any time limit. However, the article points out that the new teaching does not mean that Armageddon is any further off. It is among 'the things that must shortly take place' (Revelation 1.1), to which John the Revelator refers.

In 2008 further new insight on the Society's teachings was given. A *Watchtower* article reappraised the question of whether Jesus' use of the word 'generation' was invariably pejorative, pointing out that the text of Matthew 24 portrays Jesus as speaking to his disciples, who had approached him privately, warning them of the signs of the end and then concluding with the words, 'Truly I say to you that this generation will by no means pass away until all these things occur; (Matthew 24.34). The words 'this generation' must therefore refer to his disciples, and the article therefore infers that 'generation' denotes the anointed class which began in 1914, the 'remnant' of which will not pass away until Armageddon occurs. This was in fact the Society's position in 1927. This remnant was not confined to those who joined the organization before 1935 but could continue to be augmented (Watch Tower 2007a: 30–1). A further clarification was made in 2010, when the word 'generation' was held to denote not only the 1914 generation but also those whose lives overlapped those who received the heavenly calling and who were alive at that date. This places a time limit on the expiry of the 'generation': theoretically, if one were to assume a lifespan of 70 years, this could take us to the year 2054. However, the fact that the signs of the end are evident now – wars, famines, earthquakes, epidemics, breakdowns in human relationships – must indicate that the great tribulation is imminent. Armageddon will arrive when the last of the 144,000 have been taken up into heaven. We cannot be sure who are true claimants to membership of the anointed class, but Witnesses believe it is likely that we might find that they will suddenly have disappeared, being taken up into heaven, as a prelude to Armageddon.

Biblical prophecy in popular understanding

This book's focus is on what it means to be a Jehovah's Witness, and it may be asked whether the average Witness would be familiar with the complexities of biblical understanding that this chapter has outlined. Present-day Witnesses would be less familiar with the ideas of Russell and Rutherford, although critics continue to cite the dates of 1914 and 1925 as failed prophetic dates. Many of my informants still remember 1975, and all of the topics mentioned in this chapter have received recent coverage in Watch Tower literature, and key figures like Ezra, Nehemiah and Daniel all have video introductions that can be accessed on the JW.org website. Topics such as the Kings of the North and South have featured prominently in a recent *Watchtower* study article, and, although Witnesses might falter on the precise dates in the chronology, they are certainly familiar with the kings and kingdoms referred to in Daniel and Revelation, and how they relate to current events. One Witness recently commented to me that Britain's withdrawal from the European Union may have significance in helping to cement the Anglo-American alliance to which these two books are believed to refer. These somewhat complex explanations of Daniel are set out in detail in *Pay Attention to Daniel's Prophecy!*, which was conscientiously studied at weekly home study meetings, and, in common with all Watch Tower literature, the book contains questions that were put to members to check comprehension. These included questions such as 'When did the word "to restore and to rebuild Jerusalem" take effect?', 'When did the "seventy weeks" begin?' and 'What evidence points to the accuracy of the dates for the beginning and the end of the "seventy weeks"?' (Watch Tower 1999a: 190 n20). Witnesses receive detailed biblical instruction, but it is not mere theoretical knowledge: living 'in the world' as they do, they take an interest in world events, seeing them as confirmation that we are living in the last days of the present system and are harbingers of Armageddon.

9

Opposition

The Society's opponents

Throughout its history, the Watch Tower Society has experienced considerable opposition, which has taken a variety of forms. Its milder varieties take the form of written critiques, of which there are many – too many, in fact, to discuss in any detail in a single chapter. The much harsher form of opposition is political, and in various countries Jehovah's Witnesses have been subjected to bans, arrests, imprisonment, torture and even death. In the English-speaking world, the most visible opposition generally comes from two main, and slightly overlapping, sources: mainstream Christians – mainly (but not exclusively) Protestant evangelicals – and ex-members who recount their experiences within the organization and how they disengaged.

Of the countercult Christian literature that targets Jehovah's Witnesses, criticism has targeted the Society's Christology and soteriology, and its New World Translation of the Holy Scriptures. Of the countercult critics, probably the best known and most influential is Walter R. Martin, whose *The Kingdom of the Cults* was first published in 1965 and sold over half a million copies by 1986. His chapter on Jehovah's Witnesses started life as a short booklet, written with Norman H. Klann, titled *Jehovah of the Watchtower* (1953). Also well known is Anthony A. Hoekema's somewhat more measured *The Four Major Cults* (1963), and critics who focus on their New World Translation include Robert H. Countess (1982), David A. Reed (1986), Ron Rhodes (1993) and Robert M. Bowman (1996). There are many others. Mention should be made of Doug Harris, who lived in Twickenham, England, in 1981, where the Witnesses held their conventions. Being an evangelical Christian, he felt the need to challenge the attendees and persuaded some friends to join him in displaying placards and distributing leaflets. This led to the formation of the Reachout Trust, which produced Christian apologetic literature and offered seminars countrywide. (See e.g. Harris and Browning 1993. The organization's aims subsequently widened to target a variety of 'cults'.)

In recent times, a different form of opposition emerged from ex-members, assisted by the rise of the internet, who have organized themselves and formed networks. Since the more vociferous ex-members have the highest visibility, it is easy to assume them to be typical of ex-members more widely, but the evidence suggests otherwise (Chryssides 2019: 371–92). Some have expressed their experiences in autobiographies and novels, of which there are now over fifty. Ex-member testimony should not be discounted, and these narratives often highlight details of what is involved in belonging to the organization; however, it is difficult to assess their veracity, since ex-members frequently collude, misremember and become influenced by the anticult organizations and the media.

Christology and soteriology

Most of the countercult critics focus on Jehovah's Witnesses' understanding of the person of Christ and their doctrine of atonement. Mainstream Christians, particularly in the Protestant tradition, have taught that Jesus' death was a 'once for all' sacrifice, entailing that nothing further was needed to save humanity from sin; believers are 'saved through faith ... not a result of works' (Romans 6.10; Ephesians 2.8-9). By contrast, Witnesses have been accused of teaching salvation by works rather than faith, emphasizing the importance of house-to-house evangelism, attending congregation meetings, and studying Watch Tower literature.

Some clarification is needed about the Jehovah's Witnesses' position on salvation. Ian Brown construes it thus, purportedly summarizing a section of Rutherford's *The Harp of God*:

> Watchtower doctrine decrees that Christ alone cannot save. His atonement does not provide salvation; it is merely a ransom paid to Jehovah God by Christ in order to remove the evil effects of Adam's sin on mankind. Man may then EARN his own salvation by faith and good works. (Brown 1999: 39; caps. original)

Clearly Brown has not read Rutherford with sufficient care. Rutherford actually writes, at precisely the location Brown identifies,

> The cross[1] of Christ is the great pivotal truth of the divine arrangement, from which radiate the hopes of men. When all men come to a knowledge

---

[1] *The Harp of God*, being one of Rutherford's early writings, continues to use the word 'cross' and not 'torture stake', as Rutherford came to prefer.

of this fact and all the obedient ones have profited by the value of the ransom sacrifice, there will be great rejoicing amongst the human race. (Rutherford 1920b: 141)

The Jehovah's Witnesses' position is that Christ's sacrificial death brought about atonement but, in common with the majority of Protestants, requires the believer's faith, which is to be perfected by works. The Watch Tower position is clear, that no amount of good works can bring about atonement for Adam's sin: 'We do not earn salvation by doing these things, for no human could ever do enough to merit such an astounding blessing' (Watch Tower 1996a: 8). However, perseverance in good works is needed: 'The one who has endured to the end will be saved' (Mark 13.13).

The substantial point of difference between Watch Tower and mainstream soteriology is that mainstream Christian theology insists that Christ's full deity is necessary for atonement for sin: God himself must make the sacrifice through Jesus Christ, who was both fully God and fully human. By contrast, the Watch Tower position is that Jesus was a perfect man, not a divine being, although he pre-existed in spirit form. Mainstream Christians hold that, although the doctrine of the Trinity may not be explicitly stated in the Bible, the Holy Spirit is not merely an active force but a person. The Bible endows the Holy Spirit with personality in various places: the Spirit is a helper (or counsellor), who can teach, guide, bear witness, speak and hear (John 14.16; 16.13; 15.26; 16.13; Rhodes 1993: 209). This contrasts with the Society's view that these descriptions are personifications, just as concepts such as wisdom are portrayed as crying aloud, watching and protecting (Proverbs 1.20; 4.6).

Jehovah's Witnesses' understanding of Jesus' resurrection follows from their soteriology. As previously mentioned (Chapter 4), they teach that Jesus rose as a spirit being, rather than in physical form, since he could not have paid the ransom sacrifice for sin if he had taken back his physical body again. As one Watch Tower publication states, 'The human body of flesh, which Jesus Christ laid down forever as a ransom sacrifice, was disposed of by God's power … and put out of existence, so not corrupting' (Watch Tower 1965: 354). By contrast, mainstream Christians affirm Jesus' bodily resurrection, pointing out that he was able to be touched and that he could eat and drink like other physical human beings. The notion that, as a spirit being, he could miraculously materialize a physical body is regarded as speculation, which is not supported by scripture (Reed 1986: 70).

The Watch Tower Society's teaching on life after death also incurs much criticism. The Bible does not seem to give an unequivocal answer on whether the dead are asleep awaiting resurrection or are already with Christ, and whether our condition after death will be in physical or in spiritual form. Jehovah's Witnesses resolve such problems by distinguishing between the

144,000 anointed ones and the great crowd who belong to the earthly class, the former having spirit bodies in heaven, while the latter are expected to live physically in the restored earth. Two New Testament passages seem to run counter to this interpretation, however. The story of the rich man and Lazarus (Luke 16.19-31) portrays heaven and hell as taking place simultaneously with human life on earth, and Jesus' words to the dying thief are, according to most translations, 'Truly I tell you, today you will be with me in paradise' (Luke 23.43).

The story of Lazarus can be dismissed on the grounds that it is merely a parable, and its importance is to commend compassion for the poor, rather than to present an account of the afterlife. The incident of the dying thief is more difficult, but Watch Tower literature suggests that the comma is misplaced in mainstream translations, and Jesus' words should read, 'Truly I tell you today, you will be with me in paradise,' thus escaping the conclusion that paradise was then open. The original Greek manuscripts did not have punctuation, so it is a matter of judgement where any comma is best placed. However, critics have replied that the New World Translation's rendering lacks plausibility, since Jesus used the phrase, 'Truly I tell you' on numerous occasions without adding the word 'today', which would have been superfluous (Rhodes 1993: 329).

Protestant evangelicals have sometimes compared Watch Tower teachings with their own version of Christianity, sometimes using parallel columns marked 'Truth' and 'Error' (e.g. Brooks and Robertson 1985). However, drawing attention to such differences only serves to highlight the Jehovah's Witnesses' conviction that many of their teachings differ from a version of Christianity that they reject, believing it to have become apostate. Jehovah's Witnesses do not deny these contrasts but believe themselves to be in the truth and their critics in error.

The New World Translation

In order to ensure that the Society's teachings have biblical warrant, the Society commissioned publication of its own translation of the Bible, *The New World Translation of the Holy Scriptures*, which commenced in 1950 and was published as a single complete volume in 1961. However, this facilitated new opposition to the Society's teachings. Up to that time, the Society used mainstream versions of the Bible, mainly the King James Version and the American Standard Version. The first edition's foreword highlighted the importance of having a translation in modern speech, which was somewhat innovative at the time, since mainstream churches continued to read the Bible in the archaic language of these older translations. In the UK, the use of modern language versions gained gradual acceptance after the publication of the New English Bible in 1961, so Jehovah's Witnesses were ahead of the times in that respect. The Society also wanted a version that was 'not colored by the creeds and traditions of Christendom' (Watch Tower 1993a: 609), and certainly versions like the King James contained errors that privileged mainstream theology; for example, 1 John 5.7 reads, 'For there are three that bear record in heaven, the Father, the Word, and the Holy Ghost: and these three are one,' which not only serves to legitimate Trinitarian theology but also is an incorrect translation of the original Greek text. In addition, the translators wanted to reintroduce the name 'Jehovah' as a rendering of the tetragrammaton YHWH in the Hebrew scriptures and its presumed equivalent *kurios* in Greek. Jehovah's Witnesses are proud of the fact that they have restored 7,216 occurrences of the divine name. They also wanted to clarify the translation of *parousia*, which they have insisted, right from the time of Russell, means 'presence' rather than 'coming' and refers to Christ's invisible presence which they believe began in 1914.

A number of prominent biblical scholars expressed their evaluation of the New World Translation. William Barclay (1953: 31–2) described it as 'a shining example of how the Bible ought not to be translated', although his short article in *The Expository Times* does not identify any specific deficiencies. Bruce Metzger (1953: 65–85) provided a much more detailed critique, mainly focusing on how the translation addresses Christological issues. Like many subsequent critics, he takes issue with the rendering of John 1.1 as 'the Word was a god' and takes exception to the translation of Colossians 1.15-17: 'He is the image of the invisible God, the firstborn of all creation, because by means of him all other things were created in the heavens and upon the earth.' As he points out, the word 'other' does not appear in the Greek text, and the Watch Tower translators insert it because it supports their view that Jesus Christ is the first created being, rather than, as mainstream Christian theology asserts, 'eternally begotten of the Father'. Again, in common with many other critics, he questions the use of the name 'Jehovah', either as a rendering of Yahweh or as a legitimate translation of *kurios* ('Lord') in the Septuagint (the Greek translation of Hebrew scriptures).

One postscript concerning the New World Translation is worth mentioning. Some critics have alighted on the Society's use of Johannes Greber's (1874–1944) translation of the Bible, which appeared in 1937. Greber was a Roman Catholic priest who joined a spiritualist group, and his translation allegedly involved the help of the spirit world. The Watch Tower Society referred to him in a small number of articles in the 1950s and 1960s, expressing approval of his translation of John 1.1 and Matthew 27.51-53, which I have discussed elsewhere (Chryssides 2016: 169–70). Greber's translation of John 1.1-3 was quoted in full in a 1962 booklet titled ' "The Word" – Who Is He? According to John'. The Society ceased quoting Greber, recognizing his occultist connections, but this detail of the Society's history continues to haunt it: its critics contend that not only are Jehovah's Witnesses really occultist at heart but hypocritical as well.

Criticizing Watch Tower history

The second line of criticism comes from detractors who do not have a theological agenda and therefore focus on the lifestyle and the history of Jehovah's Witnesses. Mention has already been made of the Society's disfellowshipping and shunning (see Chapter 6), and their stance on blood will be considered in the next chapter, so I shall not repeat the criticisms of these practices. One particular focus concerns events in the Society's history, and even though several of these occurred a century or more ago, they continue to be cited. One frequently mentioned incident is the so-called miracle wheat scandal. In 1911, J. A. Bohnet, one of the Society's directors, purchased wheat that had a remarkably high yield and which was thought to be a fulfilment of Ezekiel's prophecy that 'the earth shall yield her increase' (Ezekiel 34.27). The wheat was subsequently found to be unremarkable, and *The Brooklyn Daily Eagle* took up the story, publishing a cartoon depicting Russell as a robber. Russell sued for libel and lost. Another matter that is frequently recounted is Russell's divorce (more accurately, separation) from his wife Maria, which is surrounded by allegations of sexual impropriety with their foster child Rose Ball. Yet another topic brought up by critics is Russell's study of the Great Pyramid of Giza: Russell regarded the Pyramid as the stone pillar mentioned by the prophet Isaiah (Isaiah 19.10-20) and held that its dimensions provided confirmation of dates of events mentioned in scripture and the dating of end-time events.

A further charge against Russell is the allegation that he was a Freemason – an accusation that is frequently employed against religious leaders whom their critics dislike. This accusation is fuelled by a book entitled *The Watchtower and the Masons* (1990) by a conspiracy theorist by the name of Fritz Springmeier (born Viktor E. Schoof). Springmeier claims to find thirty-five points of affinity between Russell and Freemasonry, including the use of the name 'Jehovah', his interest in the Great Pyramid, the Society's cross and crown symbol, and his alleged notion that the Bible is an encoded book, whose secrets he claimed to divulge. The author also draws attention to a discourse that Russell delivered in San Francisco in 1913, when a convention was held in a Masonic Hall in that city. The title of Russell's speech was 'The Temple of God', in which he said, 'I am a Free Mason … I am a free and accepted mason' (Russell 1913: 112).

It is not possible to discuss these criticisms in detail; readers who wish an in-depth discussion of each of them can refer to Charles F. Redeker's biography of Russell. However, critics tend not to recount the full story of these incidents. Regarding miracle wheat, Russell's involvement was merely allowing *The Watch Tower* magazine to advertise the product, and purchasers were offered a full refund, which no one ever requested. While Russell was interested in the Great Pyramid, this was no eccentric obsession with pyramidology, as is sometimes implied; the Pyramids of Egypt were a source of speculation, and Scotland's Astronomer Royal, Charles Piazzi Smyth, attached religious significance to the edifices and corresponded with Russell, highly commending his work on the theme. No accusations of sexual impropriety were upheld in the court proceedings relating to the Russell's divorce.

Regarding Freemasonry, there is no evidence at all of Russell's inclusion on any list of Masonic Lodge members, and not even vociferous critics like Lloyd Evans and M. James Penton support the allegation. As Redeker rightly points out, Russell's apparent statement that he was a Free Mason has been severely wrenched out of context. Russell based his lecture on the text 'For the Temple of God is holy, which temple ye are' (1 Corinthians 3.17) and went on to speak about Solomon's Temple and, drawing on Masonic imagery, spoke of Christ as the Master Builder who is building up his Church to its final completion as the Temple, with Jesus Christ as the high priest and his followers as his 'royal priesthood' (Hebrews 4.14; 1 Peter 2.9). He went on to say,

> If you think it is the will of God you should join the Odd Fellows, and don't feel you are Odd Fellow enough in becoming a follower of the Lord, go and join the Odd Fellows. If you feel that you want to become a member of the Free and Accepted Order of Masonry, and do not feel free and Masonic enough as a follower of Christ, God bless you, use your judgment; that is yours to decide, not mine. But now I am talking about this great order of masonry of which Jesus is the Grand Master. (Russell 1913: 361)

'Flip-flops'

Exploration of the Society's history has also caused numerous detractors to draw attention to doctrinal changes – sometimes pejoratively referred to as 'flip-flops' (Watchtower Society Quotes n.d.). Examples include attitudes to medical procedures such as vaccination and organ transplantation: many *Golden Age* articles in the 1920s and 1930s vehemently opposed vaccination, but after 1952 it was stated that individuals should decide on their medical treatment; organ transplants were regarded as matters of conscience in 1961 but condemned from 1967 to 1975, then declared acceptable in 1980. Acceptance of blood derivatives was regarded as unacceptable in 1961 but acceptable by 1964. Other flip-flops relate to doctrinal matters: obedience to 'superior authorities' (Romans 13.1) was regarded as an injunction to obey civil authorities in 1962; in 1943 the superior authorities were reckoned to be Jehovah and Christ; then in 1964 the Society interpreted the verse to enjoin obedience to governments once again. Changes in understanding of end-time chronology and the notion of the generation that would not pass away (Mark 13.30) have been discussed elsewhere, but matters relating to the final judgement seem also to have vacillated over time: will the sheep and goats be separated before or after the great tribulation? Further vacillations have taken place over the judgement of Sodom and Gomorrah. The Society has taught that there have been times when God has already given a final judgement on some of the wicked and that such people will not need to stand trial again after Armageddon. (This is because it would seem pointless for God to resurrect those he had already condemned in order to send them back into oblivion.) One example is the people of Noah's time, who were destroyed by the flood, on which the Society has maintained a consistent stance, but a more problematic example involves Sodom and Gomorrah, the two wicked cities that were destroyed by fire (Genesis 19.24-25). However, other biblical passages seem to suggest there might still be hope for the cities' inhabitants (Ezekiel 16.55; Matthew 10.15; 11.24). This ambiguity has caused the Society at times to regard the destruction of the cities as a final judgement, and at other times the opposite (Chryssides 2016: 258–62).

One *Watchtower* article defends such vacillations by comparing them to a sailing boat's tacking manoeuvres. Faced with an unfavourable wind, the captain will steer the boat in a zigzag motion, in order to enable it to progress towards the harbour (Watch Tower 1981: 26–7). However, as Raymond Franz (2000: 358) objected, the analogy only works if the boat moves forward; good sailors should not find themselves back where they were. When I put this objection to a Jehovah's Witness, he suggested that there might be benefits in moving forward then back: perhaps one learns something in the process, just as during the recent Covid epidemic scientists were changing their views, sometimes returning to a previously abandoned idea, but nonetheless learning and progressing. However, my informant did not specify what precisely has been learned from the Society's zigzag manoeuvres.

Political opposition: Nazi Germany

Jehovah's Witnesses generally disregard such attacks on their beliefs and practice. However, physical opposition cannot be so readily ignored, and Jehovah's Witnesses have suffered considerably for their faith in the course of their history. Undoubtedly, the gravest form of opposition was in Nazi Germany during the 1930s and 1940s. Jehovah's Witnesses – or Bibelforscher (Bible Students) as they were called in Germany – defied the ban on their house-to-house evangelism and literature distribution, declined to salute the national flag or to give the greeting 'Heil Hitler' and refused to accept military service. Despite the dearth of academic literature on Jehovah's Witnesses, this part of the Society's history is well documented. The Bible Students were barred from government employment, refused state benefits and had their businesses boycotted; children were forcibly separated from their parents, and members were arrested and beaten. Around 13,400 Bibelforscher were sent to prisons or camps. They were the one Christian group that were given their own distinctive symbol, the purple triangle, which they were obliged to wear, just as Jews were required to wear the Star of David. Unlike the Jews, however, the Bible Students were not automatically sent to gas chambers, and, uniquely, they were given the opportunity to be released by signing a document renouncing the Watch Tower organization and undertaking to take no further part in their activities, transferring their allegiance to the State. Since they were judged to be 'ideologically unfit' rather than biologically inferior, renouncing their faith was regarded as more important than extermination. Very few Bible Students, in fact, accepted this option, and as a result 2,000 failed to survive, and 271 German and Austrian Witnesses were executed because of their stance on war.

Opposition after the Second World War

Although Jehovah's Witnesses gained religious freedom in Germany after the war, this did not end persecution. A recent report by the United States Commission on International Religious Freedom states that 'more than many groups, Jehovah's Witnesses tend to bear the brunt of official and societal persecution' (Morton et al. 2020). Two main issues persistently arouse antagonism: their refusal of military conscription and their insistence on enthusiastic proselytizing. Numerous states that allowed limited religious freedom devised methods of controlling minority religions, which did not involve direct physical confrontation, but ensured that a religious organization could only function with state approval. One common method has been to require religious groups to register with the state, but frequently the criteria for registration discriminate against these new forms of spirituality. Eligibility to register is typically related to numerical strength or to the length of time the group has existed in the country, or to both. In measuring numerical strength, foreign missionaries are frequently excluded, and the threshold for registration can sometimes be as high as 10,000. Since new religions, by definition, are newcomers, starting from a low numerical base, it is often impossible for registration criteria to be satisfied. Registration can secure a variety of benefits for religious organizations, but Jehovah's Witnesses particularly desire the right to congregate and worship, the right to own property and the right to evangelize. As far as military service is concerned, Jehovah's Witnesses are amenable to undertaking alternative service, but not every state affords this option, thus bringing Witnesses into conflict with the civil authorities.

Jehovah's Witnesses are banned in numerous countries, principally Russia and several countries that were once part of the Soviet Union, the Islamic states, China, Vietnam and Laos (Radio Free Europe / Radio Liberty 2021). They have been banned in the past in Canada, Spain and Australia. Where countries have banned Jehovah's Witnesses from meeting or from proselytizing, bans have not deterred them. One of their strategies is 'informal witnessing'. In her book *Leaving the Witness* (so titled because the author finally disassociated), Amber Scorah describes how she arrived in China, carried Watch Tower publications wrapped in brown paper so that they would not be visible, and attempted to strike up conversations with people in places like book stores, since readers were likely targets. Having forged a friendship with one woman by this strategy, she then introduced her to the Society's teachings.

Greece

One landmark case about proselytizing in Greece involved Minos Kokkinakis (1919–1999), who was a shopkeeper in Crete and became a Witness in 1936. Two years later he was convicted for defying a ban on proselytizing, but he persevered, incurring more than sixty subsequent arrests and numerous prison sentences. (He was also sentenced to serve in an Athenian military prison in 1941, having refused military service.) In 1986 he and his wife called at a house where they were met by a Greek Orthodox cantor's wife, who called the police. After losing their appeal, the Kokkinakis case finally came before the European Court of Human Rights in 1993, when it was determined that the Greek government had violated Article 9 of the European Convention on Human Rights, which affirms the right 'in public or private, to manifest [one's] religion or belief, in worship, teaching, practice and observance' (European Court of Human Rights 1950: 7). This decision not only benefited Witnesses in Greece but also set a precedent for the right throughout the European Union for any religious group to promote their beliefs publicly. Although Jehovah's Witnesses have acquired the reputation for being litigious, they point out that utilizing the full extent of the law is conducive to spreading their teachings and note that, when Paul was brought before the governor Festus, he asserted his right as a Roman citizen to appeal to Caesar's higher court rather than stand trial at Jerusalem (Acts 25.11).

China

China's Cultural Revolution in the 1960s had a serious impact on all forms of religion, especially Buddhism. In the 1990s specific groups became targeted, and a list of *xie jiao* ('evil cults') was drawn up, consisting of organizations that were deemed to be either dangerous or 'heretical'. Heretical groups were those that did not belong to the officially sanctioned forms of religion in China, namely, the Three-Self Patriotic Movement of the Protestant Churches in China, Roman Catholicism, Buddhism, Daoism and Islam. Although Jehovah's Witnesses were not among the twenty *xie jiao* that were listed in 2017, eighteen Jehovah's Witnesses were arrested in Xinjiang the following year for evangelizing. On 15 April 2019 they were indicted 'on the suspicion of organizing and using a *xie jiao* organization to undermine law enforcement' and given heavy fines and prison sentences ranging from 2.5 to 6.5 years. The physical punishment to which they were subjected included the use of conjoined handcuffs and 'hug handcuffs' (handcuffs linked with a chain to a heavy shackle), which were kept permanently locked, even when the prisoners ate, washed and used the toilet.

South Korea

South Korea has been the seedbed of many new religions, and therefore there was no inherent objection to the presence of Bible Students when Watch Tower colporteurs began to visit in the early twentieth century. Problems arose, however, on account of the country's military policies and the Jehovah's Witnesses' stance on armed conflict. Having experienced military conflict with Japan, and subsequently between North and South, South Korea has one of the largest military forces in the world and allowed no exemptions for military service, not even for clergy or conscientious objectors. In 1948 the Military Service Act designated objectors as criminals, and from the end of the Korean War in 1953, some 19,000 Jehovah's Witnesses were imprisoned. When Park Chung Hee became president in 1963 he required 100 percent compliance, and when a state of emergency was declared in 1971, national security became prioritized over religious freedom. Soldiers sought out congregations, and offenders were brought before military rather than civilian courts. Prison conditions were harsh, family visits were not permitted and at times methods of torture were employed, resulting in the deaths of five young men. In 2001 affairs started to improve. The United Nations Human Rights Committee put pressure on the government to bring objectors before civilian courts, and in 2018 the right of conscience was formally acknowledged and alternative service was allowed. On 29 November 2018, fifty-eight Jehovah's Witnesses were released from prison, with only five remaining at the time of writing.

Eritrea

Eritrea has been a particular cause of concern. Most of the population adhere to either Sunni Islam or the Eritrean Orthodox Tewahedo Church, the Eritrean Catholic Church and the Evangelical Lutheran Church, all of which are officially recognized. Other forms of religion must register in order to have permission to worship. New and radical expressions of Christianity and Islam have proved to be unwelcome. From 1991 Jehovah's Witnesses were targeted, and in 1994 President Isaias Afwerki declared that they should have their citizenship revoked because they refused to participate in a referendum and would not undertake military service. The country has no provision for alternative service. Witnesses could no longer hold government office, and business licenses and ID cards were revoked; additionally, youths could not complete their education beyond eleventh grade, since further progression involved registration at the Sawa military camp, where they would receive military training. Arrests began in 2008, including those of elderly members, and those arrested were denied any defence or right of appeal. Alleged offences included attending religious gatherings, and on one occasion in 2012, three Witnesses were arrested for preaching at a funeral. Prison conditions are harsh, and five Witnesses died in custody. Some Witnesses have gone into hiding, while others have managed to flee the country.

The government's policies have been condemned by various human rights organizations, including the United Nations Human Rights Committee, the African Commission on Peoples' and Human Rights, and the African Committee of Experts on the Rights and Welfare of the Child. In 2016 the UN Commission of Enquiry on Human Rights in Eritrea accused the government of 'crime against humanity' on account of 'persecution on both religious and ethnic grounds' of Jehovah's Witnesses and other communities.

Russia

In Russia the 1917 Bolshevik Revolution resulted in serious repercussions for religious believers in general, not merely Jehovah's Witnesses. In 1929 Russian members were able to hear broadcasts transmitted from Estonia, but the authorities put an end to this in 1934. When war broke out, Jehovah's Witnesses refused conscription for military service, preferring to be sent to labour camps or prisons rather than to kill fellow human beings. In 1949 Witnesses in the Ukraine petitioned to register as a religious organization but were arrested. Because of their refusal to be conscripted, their persistent evangelism and denunciation of secular society, Witnesses were declared to be 'enemies of the state', and, following two secret operations in 1949 and 1951, Stalin ordered many Witnesses to be exiled. However, even in exile they continued to meet as a clandestine movement, with smuggled magazines and secret printeries to make their literature available to small groups of members. Informal witnessing was used to spread the message: they would visit strangers' homes on the pretext of asking whether they had livestock for sale and, if an opportunity presented itself, they would begin to talk about their faith.

Conditions appeared to become more favourable after 1986 with the announcement of perestroika. In 1990 Governing Body members Milton Henschel and Theodore Jaracz arrived from New York, as part of a delegation to meet with the Chairman of the Council for Religious Affairs. According to Watch Tower accounts, the meeting was cordial, and they convinced the Chairman that the organization presented no threat to the state, since they were politically neutral, seeking only to advance Jehovah's kingdom. The following year the Society was allowed registration in the republics of Russia and Ukraine.

However, it was not long before events turned against the Witnesses again. In 1997 a new law, 'On Freedom of Conscience and Religious Associations', was introduced, requiring state registration of religion. The law denied registration to organizations that were believed to threaten public order and safety, undermining family life, endangering health, inciting the public to forsake their civic obligations or to undertake 'extremist' activities (Baran 2014: 227). The 9/11 Al Qaeda attack on New York's World Trade Center intensified concerns about overzealous religious organizations, instilling a fear of religious terrorism from religious groups that could be considered 'extremist'. On 25 July 2002, the law 'On Combatting Extremist Activity' was passed. An extremist group was defined as any that disseminated 'propaganda of exclusivity, superiority or inferiority of a person on the basis of their religious affiliation or attitude towards religion' (SOVA Center for Information and Analysis 2010: 5). At first, an organization had to be suspected of violence in order to be classified as extremist, but in 2006 a modification was made to the legislation, enabling action to be taken against groups that did not explicitly incite violence. From 2008, conventions were prevented and disrupted, the organization's premises inspected and accounts scrutinized, with allegations of tax evasion; house-to-house publishers were arrested, and literature was seized.

Particularly instrumental in the opposition to Jehovah's Witnesses was Aleksandr Dvorkin, an Orthodox scholar who had trained in the United States. He had become quite prestigious in matters relating to Orthodox theology but became a self-styled expert on 'cults'. Dvorkin established the Saint Irenaeus of Lyons Information and Advisory Center, Russia's first anticult organization, backed by the Patriarch of Moscow, and from 1999 until 2012 he was head of a department for studying cults at Saint Tikhon's Orthodox University in Moscow. At first the Information and Advisory Center targeted a few small minority groups, but Dvorkin soon turned his attention to larger minority religions, such as Scientology, the Hare Krishna organization and Jehovah's Witnesses (CAP 2019). In 2009 an 'expert study' from Kemerovo State University was published, which, while not accusing Jehovah's Witnesses of incitement to hostility, nevertheless concluded that their literature was disrespectful to the Christian religion. Subsequently, the Federal List of Extremist Materials listed ninety-three Watch Tower publications as extremist literature, including the Society's *New World Translation*, *The Greatest Man Who Ever Lived* and, perhaps surprisingly, *My Book of Bible Stories*, which is a children's book of favourite Bible stories. The objection, apparently, to *The Greatest Man* and the Bible story book was the way in which priests were represented (even though they were ancient Jewish priests and not Russian Orthodox ones): they were perceived as sinister, not portraying religious authorities in a favourable light. It is also worth noting that, although the Russian Orthodox Church was no longer the state religion, it had close associations with the Communist Party. Michael Bourdeaux, who founded the Centre for the Study of Religion and Communism in the UK, commented in 2008 that 'the Moscow Patriarchate acts as though it heads a state church, while the few Orthodox clergy who oppose the church-state symbiosis face severe criticism, even loss of livelihood' (Bourdeaux 2008). The Jehovah's Witnesses' opposition to the Church could readily be perceived as opposition to the state. In April 2017 the 2002 legislation was invoked, ensuring that all Watch Tower activities were banned, properties confiscated and assets liquidated. Armed police raided over a thousand private homes, imposed restrictions on members' travel, placed many members under house arrest, imposed prison and community service sentences, and subjected numerous prisoners to torture. At the time of writing, this state of affairs continues.

Their opponents never seem to learn the strength of allegiance that Jehovah's Witnesses show to their faith, and they have continued to meet, to preach and particularly to celebrate the annual Memorial. As Emily Baran notes, during the Soviet period, instead of the usual high-profile baptisms at conventions, baptisms would take place in rivers or lakes, often in the early morning or late evening, when they would attract less attention. Another tactic was to mingle among groups of swimmers, when an elder could surreptitiously baptize a few candidates. Baptismal candidates were often required to wait for two or three years before baptism took place, to ensure that they were not infiltrators. Weddings and funerals could be used as opportunities for preaching, and quite large printing operations to distribute *The Watchtower* were carried out in basements. Not all remained loyal, however; in particular, numerous second-generation youths wanted to ensure that their educational and employment opportunities did not suffer. The majority who remained faithful devised ways of continuing to show loyalty to Jehovah. The organization's inability to register counted in their favour in certain ways: for example, the state could not require them to submit lists of members; also, their avoidance of celebrating Christmas and Easter made them seem less like a new schismatical Christian organization. Witnesses had only a limited number of Kingdom Halls: in 1997 around 85 per cent of Jehovah's Witnesses had no permanent meeting place, and therefore met in private homes, making their worship less visible to the authorities.

Other countries

These countries are by no means the only ones in which Jehovah's Witnesses have experienced persecution. Mention might be made of Malawi, where Jehovah's Witnesses refused to buy party membership cards in 1967, resulting in beatings, imprisonment, dismissals from employment, the destruction of around 100 Kingdom Halls and 1,000 private homes, and the deportation of missionaries. In Rwanda, some 400 Jehovah's Witnesses were murdered as a result of the 1994 genocide, either because they belonged to the Tutsi minority or because they attempted to protect them from attack. In other countries today, the main ground of state opposition is the refusal of Witnesses to accept military service. Whatever attempts are made to force them to abandon their faith, Jehovah's Witnesses have remained faithful; Jesus predicted, 'People will hand you over to local courts, and you will be beaten in synagogues and be put on the stand before governors and kings for my sake, for a witness to them' (Mark 13.9). Persecution has tended to be counterproductive, since it only serves to reinforce their beliefs and strengthen their determination.

10

Pressures to reform

Attitudes to change

The Watch Tower organization has been amenable to change in the course of its history. However, changes in its beliefs, organization and arrangements for meetings have all been introduced by the Society's presidents or the Governing Body, as Jehovah's representatives on earth. The Society runs on theocratic, not democratic, principles; therefore, change must be brought about appropriately, and it is highly important to maintain the unity of the organization rather than to allow different practices by different congregations, or rival teachings to circulate or to be debated (1 Corinthians 1.10). Doubts are 'the sin that easily entangles us', and Jehovah should never be doubted (Hebrews 12.1; Watch Tower 2009a: 8–9; 2013b: 13). While one might discuss one's doubts with elders, different opinions should not be expressed publicly within a congregation and should certainly not be promoted as if they were the Society's teachings. Nevertheless, there have been occasions where members have championed rival ideas and sought to bring about change, and have found themselves disfellowshipped as a consequence.

Insider attempts: Carl Olof Jonsson

One attempt to change the Society's thinking came from Carl Olof Jonsson (b. 1937), a Swedish elder, who called into question the Society's biblical chronology. Jonsson became a Jehovah's Witnesses in the mid-1950s, and was a full-time pioneer. While engaging in his work, he was challenged about the Society's historical dating. Not having a ready defence, he promised to look into the subject and became concerned that the Society might not be correct. In 1975 he began to discuss his findings with friends and started to write a treatise, in which he claimed that the destruction of Jerusalem by the Babylonians was not in 607 BCE, as the Society taught, but in 587/586 BCE, as claimed by the majority of historians. In 1977 he sent a copy to the Governing Body, who were unimpressed and cautioned him not to disseminate his findings. The following year, Governing Body member Albert D. Schroeder held a meeting in Europe with branch office representatives to inform them that there were plans to overthrow Watch Tower chronology, but that the organization had no intention of revising its dating (Jonsson 1998: 8–10).

In the same year, Jonsson was invited to a hearing before two Swedish Watch Tower office-bearers, who told Jonsson that the Brooklyn leaders were concerned about the treatise, that he should not disseminate his ideas and that Jehovah's Witnesses should not be engaging in such research. In the wake of this meeting, Jonsson decided to resign as an elder, and his reasons for stepping down became known. Eventually, Bengt Hanson, who coordinated the Society's work in Sweden, wrote to the Governing Body, reminding them that Jonsson was still hoping for a reply, and finally in 1980 Jonsson received a letter which addressed the issues he had raised. Jonsson was unimpressed, claiming that the response merely reiterated the Society's original position. The following year saw the publication of the Society's *Let Your Kingdom Come*, which contained an appendix dealing with biblical chronology, reaffirming the Society's stance against that of its critics, while not mentioning anyone by name. This made Jonsson all the more determined to publish his work: he wrote, 'My plan was to publish my treatise as a public farewell to the movement' (Jonsson 1998: 17). However, the plan was overtaken by events: he was summoned to a judicial committee and disfellowshipped on 9 June 1982. Jonsson appealed, hoping that this would buy extra time, but the appeal was turned down the following month, before *The Gentile Times Reconsidered* appeared in 1983.

The evidence which Jonsson presents is too detailed to explain here, and on Jonsson's own admission it is complex and technical (Jonsson 1998: 91). It is sufficient to say that Jonsson questions the Society's interpretation of the concept of the Gentile Times and regards much of its numerological interpretations as speculative. Jonsson rejects the notion that the dating of ancient biblical events can be determined simply from scripture, since the Bible does not give absolute dates but provides dating that relates to the accession and death of various kings of Israel and Judah. Jonsson therefore appeals to extraneous evidence, particularly Neo-Babylonian Chronicles, Ptolemy's Canon (also known as the Royal Canon, which lists Babylonian and Persian kings) and astronomical evidence: eclipses, for example, can be dated with absolute precision. Jonsson contends that this cumulative evidence suggests a 587 BCE date for Jerusalem's destruction rather than 607 BCE – the date which the Watch Tower Society continues to champion. The dispute is not merely about ancient history: the 607 BCE date is important to Jehovah's Witnesses, because the year 1914 lies at the end of the 2,520-year period of Daniel's 'seven times' prophecy (Daniel 4.32). On the assumption that a 'time' means a Jewish year of 360 days, seven times is therefore 2,520 years before 1914; hence, the 607 BCE date is crucially important to the Watch Tower organization. If the 607 BCE date were abandoned, then this would have serious repercussions for the Society's teachings regarding the key date of 1914.

More insider attempts: Christian Witnesses of Jah

A different line of criticism comes from Greg Stafford. Stafford was born in 1972 and baptized in 1990, after which he spent two years as a pioneer. Stafford founded Elihu Books in 1997 as a small publishing house for scholarly titles defending the beliefs and practices of Jehovah's Witnesses. The name 'Elihu' comes from the book of Job in the Bible: after Job's 'comforters' persist in claiming that Job's misfortunes are due to sin, Elihu arrives late in the discussion and is presented as Job's friend rather than accuser (Job 32.2–37.24). Elihu Books therefore set itself up as a friend of Jehovah's Witnesses, and Stafford's substantial volume, *Jehovah's Witnesses Defended* (2000), was an attempt to uphold the Society's beliefs and practices for the benefit of scholars and for those who were undecided about accepting Watch Tower teachings. Elihu was a debater, and Stafford, together with a few other like-minded Witnesses, are amenable to debate. However, when Stafford came to revise the work, he began to have doubts about the Society's teachings and policies. He became critical of its blood doctrines, arguing that the biblical references to blood were about eating and drinking, not transfusing, and that present-day medical procedures such as transfusion were not known in biblical times and therefore not referred to.

More generally, Stafford believed that the Society was too rigid, and his website takes the organization to task for having an inflexible structure of worship, meeting schedules, dress codes and the like. He questions the Society's prohibition of so-called pagan festivals: Paul, he notes, cautions against judging those who celebrate such events. Paul writes, 'One man judges one day as above another; another judges one day the same as all others; let each one be fully convinced in his own mind. The one who observes the day observes it to Jehovah' (Romans 14.5-6). Honouring Jehovah, he argues, is the key criterion regarding celebration, and he contends that the celebration of Christmas on 25 December is an occasion where people are specially inclined to hear the story of Jesus, and this might legitimately be encouraged. It should be a matter of conscience – not necessarily a festival to be placed in a congregation's calendar but a topic on which divergence is healthy. Paul notes the inevitability of having different factions within the early church, believing that those that merit approval will prevail over those that do not (1 Corinthians 11.19). Even Halloween, Stafford believes, should be a matter of conscience: if one wants to educate one's child on the varieties of malevolent beings such as ghosts, goblins, ghouls and demons, the festival might be an appropriate way to do this if one's conscience allows.

Stafford also adopts a lenient attitude towards reciting the Pledge of Allegiance to the state and saluting national flags. These are symbols of the nation and, as he points out, the Pledge of Allegiance mentions 'one nation under God', thus implying that God has precedence over the state, and not prioritizing one's country above God. Although Stafford agrees that one should not take sides in armed conflicts, he does not rule out the possibility of God using a nation to suppress what is evil.

Stafford sent three successive letters to the Governing Body in 2007, outlining his concerns about blood doctrine, but received no response. In the same year he formally disassociated himself and founded the Christian Witnesses of Jah, which operates largely online. The name 'Jah' is an abbreviated form of the tetragrammaton, which Stafford believes is less contentious than the disputed rendering 'Jehovah' (Stafford 2007: 6–7). Despite disaffiliating, Stafford continues to regard himself as 'one of Jehovah's Witnesses' – in other words, someone who continues to witness for Jehovah, accepting basic teachings regarding biblical inerrancy and non-trinitarianism, but does not belong formally to the Watch Tower organization.

Further insider attempts: Rolf Furuli

The most recent internal attempt at questioning the Governing Body comes in 2020 from Rolf Furuli (b. 1942), who published a book entitled *My Beloved Religion – and the Governing Body*. Furuli is one of a very few Jehovah's Witnesses who has held an academic position: he was a lecturer in Semitic Studies at the University of Oslo – a post which he held until he retired in 2011. He had been an elder for fifty-six years, having undertaken various assignments for the Society, including the roles of Circuit Overseer and District Overseer. It is ironic that Furuli's book should have led to his disfellowshipping, since at least two of his earlier works were detailed analyses of ancient chronology, defending the Society's dating against the generally accepted views of secular historians (Furuli [2003] 2007). Furuli's criticisms are not about Jehovah's Witnesses' fundamental teachings: he fully accepts the complete inspiration and authority of the Bible, the key doctrine of the ransom sacrifice, the 'two hopes' of the 144,000 and the great crowd, the authenticity and importance of the name 'Jehovah', the Society's interpretation of biblical and end-time chronology, and its policies on blood. His main concerns relate to the role of the Governing Body, as it has developed since 1938, after Rutherford's restructuring. At that point the Society's history moved from a democratic to a theocratic system, but now, Furuli believes, it has become an autocratic organization, with the Governing Body increasingly controlling aspects of members' personal lives and congregational affairs.

The term 'Governing Body', Furuli argues, is not biblical, and indeed the name first appeared in *The Watchtower* in 1944 (Watch Tower 1944a: 197). Although it regards itself as the 'faithful and discreet slave', the Society's understanding of the term has changed over the years, and he believes that the phrase's correct referent is the totality of Christians who watch for Christ's coming when he comes to judge the world at the great tribulation. The faithful and discreet slave is therefore a group that will be evident in the future, not an elite that exists in the present. Furuli contends that the Governing Body's authority now resembles that of the Roman Catholic Church, where hierarchical organization is paramount.

This small elite, he argues, has progressively intruded on the lives of Jehovah's Witnesses. One example Furuli cites is the use of tobacco, which was initially regarded as a matter of conscience, although disapproved of in the Society's literature. Today it is classed as 'gross uncleanness', together with recreational drugs, and is a practice that could merit disfellowshipping. Another example relates to blood transfusion: in previous years a nurse was permitted, if required, and if conscience allowed, to assist with medical procedures involving blood, but in 2018 the Governing Body ruled that such involvement was 'so closely linked with an unscriptural practice' that the nurse was complicit in wrongdoing, and that administering a blood transfusion under any circumstances was wrong (Furuli 2020: 10–11, 166).

Being an academic with high qualifications, Furuli sees the value of higher education, unlike the Society, which has tended to discourage its members from going to university. He cites Governing Body member Gerrit Lösch, who gave a talk to members in Italy in 2007, in which he encouraged students who were already in higher education to drop out, in order to give their lives to the Society's service. Furuli questions the Society's reasons: university life, he argues, need not lead to harmful associations involving sex, drugs and alcohol. Indeed, Furuli believes that the Governing Body, whose members did not undergo higher education themselves, hold on to a stereotype of college life. Although the Society views those who pursue higher education as materialistic, seeking high salaries, Furuli points out that in the present economic climate those who pursue trades rather than professions often earn more than university graduates.

Furuli also targets the practices of disfellowshipping and shunning. The elders' handbook 'Shepherd the Flock of God' itemizes thirty-nine offences: the majority of these, he believes, are non-biblical but have been invented by the Governing Body. In 1965 only seven offences were mentioned, rising to eighteen in 1977 and thirty-nine in 2019. Only eleven, according to Furuli, have any scriptural basis. He discusses the meaning of the original words aseēlgeia ('loose conduct'), porneia ('sexual immorality') and akatharsia ('uncleanness'). The word porneia, he argues, does not refer to the kind of action in which young courting couples often engage, such as touching intimate parts of the body, which the Society includes within the concept. Such practices may be wrong, and an elder may legitimately counsel the couple on their behaviour, but, he writes, 'In the NT, porneia is only used as a broad term, referring to sexual relations with a person to whom one is not married, with no specification of the manner or nature of the sexual actions' (Furuli 2020: 154). Furuli agrees that the biblical concept of akatharsia covers action such as lewd conversations on the telephone, viewing pornography, misusing tobacco and marijuana, and extreme physical uncleanliness but questions whether there is any biblical support for using disfellowshipping as a sanction (Furuli 2020: 166). According to biblical teaching, disfellowshipping is to cleanse the congregation from 'evil' people – that is to say, those whose lives are permeated with evil practices – not for those who have succumbed to smaller minor offences.

Regarding the consequence of disfellowshipping, which is shunning, Furuli acknowledges that there is biblical precedent for breaking all contact with those who are deceivers or 'antichrists':

> If anyone comes to you and does not bring this teaching, do not receive him into your homes or say a greeting to him. For the one who says a greeting to him is a sharer in his wicked works. (2 John 1.10-11)

However, John is referring to those who are evil and deceitful, not merely someone who, for example, decides to write a letter of disassociation to the Society. Further, shunning need not involve total refusal to speak to a disassociated or disfellowshipped member. If an apostate phones up a family member, the Society's expectation is that one should not pick up the phone; however, Furuli suggests that the caller might be in some difficult situation, such as depression, or even contemplating suicide. Just as one would not refuse to save someone from drowning, on the grounds that he or she was disfellowshipped, discipline should be tempered with compassion.

A further criticism relates to the Society's scriptural exegesis, as it appears in its publications. Instead of probing the meaning of scripture, using scholarly tools such as analysis of language, the authors of Watch Tower literature simply resort to subjective interpretations about ideas of which biblical passages remind us. Furuli cites the example of Ezekiel's vision of the Temple's perimeter wall (Ezekiel 42.20) in the 2018 publication *Pure Worship of Jehovah – Restored At Last*, which reminds the author of the need to maintain high standards of conduct in order to engage in pure worship of Jehovah. This, Furuli maintains, is a subjective allegorical interpretation, an 'association game' (Watch Tower 2018c: 154; Furuli 2020: 240), rather than discussion of Ezekiel's role as a prophet and the end-time events his words foreshadow. Furuli compares this with the Society's literature in the early 1970s, where, he believes, its authors engaged in a much more incisive approach to biblical exegesis.

In addition to exercising greater control over members' lives, Furuli criticizes the Society for increasingly taking control over the organization's assets. Back in 1972, a congregation could exercise its own discretion about constructing a Kingdom Hall. The elders would set up a building committee, who would decide on the design and the necessary building work for the project. The congregation would then own its own premises. Between 1972 and 2014, congregations had the autonomy to decide about buying and building their Kingdom Halls, and could vote on the matter. They could, where necessary, and subject to approval, acquire a loan from the Kingdom Hall Fund. In 2014 things changed, however. Soon after, congregations were required to transfer the ownership of their Kingdom Halls to the branch office, enabling the Society to sell off some of its properties, requiring congregations to merge or be redefined, or to share the same Kingdom Hall. Monies acquired from the sales were sent to the branch office, rather than retained by the congregations who had raised the money in the first place. From 2014, there was a drive to undertake substantial building work, and the Society planned to construct an additional 13,000 Kingdom Halls and thirty-five Assembly Halls worldwide. This would require fairly massive funding, and all members were asked to estimate how much they were likely to give each month. This was not a pledge, but an estimate. The estimated monies would then be sent to the branch office, together with any surplus. Before 2019 it was standard practice for circuits to use the Assembly Hall for twice-yearly assemblies without charge, but from then on there would be a rent of $13,000 payable to the branch office. As Furuli points out, a key principle at the inception of the Watch Tower organization was that it was the church without a collection, and Furuli believes that the drive to obtain funds not only contradicts the Society's original policy but is also contrary to scripture, which advocates freely giving of one's resources.

Perhaps predictably, a judicial committee was set up in Furuli's congregation, and on 17 June 2020 the announcement was made that Rolf Furuli was no longer one of the Jehovah's Witnesses. The announcement was made online, through Zoom, since the Covid-19 pandemic was then at its height, and Kingdom Halls were closed.

Advocates for Jehovah's Witness Reform on Blood

Another issue on which some Jehovah's Witnesses have sought reform is the issue of blood. On 27 January 1997 an elder wrote a letter to Governing Body member Dan Sydlik. He prefers to remain anonymous, simply calling himself J. W. Elder, identifying himself as a third-generation member and an elder of around ten years' standing. The letter contained a treatise that the elder had written, and a request for an online conversation with Sydlik, who was invited to do this either by leaving a message on a designated website, or entering a secure internet chat room at a mutually agreed time, when they could discuss the issue. No doubt Sydlik was wary of entering into a discussion with someone whose identity could not be verified, and on such a controversial subject. Predictably, Elder received no response, and consequently decided to launch a new website entitled 'New Light on Blood' (Elder 2014).

Elder's treatise provides detailed biblical exegesis on the topic of blood, questioning the Society's interpretation of God's command to Noah and arguing that these ancient laws belong to the old covenant and that Christians today are not under the Mosaic law. The web pages also contain detailed medical information about blood transfusion – the risks involved and the corresponding risks of alternatives. Elder also points out that the Society has received 'new light' in the past regarding its teachings, including details of its blood policy, and that its stance on blood is therefore an issue that could legitimately be reappraised.

Lee Elder (as he is now more frequently called) has a number of supporters who call themselves the Advocates for Jehovah's Witness Reform on Blood (AJWRB) and have set up a detailed website giving information about blood, explaining why they believe reforms are needed to the Society's stance on the subject. The AJWRB make it clear that they are not opposed to the Watch Tower organization. They are not external or ex-member critics but are fully committed Jehovah's Witnesses, who wish to see the Society reformed from within on the matter. They wish to remain anonymous, because identification would undoubtedly cause them to be disfellowshipped, and being outside the Society, they believe, would be less conducive to seeking the desired reforms.

Responses

The Society does not engage in dialogue with such critics, and Jehovah's Witnesses are cautioned to avoid reading apostate literature. However, some of their researchers made comments to me about these challenges. First, they questioned whether such changes should properly be described as reforms, believing that they would not be improvements to the organization. Regarding Furuli's points about abandoning solid biblical exegesis, they responded that the Society's change was deliberate: understanding and applying biblical teachings is more important than incisive scholarly study. Regarding financing, congregations are independent organizations in law and could choose whether or not to transfer property ownership, and individual members pledging monies continued to do so on an entirely voluntary basis. On the topic of blood, they regarded bloodless medical treatment as the gold standard, contending that alternative medical procedures should not be viewed as inferior substitutes, since they avoided problems involved in blood transfusion, which has at times caused infections and even deaths. On the subject of chronology, they believed that the Society had already given ample and detailed justification for its views on biblical dates in its plentiful literature.

Sexual abuse

As the subject of sexual abuse came to public attention, it was inevitable that the spotlight would turn to religious organizations, including Jehovah's Witnesses. In 2000, a former elder in a Kentucky congregation, and previously a Bethelite, invited victims of abuse to get in touch with him through the internet, and he drew on their experiences to set up Silentlambs.org – which became an incorporated organization in 2001 (Quenqua 2019). The organization does not exclusively focus on Jehovah's Witnesses, but the Watch Tower organization is described in its pages as a 'pedophile paradise'. Between 2007 and 2014 a number of cases were brought before US courts, and the Watch Tower organization gained a great deal of negative publicity on account of the compensation it was ordered to pay – sums amounting to millions of dollars. In the UK in 2013 and 2014 two cases attracted publicity in which victims had to face the perpetrator.

There have been several investigations into the Watch Tower organization in various countries. In 2015 an Australian Royal Commission investigated sexual abuse, not exclusively among Jehovah's Witnesses but in a variety of religious and secular organizations, including Anglicans, Roman Catholics and the Salvation Army. The report revealed that the Jehovah's Witnesses'

Australian branch held 1,006 files on alleged perpetrators, dating back to 1950. There were 579 cases in which the perpetrator admitted the offence; 108 were elders or ministerial servants, and 28 were appointed after allegations had been made. Of the accused, 401 were disfellowshipped (78 more than once) and 230 later reinstated; 383 were dealt with by the police and 161 convicted. The Watch Tower Society points out that the 1,006 total relates to the number accused and not necessarily the number who are actually guilty; it also spans a period of 65 years, which would equate to fifteen alleged cases countrywide per year.

The Society's internal policy has been to deal with such incidents by forming a judicial committee where there is sufficient evidence against the accused. In all cases, accusations of paedophilia are reported to the branch office, and a record is permanently kept both in congregational records and by the branch. The required evidence is the testimony of two or more witnesses, which is a particularly difficult criterion in the case of sex offences, which are normally clandestine. However, the Society has interpreted the biblical 'two witness' rule to allow evidence from two victims concerning similar offences by the same alleged perpetrator, not necessarily in connection with the same offence. There is no biblical precedent for considering factors such as forensic evidence, even if elders had the knowledge and facilities to do so: such evidence is for the police and the civil authorities. It has been alleged that children who have complained against members have often not been believed and that any baptized members making unsubstantiated accusations could themselves run the risk of judicial sanctions, if an accusation was construed as malicious.

Some have found it a daunting experience to face a judicial committee, even as an accuser or a witness. One may not be accompanied by a companion or any legal representative (with the exception of minors, who are normally present with a parent), and women have often been subjected to questioning about quite intimate particulars regarding which parts of the body were touched and in what way, what they were wearing and other highly personal details. If the accused denies the accusation, the elders may ask the accuser (unless he or she is a minor) to face the accused directly – something that can be highly threatening, although elders are advised to use discretion about the desirability of such a meeting (Watch Tower 2010a: 5.39; 2020a: 12.41; Royal Commission 2016: 3.2).

The Commission was not satisfied that Jehovah's Witnesses had responded adequately to the issue of child abuse, and it made a number of recommendations. It strongly criticized the 'two witness' rule, accusing the Society of outdated policies that were over 2,000 years old. It accused congregational elders of insufficiently focusing on the victims, by employing an all-male judicial committee to determine the accused's guilt rather than supporting the victim. The Commission believed that the sanctions were weak, enabling offenders to return to the community, with the risk of repeating such offences. Finally, comment was made on failure to report sexual abuse to the police or other relevant authorities. The Final Report made three main recommendations: (1) the two-witness rule should be discontinued; (2) women should be involved in the judicial investigations relating to child sexual abuse; (3) the practice of shunning those who dissociate or are disfellowshipped should not be an appropriate sanction.

Holly Folk, a well-accredited scholar of new religious movements, has criticized the Australian report on a number of grounds. She argues that the report does not distinguish between family child sexual abuse and institutional abuse (Folk 2021). The statistic of 1,006 reported allegations is the totality of reports, whether proven or unproven, and the statistic itself does not tell us how many perpetrators there were, since there may well have been multiple victims. Half of these were cases of incest, while a further proportion was abuse by relatives of the victims. Of the 1,006, 902 did not involve any Jehovah's Witness office-bearer, and of the remaining 104, 54 related to familial abuse by elders. Of course, this does not mean that all is well in the Watch Tower organization. One has a right to expect members of religious organizations to live up to the standards that their faith requires; even one instance of sexual impropriety is one too many.

As a follow-up to the report, the Australian government set up a National Redress Scheme for victims of institutional sexual abuse, to which institutions such as charities and religious organizations were encouraged to subscribe. Victims could apply to have their case assessed and to determine the amount of compensation they should receive. Initially, Jehovah's Witnesses in Australia declined to participate in the Scheme, stating that 'the religion of Jehovah's Witnesses does not have the institutional settings that the voluntary National Redress Scheme is designed to cover' (Kelly 2020) and arguing that the Royal Commission previously acknowledged that there were no situations in which they were responsible for the care of children, or separated children from adults. However, faced with the prospect of losing their charitable status, they subsequently agreed to take part (Gredley 2021).

Investigations in other countries

Two other government reports followed that of the Australian Commission: in Belgium and in the Netherlands. The Belgian report was undertaken by the Centre for Information and Advice on Sectarian Organizations (CIAOSN), which is a cult-monitoring organization set up by the Belgian government in 1998. The report was prompted by a number of articles that appeared in

2017 in the newspaper *Trouw* (meaning 'Truth'), which is sponsored by the Reformed Church in the Netherlands. The journalists drew substantially on information from Reclaimed Voices, an organization set up in early 2018 in the Netherlands, with a view to providing assistance to sexual abuse victims and aiming to change the internal procedures offered by Jehovah's Witnesses. The body spread to Belgium, where in December of that year the Belgian Parliament gave approval to the CIAOSN investigation. The Belgian report substantially relied on the media coverage, and as Folk comments, 'the report fails to meet even basic standards for social science research' (Folk 2021).

In 2019 a motion passed by the Dutch Parliament initiated the survey by the Ministry of Justice and Safety in Utrecht, resulting in a report exclusively targeting Jehovah's Witnesses. The investigators set up a section of the University of Utrecht's website, containing a survey which provided basic information about the research and in which victims of sexual abuse by Jehovah's Witnesses could relate their experiences, positive as well as negative. Public attention was drawn to the research through a press release on the university's website, and on the media. The Jehovah's Witness organization in the Netherlands cooperated by sending a letter to congregations, suggesting that members of congregations might participate. The number of responses was reported as 751, which might suggest a high level of abuse. However, 422 respondents in all gave accounts of sexual abuse – 214 of abuse they claimed to have personally experienced and 208 of experiences of others. Of these, 84 per cent were of multiple incidents. Most of these occurred between 1970 and 2009, which may suggest that the problem has declined in the past decade; however, the researchers suggest that, since children are often the victims, they may not yet have reached an age to report such incidents. Approximately half of the cases involved family members, just over a quarter by fellow members and 4 per cent by office-bearers. Interpreting the data is hampered by the fact that there are overlapping categories: some victims may have had multiple perpetrators, for example, and those reporting personal experiences may also have had the incidents reported by another respondent.

The report's recommendations included a need to give more attention to victims, to ensure that they did not risk the congregation's disciplinary procedures and that there should be a merging of their internal regulations with external criminal law. Elders should always advise victims of the right to report offences to the authorities. It was also recommended that there should be an internal desk for hearing reports of sexual abuse and for affording access to counselling facilities, and that elders should undertake relevant training in how to handle reports of abuse. Consideration should be given to admitting women to the community's hierarchy, particularly in view of the fact that the majority of victims were female.

The report has been criticized on a number of grounds. As the authors themselves acknowledge, 'the research presented in this report was not submitted to truth-finding' (University of Utrecht 2019: 7.4), and they are unable to verify the veracity of the responses. The report also does not compare Jehovah's Witnesses with other religious organizations; hence, it cannot be determined whether they have a better or worse track record than other spiritual communities or secular organizations. A more serious deficiency, for which the report has been criticized, is its methodology, which employed self-selection of respondents, whose testimony was provided entirely online. There were no checks to ensure that different reports did not come from the same IP address, for example, and it would have been all too easy for opponents of Jehovah's Witnesses to fabricate reports, or for the same person to send multiple accounts, purporting to come from different sources (Folk, Introvigne and Melton 2020).

Watch Tower responses

Jehovah's Witnesses do not turn a blind eye to sexual impropriety, however. Numerous articles from 1982 on in *The Watchtower* and *Awake!* magazines have deplored sexual abuse, and offered advice on alerting children to potential abusers and how to support victims (Watch Tower 1982). Despite criticisms that the accusations of minors go unheeded, one *Awake!* article affirms that children seldom lie or fantasize about such incidents (Watch Tower 1993c: 6). Regarding the criticism that the congregational elders do not inform the civil authorities, the Society points out that, as Jehovah's organization, its role is to apply theocratic law, which is not the same as civil law. As one Circuit Overseer put it to me, 'The law deals with crime; we deal with sin.' The police and the law courts uphold the law of the land and are able to examine evidence and determine penalties that are not available to congregational elders. The Society has no objection to that: it is not a law enforcement agency, although Jehovah's Witnesses are committed to compliance with the law, and if a state requires child sexual abuse to be reported to the authorities, the elders will do that, and they will advise victims and their parents that they should report the offence to the police.

The 'two witness' rule, all-male leadership and sanctions such as disfellowshipping and shunning are aspects of theocratic law. Those outside the Society may well disagree with them, but scholars such as Massimo Introvigne and Alessandro Amicarelli have pointed out that recommendations to abandon such principles, as the Australian Commission and the Dutch government have made, are attempts to interfere with religious freedom (Introvigne and Amicarella 2020: 3). If someone voluntarily belongs to an organization, Introvigne and Amicarelli argue, they signal agreement to be bound by its rules. Regarding the role of women in counselling victims, the elders' manual 'Shepherd the Flock of God' acknowledges that a victim may require assistance beyond the 'spiritual shepherding' that the elders provide and suggests that a child could approach an 'empathetic sister' for support and, where appropriate, seek professional advice from medics and professional counsellors (Watch Tower 2020a: 14.17).

On the issue of reinstatement, the Society has been accused of allowing sex offenders to return to the congregation, where they can continue to perpetrate their offences. The Christian faith has always allowed for, and indeed welcomed, repentance, teaching that even the most loathsome sinner is not beyond God's grace. This belief inevitably presents problems in exercising discipline, and hence judicial committees allow for the possibility that the offender is contrite. However, reinstatement does not mean that the offender is accepted back as things were before. The repentant offender will be deprived of privileges and may also be barred from contributing comments at meetings, at which the meeting conductor will ignore them if they raise a hand. The elders will decide whether and when such a privilege will be restored.

It is possible that an offender may try to move to another congregation, and there have been instances where this has occurred. The Society keeps meticulous records about baptized members, and if they attempt to attend another Kingdom Hall, an elder in the previous congregation would write a letter of introduction: this is standard practice for all transferring members and not merely for offenders. Where there are issues regarding past disciplinary action, this would be mentioned. In the case of sex offences, elders are instructed to notify the branch office immediately, where a record of the accusation is retained; this is the case whether or not disciplinary action is taken.

In addition to the various Watchtower and Awake! articles on child abuse and child protection, a document was made available in December 2020 to all congregations and placed on the Society's website, titled 'Jehovah's Witnesses' Scripturally Based Position on Child Protection' (Watch Tower 2021b). The statement reiterated the Society's position that child protection was a matter of serious concern and directed elders to listen carefully and sympathetically to reports of abuse. Where accusations of sexual abuse are made, the branch office should be consulted, in order to ensure that they are complying with laws relating to reporting obligations; parents and guardians should be informed of their right to report such matters to the police, and, if a child is believed still to be in danger, the elders should automatically report the matter to the authorities. The accuser should not be made to confront the alleged perpetrator, and when presenting an accusation, a child has a right to be accompanied by a confidant of either gender, or alternatively to present a written statement. Offenders who are unrepentant should be disfellowshipped, and if they persuade the elders that they are genuinely repentant, they might be readmitted to the congregation but with restrictions imposed and privileges withdrawn, and they should not be eligible for any office 'for decades, if ever' (Watch Tower 2021b: 3). The document concludes by itemizing the various Watch Tower publications that have addressed the issue from 1983 to the present (Watch Tower 1983b; 1991; 1993c; 2007b; 2016a; 2019c,d,e).

The topic of sexual abuse is an extremely sensitive one, particularly for those who have been affected by it. Sexual abuse has undoubtedly taken place on many occasions within the organization, and it is to be deplored, wherever it occurs. Some time ago I was asked to write an expert witness report on a historical sex abuse case. This involved examining the victim's detailed witness statement, which provided considerable and unpleasant detail about multiple locations in which she was fondled and sometimes raped by a ministerial servant over a period of several years. For reasons of confidentiality I cannot give more detailed information, except to say that the press reports were not wholly accurate: they implied that the abuse had taken place in Kingdom Hall premises, when all the incidents took place at her home. Of course, the venue does not make the offence any less serious.

To criticize official reports on sexual abuse is not to condone such offences. All interested parties should wish to see proper investigation, which involves using appropriate methodology in researching this important issue. It is certainly not in the interests of the victims if research is seriously flawed. Although sexual abuse is to be strongly condemned wherever it occurs, it is important neither to exaggerate nor to minimize the extent to which it happens among Jehovah's Witnesses, and without good evidence it should not be implied that such offences are more or less prevalent than in other religious groups and secular organizations. Those who believe that a Kingdom Hall is a paedophile paradise have either never visited one or have succumbed to malicious rumours. Whatever the failings of the Watch Tower Society, this description is wildly inaccurate, particularly in view of the fact that there are no separate premises or activities for children in the Watch Tower Society. As to the suggestion that paedophiles deliberately join the organization for this purpose (Hovaland 1998), this seems highly unlikely in view of the stringent requirements that need to be satisfied to be eligible for baptism.

Shunning

Some final comments should be made on the issue of shunning. A number of legal cases have been brought against the Society by ex-members who have claimed to have experienced emotional harm by being ostracized. The first to attract publicity was in 1987, when Janice Paul, who wrote a letter of disassociation to the congregation at Ephrata, Washington, in 1975. Finding herself shunned by former acquaintances, she claimed tort damages against the Society. However, the court refused to uphold her case on the grounds of 'ecclesiastical abstention', regarding the Society's policy as a matter of religious freedom, invoking the US Constitution's First and Fourteenth Amendments, which entailed that the judgements of religious courts take precedence over civil ones (*Paul v. Watchtower Bible Tract Soc. of N. Y* 1987). A similar judgement was made in subsequent litigation in Tennessee in 2007, and courts in Berlin and Italy in 2010 and 2017, respectively, decline to adjudicate on matters they regarded as essentially religious.

However, in March 2021, the Criminal Court of Ghent, Belgium, took a different view, when sixteen ex-members decided to bring an action against the Christian Congregation of Jehovah's Witnesses, claiming that the shunning they had experienced constituted discrimination and hatred, in violation of Article 22 of the Anti-Discrimination Act, and that they had experienced emotional and economic harm as a consequence. The investigation lasted over four years and, notwithstanding considerations of religious freedom, the Society was required to pay a fine of €13,000, plus compensation to the plaintiffs. At the time of writing, it is unclear whether an appeal might reverse this verdict, but Jehovah's Witnesses to whom I have spoken are adamant that their policies of disfellowshipping and shunning are in accordance with biblical teachings, and, whatever human courts decide, they will continue to implement Jehovah's law, as they interpret it.

11

Prospects

Armageddon

Jehovah's Witnesses, of course, believe that their future, and indeed the future of humankind, will be in fulfilment of biblical prophecy, and that they will experience an everlasting paradise in the new world after Armageddon. Various signs indicate that the Battle of Armageddon is about to begin. Signs of the end include wars, plagues, natural disasters such as earthquakes and floods, and breakups in human relationships: although these have been in evidence for centuries, Jehovah's Witnesses believe that there has been a particular increase in recent times. Before the final battle takes place, the 'remnant' – those of the anointed class who still remain on earth – will be taken up into heaven to complete the 144,000.

Armageddon features prominently, both in popular culture and in American Protestant fundamentalism. In popular culture it is associated with a threatened destruction of the earth, as in the 1998 film bearing the title. For Jehovah's Witnesses, however, Armageddon does not mean the earth's destruction but rather the destruction of God's enemies. In Watch Tower eschatology, it forms part of a chain of end-time happenings. The sequence is somewhat difficult to unravel, for a number of reasons. The timeline is somewhat complex, and it is not set out in one single continuous part of scripture; much of the Bible's apocalyptic imagery is obscure, and it is necessary to harmonize components that appear to conflict. Additionally, Jehovah's Witnesses' interpretation of certain details has changed in recent years. In some places the Bible suggests that Christ's return will be inconspicuous, like 'a thief in the night' (1 Thessalonians 5.1-3), but in other places it is stated that the present system will end with an ear-splitting trumpet sound from the Archangel Michael – scarcely the action of the average thief. Consequently, Jehovah's Witnesses reconcile these descriptions by noting that Paul's allusion to the silent thief is closely followed by mention of a period of peace and security, in which earthly rulers will assure the earth's citizens that all is well. This is peace and security that is offered by the United Nations, which was created to replace the League of Nations (see Chapter 8). However, this is a lie: the great tribulation will soon begin. Wars have continued in the world and Jehovah's Witnesses have continued to be persecuted for their faith. The book of Daniel mentions the King of the North and the King of the South: the latter is the Anglo-American alliance, while the former has assumed various identities as history has progressed. After 1871 when the Unification of Germany took place, the country was identified as the King of the North, on account of its opposition to Britain and America – the King of the South – during the two world wars and its hostility towards the Bible Students during that period. After the Second World War, the King of the North was Russia, as was evidenced by the Cold War and its treatment of Jehovah's Witnesses, which continues to the present.

The ensuing chain of end-time events lies in the future: the ten political powers represented in the United Nations (the ten horns of the scarlet wild beast – Revelation 17.3) will turn against all false religion, taking exception to the ways in which it has interfered with political systems. It will plunder their wealth and expose their corruption, leaving God's people – Jehovah's Witnesses – standing alone. Babylon the Great will have been destroyed.

Ezekiel states that in the period of apparent security, Gog of Magog will attack them with a vast army of horses and horsemen wielding swords (Ezekiel 38.1-12). Gog is mainly mentioned in the book of Ezekiel and once in Revelation (Revelation 20.1-2). Gog is to be understood as a coalition of nations, who have come to hate the only surviving religion and seek to destroy it. However, Jehovah's Witnesses have been well trained in cultivating the virtues of loyalty, endurance and courage, and will be able to stand firm. At the appropriate moment, Jesus Christ will come to the rescue, the remnant of the 144,000 will be taken up into heaven and the battle of Armageddon will commence. The exact way in which the battle will take place is somewhat indeterminate; the Bible mentions a number of ways in which God's enemies have been destroyed: natural calamities, such as earthquakes, hailstorms and lightning; God's enemies may turn against each other; or angels may slay the wicked.

In view of the amount of attention Armageddon has received in popular culture and Protestant fundamentalism, it may seem strange that it is only mentioned once in the Bible: 'And they gathered them [the kings] together to the place that is called in Hebrew Armageddon' (Revelation 16.16; my parenthesis). As with much of John's writing, this verse creates problems. Armageddon (Hebrew, *Har Megiddon*) literally means 'Mountain of Megiddo', but Megiddo is not a mountain but a plain, and it has a relatively small area, being 20 by 18 miles (32 by 29 kilometres), which would hardly allow sufficient space for 'the kings of the entire inhabited earth' to assemble with their armies. Indeed, no single physical space would be sufficiently large for the scale of this conflict, which will be universal, not local.

Although Megiddo is identified as the scene of numerous ancient battles (Judges 4.1-22; 5.19-21), it is inferred that the 'Mountain of Megiddo' must refer to God's mountain, Mount Zion, and that the battle will take place in supernatural rather than natural realms. Armageddon will not be a physical battle but a spiritual one between Christ (Michael in his spiritual form) and his angelic forces, and Satan with his army of demons; hence, Jehovah will not call on his followers to take part in the conflict. Although the battle will be a cosmic event, it is not to be feared by God's people for, although there will be human casualties, none of Jehovah's followers will suffer any harm. The battle ends with an angel descending from heaven with the key of the abyss, into which Satan is hurled, having been bound, and the abyss is sealed for a thousand years (Revelation 20.1-3).

Armageddon marks the beginning of the millennium – Christ's thousand-year rule. Those who remain on earth and are sick or have injuries or deformities will be progressively restored to a perfect physical state, and the earth will be gradually transformed into a perfect paradise, with the dead being brought back to life. Miraculous healing will once again return, although healing will only be accomplished through Jesus himself, perhaps with the aid of the 144,000, but not by his followers who remain on earth. If one wonders how the planet could accommodate all past generations of humanity as well as the present population of the earth, this should not be a problem. In the Society's early days, Russell performed a calculation in the first volume of his *Studies in the Scriptures*, in which he calculated that, if there were three generations for each century, some 252 billion (252,000,000,000) would have lived since the time of Adam (Russell 1886: 160). (A later Watch Tower estimate suggests a lower figure of 20 billion (Watch Tower 1989a: 340).) Even such a great number, Russell reckoned, would still be able to have standing room in a large city like Philadelphia or London. It should be remembered that in the coming world the earth's resources will be multiplied: 'the earth will yield her increase', the desert will blossom like the rose and streams and waters will break out in the wilderness and the desert (Psalm 67.6; Isaiah 35.1-6).

Further, not everyone will be resurrected immediately. Jehovah's Witnesses envisage that those who have died most recently will be resurrected first: this will enable recognition by their friends and families who were still alive at Armageddon. One can readily recognize one's deceased parents or grandparents, whom one knew during one's lifetime, and they in turn will be able to recognize those who belonged to generations that overlapped their lifetimes. Those who accept Jehovah and his organization will qualify to live forever in this everlasting paradise, while those who reject the truth will not be brought back to life but will simply experience nothing.

The dead who have not had an opportunity to accept the truth will be enabled to do so; one reason for the progressive resurrecting of the dead is the need to have sufficient publishers to instruct those who will be offered this prospect. Jehovah and Christ will judge who merits further instruction, and one can only rely on Jehovah's justice, rather than speculate as to who will ultimately survive. Those who have led wicked lives and deliberately rejected the truth will have no further opportunities, while those who, through no fault of their own, have been unable to hear the truth will merit instruction. Hence, in the coming new world, there will still be plenty of instruction to be given, as successive generations are brought back to life. We do not know, of course, what proportion of returners will come to accept the teachings, but it is unlikely that the earth would have to accommodate 252 billion people. The Society's teaching and preaching work will continue before and after Armageddon, so time spent on new projects will not be wasted, whatever occurs.

This is not quite the end of the story. The book of Revelation states that at the end of the millennium Satan is released for a short period. He attempts to lead an all-out attack on God's people with a large army of those who have not accepted the truth, but he is prevented by fire falling from heaven, which consumes his supporters. Satan is then hurled into a fiery lake, in which he will be imprisoned for ever. Then the everlasting paradise on earth can now commence.

Methods of instruction

How will seekers and returners be instructed? The Society has invariably made a point of updating its methods of instruction. In the past it has promoted one favoured key book for its Bible studies. In the 1920s it was Rutherford's *The Harp of God*, which was replaced in 1946 by '*Let God Be True*'. In the late 1960s *The Truth That Leads to Eternal Life* became the key text: it was reckoned to be so powerful that it was nicknamed 'The Blue Bomb' and remained in use until 1982 when *You Can Live Forever on Paradise Earth* was published. In 1995 *Knowledge That Leads to Eternal Life* became the basis for Bible study, until 2005, when *What Does the Bible Really Teach?* became available as a paperback and was prominently displayed on the literature carts. The slightly simplified *What Can the Bible Teach Us?* came to replace it in 2015.

In 2021, however, a new and innovative approach to Bible studies was announced at the Society's Annual Meeting. As Governing Body member Anthony Morris III explained, people had become more acclimatized to electronic media, and in the past many found it hard to plough through a traditional book; many people, he said, had not read a book since they left school. Further, books are not interactive and may not address specific problems that students experience. The standard study text was therefore to be replaced by an ambitious electronic package, which would be available in electronic and in print format. Its title is *Enjoy Life Forever!: An Interactive Bible Course*. The package had been piloted by 100 publishers worldwide: in print form it is 256 pages in length, containing sixty lessons, including instruction on all the questions that are put to baptismal candidates. The material contains hyperlinks to videos, allowing the student to select particular items of relevance. So as to avoid making the package too daunting for the new seeker, a brochure containing the first three lessons is available to students. This serves as a sample for those who wish to undertake the full programme and avoids the cost of distributing the full print text, since students may become tired of study after a short period and wish to discontinue. Those who receive the brochure in paper format can request a Bible study from the Witness who gave it, and those who download it online are directed to the JW.org website, where they can request a visit from one of the publishers. In the past, Watch Tower books contained mainly text and displayed footnotes containing questions which are designed to check comprehension. By contrast, *Enjoy Life Forever!* is copiously illustrated, and the questions posed are intended to elicit discussion rather than recollection. For example, the first lesson, 'How Can the Bible Help You?', asks open-ended questions like 'How do you view the Bible?' as well as ones that check recall.

Life in the new world

The coming new world will be a perfect paradise. Although no doubt it is not possible to envisage all its features from the standpoint of the present system of things, Watch Tower publications enumerate several benefits that the faithful can hope to experience. Life will be everlasting: war will be a thing of the past, death will have been abolished and there will be no sorrow, sickness, disability or pain. Its inhabitants will all live in proper housing and enjoy ample food (Psalms 37.29; 46.9; Isaiah 33.24; 35.5-6; Revelation 21.4; Isaiah 65.21; Psalm 72.16). In order to bring about this perfect paradise, one important task will be to transform the planet Earth from its polluted state to a world with clean air, pure water, restored rainforests and a properly balanced ecological system. Current problems such as climate change, global warming, a shrinking ozone layer, toxic waste and over-exploitation of natural resources are all due to humanity's subjection to human government rather than theocratic rule. Jehovah's Witnesses believe that the earth has an outstanding ability for self-renewal, particularly since the new world will be free from the worst kind of pollution, namely, the human mind, whose rebelliousness against Jehovah has caused humanity's lack of responsibility for the planet. Jehovah's Witnesses find assurance in Isaiah's prophecy, 'The wilderness and the parched land will exult, And the desert plain will be joyful and blossom as the saffron' (Isaiah 35.1).

Although this world will be a perfect paradise, it will not be eternal rest, since human effort will be needed to bring about the earth's restoration after Armageddon. Rest was never an aspect of the paradise God created for Adam and Eve: they were instructed to cultivate the Garden of Eden (Genesis 2.15). However, work will be pleasant and satisfying; it is only after Adam and Eve disobey God that tilling the ground becomes laborious, and God tells them that the ground will produce weeds and that 'in the sweat of your face you will eat bread' (Genesis 3.19). Some forms of work will not be needed: there will be no armed forces or armaments industries, for Isaiah predicted, 'Nor will they learn war anymore' (Isaiah 2.4). There will be no need for doctors, dentists or opticians, and those involved in law enforcement will be obsolete, although we do not know in detail precisely which occupations will be needed. When one looks at the artwork in Watch Tower literature, one does not find depictions of high technology but rather portrayals of men and women engaged in horticulture and construction work. This, however, is not to imply that the new world will not be technologically advanced, but that the Society's writers and artists only portray aspects that have biblical warrant. Horticulture and construction are depicted because both are described by Isaiah:

They will build houses and live in them,
And they will plant vineyards and eat their fruitage. (Isaiah 65.21)

In the new world there will be perfect harmony, not only among humans, but also between humans and animals:

The wolf will reside for a while with the lamb,
And with the young goat the leopard will lie down,
And the calf and the lion and the fattened animal will all be together;
And a little boy will lead them. (Isaiah 11.6)

Despite the fact that animals will be part of the coming paradise, animals are believed not to enjoy everlasting life like humans but will live and die, as they did before Armageddon (2 Peter 2.12; Watch Tower 2018a: 110–12).

The anticipated harmony between humans and animals which Isaiah envisages might seem to suggest that animals would be companions rather than food. God tells Adam and Eve that they may eat of any plant in the Garden of Eden, apart from the tree of knowledge of good and evil, but he gives no permission to eat any of the animals, birds or fish. It is only after Noah survives the flood that God says, 'Every moving animal that is alive may serve as food for you. Just as I gave you the green vegetation, I give them all to you' (Genesis 9.3). The reference to vegetation in this instruction is an explicit acknowledgement that only plant life was permitted as food. This observation has caused Jewish vegetarians to argue that vegetarianism was the primordial diet, and the ideal, since it was God's intended practice in Eden. When one looks at illustrations in Watch Tower publications, they are invariably of men wheeling barrels full of giant marrows, vineyards yielding large crops of grapes and tables with ample loaves of bread. Families are never portrayed eating meat, and there are certainly no pictures of abattoirs, butchers' shops or people fishing. The Society's literature does not state explicitly that the new world diet will be vegetarian; one Witness with whom I discussed the question acknowledged the possibility but agreed that in our present situation this was not yet known.

A further issue involves the question of marriage and family life in the new world. Jehovah's Witnesses believe that death breaks the marriage bond, and if one's spouse dies, the remaining partner is free to remarry. Yet Watch Tower literature seems to depict conventional families in the new world; so will marriages be reconstituted? Some couples will not die at all, if they have lived through Armageddon – which raises the question of whether their marriages will remain valid. No doubt there will be some single-parent families, since there have been many instances where only one parent has accepted the truth. Also, what might happen to 'blended families', created by subsequent marriages? The Bible recounts an incident in which the Sadducees presented Jesus with a conundrum about a woman who successively married seven brothers, after each one progressively died, enquiring which husband she would have in the resurrection. Jesus' response was, 'In the resurrection neither do men marry nor are women given in marriage, but they are as angels in heaven' (Matthew 22.30). However, a 2014 edition of *The Watchtower* contained discussion about whether Jesus was referring to the earthly or the heavenly class (Watch Tower 2014f: 29). On the one hand, the Sadducees were seeking an answer about earthly resurrection, and Jesus refers to the God of Abraham, Isaac and Jacob in his answer, all of whom would be raised on earth rather than heaven. On the other hand, Jesus uses the expression 'those who have been counted worthy of gaining that system of things' in his answer, and says, 'Neither can they die any more,' and that they are like angels (Luke 20.36). The reference to angels, who are believed to be genderless, could imply that Jesus was talking about the 144,000 and not referring to life on paradise earth. However, the article concludes that one cannot be certain about the issue. If a couple are separated through belonging to the anointed and the earthly classes, respectively, they will not feel any of the sorrow of human separation, since such attachments belong to our present state with earthly emotions. Even Jesus' parents Mary and Joseph will be everlastingly separated, since Joseph is believed to have died before Jesus made his ransom sacrifice, while Mary lived on, and the anointed class will only be composed of those who outlived Jesus (Watch Tower 1987: 31).

One event that will not feature in the new world is the annual Memorial of Jesus' death. Once all of the 144,000 anointed class has taken their place in heaven, there will be no one left on earth who will be eligible to partake of the emblems. Jesus said, 'For whenever you eat this loaf and drink this cup, you keep proclaiming the death of the Lord, until he comes' (1 Corinthians 11.26), thus implying that the annual celebration would not continue indefinitely. When I have attended an annual Memorial service, members have frequently remarked that it could be the last, since Armageddon is expected soon. Although its celebration will cease, Jehovah's Witnesses expect to have fond memories of it in the new world and will continue to be grateful for Jesus' ransom sacrifice (Watch Tower 2018d; 2019b). When Jesus speaks of 'that day when I drink it [the wine] new with you in the Kingdom of my Father' (Matthew 26.29), Jehovah's Witnesses regard this statement as symbolic: the 144,000 who will rule in the kingdom of heaven will have spiritual, not physical, bodies, and hence will not consume physical substances. The reference to drinking wine refers to the joy that Jesus and his anointed ones will experience in heaven (Watch Tower 2018b: 269).

Language in the new world

What language will be spoken in the coming paradise? The Bible states that when Noah's family spread further afield, 'all the earth continued to be of one language and of one set of words' (Genesis 11.1) and that it was the building of the Tower of Babel that caused God to punish human arrogance by destroying the edifice, thwarting further such projects by causing humanity to speak different languages (Genesis 11.7-9). The miraculous happening at Pentecost, which caused Peter's multilingual audience to hear his speech in their own language, is often perceived as a contrast to Babel, and it might be inferred that, since a single language was humanity's primordial condition, the new world would revert to one single universal language. Such an expectation might seem to be reinforced by the prophet Zephaniah, when he says,

Then I will change the language of the peoples to a pure language,
    So that all of them may call on the name of Jehovah,
    To serve him shoulder to shoulder. (Zephaniah 3.9)

The book of Revelation portrays the great crowd as being drawn 'out of all nations and tribes and peoples and tongues' (Revelation 7.9), singing praises to Jehovah and the Lamb. If the great crowd sings praises in every language, then this implies not only a multiplicity of languages but also a revival of dead and dying languages. This in part explains why Jehovah's Witnesses have recently started to produce some of the literature in minority languages such as Scottish and Irish Gaelic: these tongues will also be used in praise of Jehovah and Christ in the new world.

The 'pure language' about which Zephaniah speaks is not, therefore, some universal language like Esperanto. The expression is believed to refer to 'proper understanding of the truth found in God's Word regarding Jehovah and his purposes, particularly the truth about God's Kingdom' (Watch Tower 2003: 4).

The pure language is the truth about Jehovah God and his purposes as found in his Word, the Bible. That 'language' includes a correct understanding of the truth about God's Kingdom and how it will sanctify Jehovah's name, vindicate his sovereignty, and bring eternal blessings to faithful mankind. What results from this change of language? We are told that people will 'call upon the name of Jehovah' and will 'serve him shoulder to shoulder'. Unlike the events of Babel, this change to the pure language has resulted in praise to Jehovah's name and unity for his people. (Watch Tower 2008c: 22)

Jehovah's Witnesses come from a multiplicity of backgrounds and speak many different languages, yet they are united in their love for Jehovah and his truth that is found in the Bible. The article quoted above continues by comparing life as a Witness with learning a new language. Language learning entails more than memorizing a few useful phrases; it involves acquiring fluency and often recognizing and employing new thought patterns. In order to achieve this, one must first listen and concentrate, particularly during the Society's meetings. One must imitate the fluent speakers, which means using more experienced members as role models. Language learning involves memory, and participants are encouraged to memorize key Bible texts and to acquire useful abilities, such as memorizing the names of the books of the Bible in order – a particularly useful technique when listening to Bible talks at congregation meetings and conventions, when it is customary for the speaker to direct the congregation frequently and swiftly to biblical texts. (This last skill may be obsolescent, however, with the advent of digital editions of the New World Translation.)

One Watch Tower publication, however, appears to take a different interpretation of Zephaniah and suggests that a reversal of the confusion of languages at Babel will occur in the new world. Whatever the multiplicity of languages that are used to praise Jehovah, the author suggests that linguistic barriers will exist no longer and speculates that there might be a return to the original language of Eden, which Adam and Eve spoke:

> What will become the common language of all the earthly children of the 'Eternal Father'? Will it be the original language of the first Adam, the language with which Jehovah endowed him? Likely. In any event, all language barriers will be wiped out. You will be able to travel anywhere and communicate with people. You will be able to understand them, and they will be able to understand you. There will be one language for all mankind, and it would be appropriate for the entire Bible to be available in that language. (Watch Tower 1986: 176)

For Jehovah's Witnesses, belief in the coming paradise is an important hope, and they are encouraged to contemplate this future destiny. Belonging to a kingdom involves standards of behaviour and obedience to its laws, and those who want to be subject to Jehovah's everlasting rule are members of that kingdom now, and not merely in the future. Hence, contemplating the future paradise should be a guide to how one behaves under the present system. As Paul said, 'no sexually immoral person or unclean person or greedy person, which means being an idolater, has any inheritance in the Kingdom of the Christ and of God' (Ephesians 5.5), and hence those who continue with sinful practices, such as fornication, homosexual acts, excessive alcohol consumption, gambling and smoking, must mend their ways and live as they would in the new world.

The future of the Society

It is always tempting to conclude a book by looking into the future. What might the Watch Tower Society be like in the coming decades, and what changes might we expect? For Jehovah's Witnesses the answer is simple: Armageddon is 'just around the corner', and we can expect the end-time agenda outlined above to work itself out into the expected everlasting paradise on earth, governed by Jehovah, Jesus Christ and the 144,000. But what if this does not happen? Scholars of religion are seldom convinced by the prospect of supernatural outcomes and have characteristically equated prophecy with failure. So what if Armageddon does not arrive soon? What might we expect?

Inevitably the question arises as to how long a religion can continue to expect an imminent end to the present system. Mainstream Christianity itself has survived for over 2,000 years, with many fundamentalists continuing to affirm that we are living in the end times and that Christ will return soon. Jehovah's Witnesses have placed a time limit on the arrival of Armageddon with the new interpretation of the 'generation' prophecy. If Armageddon is due within the lifetime of those whose lives overlap the 1914 generation, then this allows considerable leeway. Donald Allen (2019) takes the example of Frederick Franz, who died in 1992. Born in 1892, and baptized in 1923, he is the last-known anointed member to have lived through the year 1914. If someone aged 20 were baptized in the year Franz died, and lived as long, the overlapping generation would then extend to 2071. Of course, some of the 1914 generation may have outlived Franz, and there were no doubt slightly younger baptismal candidates in 1992, thus allowing some leeway, but not much. However, there is still ample time for prophetic expectations to be compatible with the Society's current teaching.

Minority religions have had different trajectories in the past. A number have declined, for example, the Swedenborgians, Theosophists, Christadelphians and Father Divine's Peace Mission. Others have become accepted by the mainstream, for example, Seventh-day Adventists, Pentecostals and the Worldwide Church of God: the last of these underwent a dramatic theological shift under its change of presidency in 1995. A few are expanding, for example, the Church of Jesus Christ of Latter-day Saints.

Just as one cannot predict future changes in society, both technological and political, so too one cannot predict how religious groups are likely to respond. However, it is unlikely that Jehovah's Witnesses will move towards the mainstream, for a variety of reasons. Their consistent and thoroughgoing belief that mainstream Christianity has abandoned its true nature effectively precludes any kind of reconciliation. The Society's stance on blood marks them out as different from all other religious groups, and, as Zoe Knox observes, it has become an important aspect of Jehovah's Witnesses' identity (Knox 2018: 183). A further important factor in maintaining the status quo is the Governing Body: being self-perpetuating, it is unlikely to co-opt new members with significantly different ideas, and, as has been shown in Chapter 10, it is unamenable to significant change from the grassroots. The fact that 144,000 is a finite number need not set any limit to the ability of the Governing Body to perpetuate itself, since new members of the anointed class can be recognized and accepted, and no records are kept of those who are deemed to belong to that number.

The Governing Body continues to be the defining authority for Jehovah's Witnesses, and it is difficult to see how this could change. As we have seen, any challenges from within tend to be regarded as rebellion against Jehovah's theocratic governance, and external attempts to bring about changes that are contrary to the Society's understanding of scripture are firmly rejected. The only changes the organization is likely to make are those required by law, where this does not interfere with its understanding of Jehovah's requirements. The Society has made numerous alterations to its patterns of worship and to its organizational structure in recent times, and it is certainly foreseeable that it may decide that further changes are desirable. Various changes have been prompted by the internet and cyber-technology, and, as one Jehovah's Witness recently commented to me, the use of videos at congregation meetings and conventions has created greater standardization.

For a religious organization to maintain its strength, one or both of two factors are necessary: it must retain its children or it must forcefully evangelize. Jehovah's Witnesses are strong on their evangelism but not so effective at retaining subsequent generations: it is estimated that of those who are raised as Jehovah's Witnesses, two-thirds no longer maintain their allegiance in adulthood (Lipka 2016). This compares with 65 per cent of evangelical Protestants and 64 per cent of Mormons who stated that they remained in the denomination in which they were raised. There are various possible explanations, although there is no firm evidence to explain the drop off. It is possible that children felt that congregational worship and Watch Tower material were geared towards adults, with few concessions to younger members, and availed themselves of the opportunity to leave when they were no longer under parental control. Other young Jehovah's Witnesses want to pursue further and higher education, where the real dangers to faith maintenance are not sex, alcohol and drugs but rather exposure to new and alternative ideas. Questioning authorities and recognizing the existence of different viewpoints are central to academic study, and finding that many of the authority figures are women rather than men will inevitably expose the upcoming student to new secular movements such as feminism. It is also possible that statistics about retention fail to account for degrees of commitment; perhaps it is more difficult to live up to the high level of commitment that is characteristic of Jehovah's Witnesses than to maintain a more lukewarm nominal membership of a mainstream denomination.

On the other hand, Jehovah's Witnesses are not dwindling in overall numbers. Some 65 per cent of current Witnesses are first-generation converts, which reflects a remarkable degree of success in the organization's evangelism. A comparison of numerical strength between 2009 and 2019 reveals a 20 per cent increase in the number of average publishers and a 15 per cent increase in Memorial attendance over the past decade, compared with a 12 per cent increase in global population over that period. Jehovah's Witnesses are therefore growing slightly faster than the world's population.

With regard to academia, Jehovah's Witnesses have become somewhat more favourable to contacts with the academic community. They attend some academic seminars and occasionally present papers, although these are mainly factual or historical rather than presentations that are designed to open up doctrinal debate. No doubt this change is motivated by various factors. Obtaining fair and objective portrayals is important both to themselves and to the academic community. Things have changed considerably since H. H. Stroup's attempts to engage the organization's cooperation for his research. In addition, the Society has looked to the academic community for support in times of persecution. Faced with the attempts in Russia to suppress Jehovah's Witnesses, a number of academics signed a petition which was sent to President Putin and which aimed to demonstrate that they do not pose a threat to the state. From the Jehovah's Witnesses' standpoint, there is an obvious need to have experts speak out on their behalf, while from the standpoint of academics, it is important to disseminate accurate information, in contrast to the biased and misinformed accounts which are so frequently disseminated by the anticult movement.

This book has been written during the period of the Covid-19 pandemic and reached completion shortly before the world emerged from it. As with many religious organizations, the pandemic caused some radical rethinking about how to practise one's faith and how to use technological innovations to replace traditional forms of human contact. It remains to be seen how such these fairly radical changes will shape Jehovah's Witnesses' future. The New World Translation renders the meaning of the tetragrammaton (YHWH or JHVH) – the name 'Jehovah', which God gave to Moses (Exodus 3.14) – as 'I Will Become What I Choose to Become'. The concept of becoming indicates Jehovah's direction for his people and causes his Witnesses to reflect on how the future of Jehovah's organization is being shaped. One recent *Watchtower* article challenges its readers:

> Throughout history, Jehovah has caused his servants to fulfill many different roles. What will he cause you to become? Much depends on how willing you are to exert yourself. ... If you make yourself available, Jehovah can cause you to become a zealous evangelizer, an effective teacher, a capable comforter, a skilled worker, a supportive friend, or whatever else he needs to accomplish his will. ... Jehovah can cause you to become whatever he needs to accomplish his will. (Watch Tower 2019e: 25)

Jehovah's Witnesses are restorationist in terms of their doctrines and practices, seeking to return to the faith of the first-century early Church. However, in other respects, as described in this volume, they have always been progressive and willing to adapt to what they believe Jehovah is causing them to become.

Glossary

These are brief explanations of terms used by Jehovah's Witnesses, with which the reader may be unfamiliar. Fuller explanations can be found in my *Historical Dictionary of Jehovah's Witnesses* ([2012] 2019).

anointed class the 144,000 who will rule eternally with Christ in heaven

apostate a person or community who has abandoned true religion

Babylon the Great the present system of false religion

Bethel a residential branch office, responsible for the Society's administration and literature distribution

Bibelforscher name of the Bible Students in Germany, which continued for some time after the name 'Jehovah's Witnesses' was adopted in 1931

Bible Students the name given to Watch Tower supporters before the name 'Jehovah's Witnesses' was adopted

branch a country or region in which the Society has a headquarters

brother baptized male member

canon agreed body of scriptures

circuit a group of around twenty congregations

creature worship undue veneration given to humans instead of Jehovah

demonstration short dramatization, demonstrating aspects of witnessing

disassociation resignation from the Society

elder senior man who is responsible for congregational life

field ministry evangelization, usually house-to-house or at literature carts

Gentile times Period from 607 BCE to 1914, when the Gentiles rather than the Jews are held to enjoy God's favour (Luke 21.24)

Governing Body group of men who oversee the Society's affairs at its headquarters

great crowd those who will experience everlasting life on earth after Armageddon

great tribulation final part of the last days, which is about to occur

Greek Christian Scriptures books of the Bible from Matthew to Revelation, usually called the New Testament outside the Society

Hebrew-Aramaic Scriptures books of the Bible from Genesis to Malachi, usually called the Old Testament outside the Society

holy spirit God's active force, not part of any Trinity, and always spelt in lower case

informal witnessing evangelizing that is not carried out in house-to-house ministry or literature carts, usually in informal conversations

Kingdom Hall meeting place for congregations

Memorial the annual commemoration of Jesus' final meal with his disciples, in which bread and wine were shared

millennium Christ's thousand-year rule after Armageddon

ministerial servant baptized male members who are responsible for the material aspects of the congregation

ministry an alternative term for field service

New World Translation the Watch Tower Society's own translation of the Bible

Old Covenant obligations and promises given by God to the Jews before Christ

overseer usually an elder, who has been given a specific task within a congregation, or who has oversight over designated territory

pagan pertaining to false religion

pioneer officially appointed man or woman whose time commitment exceeds normal expectations

privileges assigned tasks within a congregation

publisher one who proclaims Jehovah's message to the public

remnant members of the 144,000 who remain alive on earth

sister baptized female member

special pioneer one who undertakes assigned tasks by the branch office, with additional time commitment and usually a modest stipend

spiritual food edifying literature, principally the Bible and the Society's publications

stumbling spiritual faltering, or leading someone else astray

system of things characteristic features of an extended time period

theocracy/theocratic government by Jehovah

truth body of teaching found in the Bible, as proclaimed by Jehovah's Witnesses

Biblical chronology: A comparative table

The table below serves two purposes. Not all readers may be familiar with the biblical narrative and biblical chronology, and this brief summary may therefore assist their understanding of the Bible stories to which the main text alludes. The comparison also highlights differences between Jehovah's Witnesses' comprehension and those of the majority of mainstream scholars.

Event	Watch Tower date	Mainstream dating
Creation of Adam	4026 BCE	generally regarded as myth, not history
Noah saves his family from a great flood by building an ark	2370–2369 BCE	myth, not history
Nimrod travels to Babel, where he established a kingdom and oversees the building of a tower	c. 2239 BCE	myth, not history
Abraham	b. 2018 BCE	? c. 1900–1300 BCE/ historicity uncertain
Abraham's nephew Lot escapes Sodom and Gomorrah's destruction	1919 BCE	historicity uncertain
Jacob has twelve sons, including Joseph, and is given the name 'Israel'	1858–1711 BCE	historicity uncertain
Joseph is taken captive into Egypt, where he becomes prime minister Interprets dreams for Pharaoh	1737 BCE	? died 1445/1444 BCE

Event	Watch Tower date	Mainstream dating
Job is head of a large family and suffers many afflictions as a test of his faith but had his fortunes restored	between 1654 and 1473 BCE; writing completed by 1473 BCE	a fictional work, possibly written c. 400 BCE
Moses leads the Israelites out of Egypt, where they have been enslaved	b. 1593 BCE	? c. 1230 BCE
The Passover is the Israelites' last meal before fleeing Egypt	1513 BCE	thirteenth/twelfth century BCE (historicity disputed)
Receives the law from God on Mount Sinai	1513 BCE	thirteenth/twelfth century BCE (historicity disputed)
Joshua succeeds Moses and captures Jericho	1473 BCE	c. 1200–1100 BCE
Israel becomes a monarchy, with Saul as the first king	1117 BCE	c. 1000–985 BCE
King David succeeds Saul and establishes Jerusalem as his capital	1077 BCE	c. 985–963 BCE
King Solomon succeeds David and builds the Jerusalem Temple	construction begins 1034 BCE Temple completed 1026 BCE	c. 963–929 BCE Temple completed c. 929 BCE
Elijah and Elisha – Hebrew prophets	tenth century BCE	ninth century BCE
Babylonian King Nebuchadnezzar invades Jerusalem	607 BCE	587 BCE
Jewish exile in Babylon	607–537 BCE	586–538 BCE
Daniel is a Jew who is made an official in Babylon	618–536 BCE	of dubious historicity, written 168–165 BCE

Event	Watch Tower date	Mainstream dating
Persian king Cyrus captures Babylon and issues a decree, releasing the Jews	539; 537 BCE	538 BCE
Ezra arrives from the exile in Babylon to oversee the rebuilding of the Jerusalem Temple	515 BCE	520–515 BCE
Nehemiah's arrival in Jerusalem to reconstruct the city walls	455 BCE	439–437 BCE
Greeks rule Judaea	332 BCE	332 BCE
Romans rule Judaea	63 BCE	63 BCE
Birth of John the Baptist and Jesus	2 BCE	7–4 BCE
Baptism of Jesus	29 CE	c. 27 CE
Death of Jesus	33 CE	c. 30 CE
Pentecost	33 CE	c. 30 CE
Paul (previously named Saul) converts to the Christian faith after a vision of Jesus on the Damascus Road	c. 34 CE	c. 35 CE
Jesus' disciple Peter meets the Roman centurion Cornelius	c. 36 CE	no date given
First Jerusalem Council	c. 49 CE	c. 50 CE
John (reputedly Jesus' closest disciple) dies, thus ending the first generation of Jesus' disciples	c. 100 CE	c. 100 CE (trad.)

Bibliography

Allen, Donald P. (2019), '140 Years Strong: A Historical and Critical Analysis of the Primary Mechanisms Employed by the Jehovah's Witnesses to Thrive in a Hostile World', PhD thesis, University of East Anglia, Norwich, UK.

Anon (1984), 'Do Jehovah's Witnesses Still Hold to Their 1984 Doomsday Deadline?', *Christianity Today*, 21 September: 66–7.

Baran, Emily B. (2014), *Dissent on the Margins: How Soviet Jehovah's Witnesses Defied Communism and Lived to Preach about It*, New York: Oxford University Press.

Barclay, William (1953), 'An Ancient Heresy in Modern Dress', *Expository Times* 65 (October): 31–2.

Bauer, Walter (1958), *A Greek-English Lexicon of the New Testament and Other Early Christian Literature*, Chicago: University of Chicago Press.

Beckford, James A. (1975), *The Trumpet of Prophecy*, Oxford: Blackwell.

Betheltours (2021), 'Israel Bible Lands Tours in 2019–2020'. Available online: www.betheltours.org/israel.php (accessed 19 February 2021).

Botting, Gary, and Heather Botting (1984), *The Orwellian World of Jehovah's Witnesses*, Toronto: University of Toronto Press.

Bourdeaux, Michael (2008), 'President Putin and the Patriarchs', *The Times*, 11 January.

Bowman, Robert M. (1996), *Understanding Jehovah's Witnesses: Why They Read the Bible the Way They Do*, Grand Rapids, MI: Baker Book House.

Brooks, Keith L., and Irvine Robertson (1985), *The Spirit of Truth and the Spirit of Error* [pamphlet], Chicago: Moody Press.

Brown, Ian (1999), *Sixty Questions Every Jehovah's Witness Should Be Asked*, Belfast, UK: Ambassador-Emerald International.

CAP (Coordination of the Associations and the People for Freedom of Conscience) (2019), 'The Role of FECRIS and Anti-Cult Organization in Russia', 17 May. Available online: https://freedomofconscience.eu/the-role-of-fecris-and-anti-cult-organization-in-russia (accessed 1 March 2021).

Cetnar, William J., and J. Cetnar (1983), *Questions for Jehovah's Witnesses*, Kunkletown, PA: Joan C. Cetnar.

Chryssides, George D. (1999), *Exploring New Religions*, London: Cassell.

Chryssides, George D. (2010), 'How Prophecy Succeeds: Jehovah's Witnesses and Prophetic Expectations', *International Journal for the Study of New Religions*, 1(1): 27–48.

Chryssides, George D. ([2012] 2019), *Historical Dictionary of Jehovah's Witnesses*, Lanham, MD: Rowman & Littlefield.

Chryssides, George D. (2016), *Jehovah's Witnesses: Continuity and Change*, London: Routledge.

Chryssides, George D. (2019), 'Moving Out: Disengagement and Ex-Membership in New Religious Movements', in George D. Chryssides and Stephen E. Gregg (eds), *The Insider/Outsider Debate: New Perspectives in the Study of Religion*, 371–92, Sheffield, UK: Equinox.

Chryssides, George D. (2020), 'Jehovah's Witnesses and Covid-19', CenSAMM, 30 April. Available online: https://censamm.org/blog/jehovahs-witnesses-and-covid (accessed 30 April 2020).

Cole, Marley (1955), *Jehovah's Witnesses: The New World Society*, Aurora, MO: Stoops (later reissued as *Jehovah's Witnesses: The Global Kingdom* in 1985).

Cole, Marley (1957), *Triumphant Kingdom*, New York: Criterion Books.

Cole, Marley (1966), *The Harvest of Our Lives*, Aurora, MO: Stoops.

Countess, Robert H. (1982), *The Jehovah's Witnesses' New Testament*, Phillipsburg, NJ: Presbyterian and Reformed.

Crompton, R. (1996), *Counting the Days to Armageddon: The Jehovah's Witnesses and the Second Presence of Christ*, London: Lutterworth.

Curry, Melvin D. (1992), *Jehovah's Witnesses: The Millenarian World of the Watch Tower*, New York: Garland.

Czatt, Milton Stacey (1933), *The International Bible Students: Jehovah's Witnesses*, Scottdale, PA: Mennonite Press.

Elder, Lee (2014), 'Jan. 27, 1997 Letter to Dan Sydlik. Advocates for Jehovah's Witness Reform on Blood', AJWRB, 4 August. Available online: www.ajwrb.org/jan-27-1997-letter-to-dan-sydlik (accessed 19 February 2021).

European Court of Human Rights (1950), *European Convention on Human Rights*. Available online: https://www.echr.coe.int/documents/convention_eng.pdf (accessed 3 June 2021).

Folk, Holly (2021), 'Jehovah's Witnesses and Sexual Abuse: 2. Belgium and The Netherlands', *Bitter Winter*, 13 January. Available online: https://bitterwinter.org/jehovahs-witnesses-and-sexual-abuse-2-belgium-and-the-netherlands/ (accessed 1 March 2021).

Folk, Holly, Massimo Introvigne and J. Gordon Melton (2020), 'Expert Opinion', 7 January. Available online: www.rijksoverheid.nl/binaries/rijksoverheid/documenten/rapporten/2020/01/23/tk-bijlage-1-expert-opinion/tk-bijlage-1-expert-opinion.pdf (accessed 1 March 2021).

Franz, Raymond V. (2000), *Crisis of Conscience: The Struggle between Loyalty to God and Loyalty to One's Religion*, 3rd edn, Atlanta, GA: Commentary Press.

Furuli, Rolf J. ([2003] 2007), *Assyrian, Babylonian, Egyptian, and Persian Chronology Compared with the Chronology of the Bible*, 2 vols, Larvik, Norway: Awatu.

Furuli, Rolf J. (2018), *Can We Trust the Bible? With Focus on the Creation Account, the Worldwide Flood, and the Prophecies*, Larvik, Norway: Awatu.

Furuli, Rolf J. (2020), *My Beloved Religion – and the Governing Body*, Larvik, Norway: Awatu.

Gray, James M. (1909), *Satan and the Saint*, Edinburgh: Oliphant, Anderson and Ferrier.

Gredley, Rebecca (2021), 'Jehovah's Witnesses to Join Redress Scheme for Child Sexual Abuse Survivors', *New Daily*, 3 March. Available online: https://thenewdaily.com.au/news/2021/03/03/jehovahs-witnesses-redress-scheme (accessed 31 March 2021).

Gruss, Edmond C. ([2001] 2007), *Jehovah's Witnesses: Their Claims, Doctrinal Changes and Prophetic Speculation: What Does the Record Show?*, Maitland, FL: Xulon Press.

Harris, Doug, and Bill Browning (1993), *Awake! to the Watchtower*, London: Reachout Trust.

Harvey, Graham (2003), 'Guesthood as Ethical Decolonising Research Method', *Numen* 50 (2): 125–46.

Hoekema, Anthony A. (1963), *The Four Major Cults: Christian Science, Jehovah's Witnesses, Mormonism, Seventh-day Adventism*, Exeter, UK: Paternoster.

Holden, Andrew (2002), *Jehovah's Witnesses: Portrait of a Contemporary Religious Movement*, London: Routledge.

Hovaland, Norman (1998), 'Do You Practice Incest? Do You Molest Children?', Silentlambs, 18 August. Available online: https://silentlambs.org/news/do-you-practice-incest-essay-on-the-first-mention-of-pedophile-paradise (accessed 26 February 2021).

Introvigne, Massimo, and Alessandro Amicarelli (2020), *The New Gnomes of Zurich: The Jehovah's Witnesses, the Spiess Case, and Its Manipulation by Anti-Cult and Russian Propaganda*, Turin: CESNUR.

Jonsson, Carl Olaf ([1983] 1998), *The Gentile Times Reconsidered: Chronology and Christ's Return*, Atlanta, GA: Commentary Press.

Kelly, Cait (2020), '"Harsh Sanctions": The Organization Refusing to Join the Child Abuse Redress Scheme', *New Daily*, 25 June. Available online: https://thenewdaily.com.au/news/2020/06/25/national-redress (accessed 28 February 2021).

Kliever, Lonnie D. (1995), *The Reliability of Apostate Testimony about New Religious Movements*, Los Angeles: Freedom.

Knox, Zoe (2018), *Jehovah's Witnesses and the Secular World: From the 1870s to the Present*, London: Palgrave Macmillan.

Liebster, Max (2003), *Crucible of Terror: A Story of Survival through the Nazi Storm*, New Orleans, LA: Grammaton Press.

Liebster, Simone A. (2000), *Facing the Lion: Memoirs of a Young Girl in Nazi Europe*, New Orleans, LA: Grammaton Press.

Lipka, Michael (2016), 'A Closer Look at Jehovah's Witnesses Living in the U.S', Pew Research Center, 26 April. Available online: www.pewresearch.org/fact-tank/2016/04/26/a-closer-look-at-jehovahs-witnesses-living-in-the-u-s (accessed 3 June 2020).

Macmillan, A. H. (1957), *Faith on the March*, Englewood Cliffs: Prentice Hall.

Martin, Walter R., and Norman H. Klann ([1953] 1974), *Jehovah of the Watchtower*, Grand Rapids, MI: Zondervan.

Martin, Walter ([1965] 1985), *The Kingdom of the Cults*, Minneapolis, MN: Bethany House.

Metzger, Bruce M. (1953), 'The Jehovah's Witnesses and Jesus Christ: A Biblical and Theological Appraisal', *Theology Today* 10: 65–85.

Morton, Jason, Keely Bakken, Mohy Omer and Patrick Greenwalt (2020), 'The Global Persecution of Jehovah's Witnesses', United States Commission on International Religious Freedom, Issue Update, November. Available online: www.uscirf.gov/sites/default/files/2020%20Issue%20Update%20-%20Jehovahs%20Witnesses.pdf (accessed 1 March 2021).

Paul v. Watchtower Bible Tract Soc. of N. Y, 819 F.2d 875, 877 (9th Cir. 1987). Available online: https://casetext.com/case/paul-v-watchtower-bible-tract-soc-of-n-y (accessed 31 March 2021).

Penton, M. James ([1985] 2019), *Apocalypse Delayed: The Story of Jehovah's Witnesses*, Toronto: University of Toronto Press.

Pike, Royston (1954), *Jehovah's Witnesses: Who They Are, What They Teach, What They Do*, London: Watts.

Quenqua, Douglas (2019), 'A Secret Database of Child Abuse: A Former Jehovah's Witness Is Using Stolen Documents to Expose Allegations That the Religion Has Kept Hidden for Decades', *The Atlantic*, 5 April. Available online: www.theatlantic.com/family/archive/2019/03/the-secret-jehovahs-witness-database-of-child-molesters/584311 (accessed 1 March 2021).

Radio Free Europe / Radio Liberty (2021), 'Countries Where Jehovah's Witnesses' Activities Are Banned'. Available online: https://www.rferl.org/a/countries-where-jehovahs-witnesses-activities-are-banned/29757419.html (accessed 20 February 2021).

Rammerstorfer, Bernhard (2004), *Unbroken Will*, New Orleans, LA: Grammaton.

Redeker, Charles F. (2006), *Pastor C. T. Russell: Messenger of Millennial Hope*, Pacific Palisades, CA: Pastoral Bible Institute.

Reed, David A. (1986), *Jehovah's Witnesses Answered Verse by Verse*, Grand Rapids, MI: Baker Books.

Rhodes, Ron (1993), *Reasoning from the Scriptures with the Jehovah's Witnesses*, Eugene, OR: Harvest House.

Rogerson, Alan (1969), *Millions Now Living Will Never Die: A Study of Jehovah's Witnesses*, London: Constable.

Royal Commission (2016), *Report of Case Study No. 29*. Available online: www.childabuseroyalcommission.gov.au/sites/default/files/file-list/Case%20Study%2029%20-%20Findings%20Report%20-%20Jehovahs%20Witnesses.pdf (accessed 1 March 2021).

Russell, C. T. (1886), *The Divine Plan of the Ages*, London: International Bible Students Association.

Russell, C. T. (1904), *The New Creation*, London: International Bible Students Association.

Russell, C. T. (1913), 'The Desire of All Nations', *Pastor Russell's Convention Discourses*. Available online: https://dawnbiblestudents.com/health/10%20Convention%20Report%20Sermons.pdf (accessed 19 February 2021).

Russell, C. T. (attributed) (1917), *The Finished Mystery*, Brooklyn, NY: International Bible Students Association.

Rutherford, J. F. (1920a), *Millions Now Living Will Never Die*, Brooklyn, NY: International Bible Students Association.

Rutherford, J. F. (1920b), *The Harp of God*, London: International Bible Students Association.

Schnell, William J. (1959), *Thirty Years a Watch Tower Slave: The Confessions of a Converted Jehovah's Witness*, Grand Rapids, MI: Baker Book House.

Schulz, B. W., and R. de Vienne (2014), *A Separate Identity: Organizational Identity among Readers of Zion's Watch Tower: 1870–1887*, Milton Keynes: Fluttering Wings Press.

Scorah, Amber (2019), *Leaving the Witness: Exiting a Religion and Finding a Life*, New York: Viking.

Seibert, Gertrude (1905), *Daily Heavenly Manna for the Household of Faith*, Allegheny, PA: Watch Tower Bible and Tract Society.

Smith, Wilfred Cantwell (1959), 'Comparative Religion: Whither and Why?', in Mircea Eliade and J. M. Kitagawa (eds), *The History of Religions; Essays in Methodology*, 31–58, Chicago: University of Chicago Press.

SOVA Center for Information and Analysis (2010), 'The Structure of Russian Anti-Extremist Legislation', November. Available online: https://www.europarl.europa.eu/meetdocs/2009_2014/documents/droi/dv/201/201011/20101129_3_10sova_en.pdf (accessed 3 June 2021).

Springmeier, Fritz (1990), *The Watchtower and the Masons*, Portland, OR: Fritz Springmeier.

Stafford, Greg ([1998] 2000), *Jehovah's Witnesses Defended: An Answer to Scholars and Critics*, Huntington Beach, CA: Elihu Books.

Stafford, Greg (2007), 'Christian Witnesses of Jah', *In Medio* 2 (8): 1–9.

Stroup, H. H. (1945), *The Jehovah's Witnesses*, New York: Columbia University Press.

Tertullian ([197] 1931), *Apology*, trans. T. R. Glover, London: Heinemann.

University of Utrecht (2019), *Sexual Abuse and Willingness to Report within the Community of Jehovah's Witnesses*, Utrecht: Research and Documentation Centre of the Ministry of Justice and Safety. Available online: https://boeken.rechtsgebieden.boomportaal.nl/publicaties/9789462907782#5 (accessed 20 February 2021).

Voas, David (2008), 'The Trumpet Sounds Retreat: Learning from the Jehovah's Witnesses', in E. Barker (ed.), *The Centrality of Religion in Social Life*, 117–30, Farnham, UK: Ashgate.

Vonck, C. (ed.) (2016), *The Jehovah's Witnesses in Scholarly Perspective*, Antwerp: Faculty for Comparative Study of Religions and Humanism.

Watch Tower (1890), *Hymns and Poems of Dawn*, Allegheny, PA: Tower.

Watch Tower (1895), 'Consecration vs. the World and its Affairs', *Zion's Watch Tower*, 1 August: 1848–9.

Watch Tower (1915), 'Christian Duty and the War', *The Watchtower*, 1 September: 5754–5.

Watch Tower (1935), 'Washington Convention', *The Watchtower*, 15 April: 127–128.

Watch Tower (1936), 'Birthday Celebrations', *Awake!*, 6 May: 499.

Watch Tower (1940a), 'Octogenarians Not on the Retired List', *The Watchtower*, 1 January: 16.

Watch Tower (1940b), 'The Mending of a Heart', *Consolation*, 25 December: 19.

Watch Tower (1944a), 'Bringing Many Sons unto Glory', *The Watchtower*, 1 July: 195–204.

Watch Tower (1944b), 'The Strangers Right Maintained', *The Watchtower*, 1 December: 355–64.

Watch Tower (1945), 'Immovable for the Right Worship', *The Watchtower*, 1 July: 195–204.

Watch Tower (1946), *'Equipped for Every Good Work'*, Brooklyn, NY: Watchtower Bible and Tract Society Inc.

Watch Tower (1947), 'Marriage', *The Watchtower*, 15 January: 19–27.

Watch Tower (1948), 'Dangers of Blood Transfusion', *Awake!*, 22 October: 12.

Watch Tower (1951a), 'Questions From Readers: Is It proper to Have or Attend Celebrations of Birthday Anniversaries?', *The Watchtower*, 1 October: 607.

Watch Tower (1951b), *What Has Religion Done for Mankind?*, Brooklyn, NY: Watchtower Bible and Tract Society.

Watch Tower (1952), 'Keeping the Organization Clean', *The Watchtower*, 1 March: 131–48.

Watch Tower (1954), 'Questions from Readers', *The Watchtower*, 1 May: 286–7.

Watch Tower (1955), 'What If a Publisher Refuses to Stop Associating with a Disfellowshiped Person?', *The Watchtower*, 1 October: 607.

Watch Tower (1959), *Jehovah's Witnesses in the Divine Purpose*, Brooklyn, NY: Watchtower Bible and Tract Society of New York.

Watch Tower (1961), 'Questions from Readers: In View of the Seriousness of Taking Blood into the Human System by a Transfusion, would Violation of the Holy Scriptures in This Regard Subject the Dedicated, Baptized Receiver of Blood Transfusion to Being Disfellowshiped from the Christian Congregation?', *The Watchtower*, 15 January: 63–4.

Watch Tower (1965), *'Things in which It Is Impossible for God to Lie'*, Brooklyn, NY: Watch Tower Bible and Tract Society of Pennsylvania.

Watch Tower (1966a), *Life Everlasting in Freedom of the Sons of God*, Brooklyn, NY: Watchtower Bible and Tract Society of New York.

Watch Tower (1966b), 'A New Priesthood Begins', *The Watchtower*, 1 January: 26–30.

Watch Tower (1968), 'Why Are You Looking Forward to 1975?', *The Watchtower*, 15 August: 494–501.

Watch Tower (1970), 'It Is Not in the Bible!', *The Watchtower*, 1 November: 644–7.

Watch Tower (1972), '"They Shall Know that a Prophet Was Among Them"', *The Watchtower*, 1 April: 197–200.

Watch Tower (1973a), *God's Kingdom of a Thousand Years Has Approached*, Brooklyn, NY: Watchtower Bible and Tract Society of New York.

Watch Tower (1973b), 'Chess – What Kind of Game Is It?', *Awake!*, 22 March: 12–14.

Watch Tower (1974a), 'Maintaining a Balanced Viewpoint toward Disfellowshiped Ones', *The Watchtower*, 1 August: 466–73.

Watch Tower (1974b), 'How Are Jehovah's Witnesses Different?', *The Watchtower*, 15 October: 629–31.

Watch Tower (1975a), *1975 Yearbook of Jehovah's Witnesses*, Brooklyn, NY: Watch Tower Bible and Tract Society of Pennsylvania.

Watch Tower (1975b), 'My Life as a Famous Artist', *Awake!*, 8 July: 12–16.

Watch Tower (1976), 'A Solid Basis for Confidence', *The Watchtower*, 15 July: 438–43.

Watch Tower (1979), 'Questions from Readers: Around December 25 You Hear Much about "Three Wise Men" Being Led by a Star to Jesus. But Did They Visit Him in Bethlehem or Later in Nazareth?', *The Watchtower*, 15 December: 30.

Watch Tower (1980a), *1980 Yearbook of Jehovah's Witnesses*, Brooklyn, NY: Watch Tower Bible and Tract Society of Pennsylvania.

Watch Tower (1980b), 'Science Attests the Accuracy of the Bible', *The Watchtower*, 1 October: 10–13.

Watch Tower (1981), 'The Path of the Righteous Does Keep Getting Brighter', *The Watchtower*, 1 December: 27–31.

Watch Tower (1982), 'The New Morality – Harvesting Its Crop', *Awake!*, 22 June: 3–12.

Watch Tower (1983a), *School and Jehovah's Witnesses*, Brooklyn, NY: Watch Tower Bible and Tract Society of Pennsylvania.

Watch Tower (1983b), 'Help for Victims of Incest', *The Watchtower*, 1 October: 27–31.

Watch Tower (1984a), 'What About Music Videos?', *Awake!*, 22 May: 18–20.

Watch Tower (1984b), 'Questions from Readers: Does Jesus' Producing So Much Wine at the Marriage in Cana Indicate That Hundreds Attended That Feast?', *The Watchtower*, 1 November: 31.

Watch Tower ([1985] 1989), *Reasoning from the Scriptures*, Brooklyn, NY: Watchtower Bible and Tract Society of New York.

Watch Tower (1986), *Worldwide Security under the "Prince of Peace"*, Brooklyn, NY: Watch Tower Bible and Tract Society of Pennsylvania.

Watch Tower (1987), 'Questions from Readers: Is It Wise for a Christian whose Mate Has Died to Remain Single in the Hope of Being Reunited in the Future?', *The Watchtower*, 1 June: 31.

Watch Tower (1988), *Revelation—Its Grand Climax at Hand!*, Brooklyn, NY: Watch Tower Bible and Tract Society of Pennsylvania.

Watch Tower (1989a), *Live For Ever on Paradise Earth*, Brooklyn, NY: Watch Tower Bible and Tract Society of Pennsylvania.

Watch Tower (1989b), *Reasoning from the Scriptures*, Brooklyn, NY: Watchtower Bible and Tract Society of New York.

Watch Tower (1989c), *Should You Believe in the Trinity?* Brooklyn, NY: Watchtower Bible and Tract Society of New York.

Watch Tower ([1989] 2011, [2008] 2012), *Questions Young People Ask – Answers That Work*, 2 vols., Brooklyn, NY: Watchtower Bible and Tract Society of New York.

Watch Tower (1990a), *"All Scripture Is Inspired of God and Beneficial"*, Brooklyn, NY: Watchtower Bible and Tract Society of New York.

Watch Tower (1990b), '"Keep Seeking the Kingdom and God's Righteousness"', *The Watchtower*, 1 October: 15–20.

Watch Tower (1991), 'Healing the Wounds of Child Abuse', *Awake!*, 8 October: 3–11.

Watch Tower (1993a), *Jehovah's Witnesses: Proclaimers of God's Kingdom*, Brooklyn, NY: Watchtower Bible and Tract Society of New York.

Watch Tower (1993b), 'My Reflection as a Military Historian', *Awake!*, 22 April: 9–12.

Watch Tower (1993c), 'Protect Your Children!', *Awake!*, 8 October: 3–13.

Watch Tower (1994), 'Youths Who Have "Power beyond What Is Normal"', *Awake!*, 22 May: 9–15.

Watch Tower (1995a), 'A Time to Keep Awake', *The Watchtower*, 1 November: 20.

Watch Tower (1995b), 'Watching the World', *Awake!*, 8 November: 28–29.

Watch Tower (1996a), 'What Must We Do to Be Saved?', *The Watchtower*, 1 February: 4–8.

Watch Tower (1996b), 'Who Should Decide Family Size?', *Awake!*, 8 October: 12–14.

Watch Tower (1996c), 'A Fragile but Hardy Traveler', *Awake!*, 8 October: 15–18.

Watch Tower (1998), 'Questions from Readers', *The Watchtower*, 15 October: 30–1.

Watch Tower (1999a), *Pay Attention to Daniel's Prophecy!*, Brooklyn, NY: Watchtower Bible and Tract Society of New York.

Watch Tower (1999b), 'Is Everlasting Life Really Possible?', *The Watchtower*, 15 April: 4–9.

Watch Tower (2000a), *Isaiah's Prophecy – Light for All Mankind – I*, Brooklyn, NY: Watchtower Bible and Tract Society of New York.

Watch Tower (2000b), 'Joyful Weddings That Honor Jehovah', *The Watchtower*, 1 May: 19–22.

Watch Tower (2001), 'Could This Be the Best Career for You?', *The Watchtower*, 15 March: 20–2.

Watch Tower (2002a), 'The Bible's Viewpoint: Should Christians Share in New Year's Festivities?', *Awake!*, 8 January: 20–1.

Watch Tower (2002b), 'Christian Funerals – Dignified, Modest, and Pleasing to God', *The Watchtower*, 15 September: 29–32.

Watch Tower (2003), 'Teach Others the Pure Language', *Kingdom Ministry*, January: 4.

Watch Tower (2005a), *Organized to Do Jehovah's Will*, Brooklyn, NY: Watchtower Bible and Tract Society of New York.

Watch Tower (2005b), 'Trained to Give a Thorough Witness', *The Watchtower*, 1 January: 12–17.

Watch Tower (2005c), 'Christmastime – What Is Its Focus?', *The Watchtower*, 15 December: 4–7.

Watch Tower (2006a), 'Why Look to the Bible for Guidance?', *Awake!*, 6 January: 18–19.

Watch Tower (2006b), 'Was Jesus Really the Son of God?', *Awake!*, March: 12–13.

Watch Tower (2006c), 'Jehovah's Word Is Alive: Highlights from the Book of Job', *The Watchtower*, 15 March: 13.

Watch Tower (2006d), 'What Was the Original Sin?', *Awake!*, 6 June: 28–9.

Watch Tower (2006e), 'Weddings That Are Honorable in the Sight of God and Man', *The Watchtower*, 15 October: 18–22.

Watch Tower (2006f), 'Increase the Joy and Dignity of Your Wedding Day', *The Watchtower*, 15 October: 28–31.

Watch Tower (2007a), 'Questions from Readers: When Does the Calling of Christians to a Heavenly Hope Cease?', *The Watchtower*, 1 May: 30–1.

Watch Tower (2007b), 'Keep Your Children Safe', *Awake!*, October: 3–11.

Watch Tower (2007c), 'Can You Trust the Bible?', *Awake!* (Special Issue), November.

Watch Tower (2007d), 'Honorable Marriage in God's Sight', S-41-E [Wedding service outline, 2 pp.], Brooklyn, NY: Watch Tower Bible and Tract Society of Pennsylvania.

Watch Tower (2008a), 'Was It Designed?: Spider Silk', *Awake!*, 8 January: 24.

Watch Tower (2008b), 'Was It Designed?: Gecko Adhesive', *Awake!*, 8 April: 29.

Watch Tower (2008c), 'Are You Speaking the 'Pure Language' Fluently?', *The Watchtower*, 15 August: 21–5.

Watch Tower (2008d), 'Was It Designed?: The Seagull's Leg', *Awake!*, 8 September: 25.

Watch Tower (2008e), 'Was It Designed?: The Navigational System of the Butterfly', *Awake!*, 8 November: 10.

Watch Tower (2009a), 'Face Your Doubts', *The Watchtower*, 1 May: 3–9.

Watch Tower (2009b), 'Lunar New Year – Is It for Christians?', *The Watchtower*, 1 December: 20–3.

Watch Tower (2010a), *'Shepherd the Flock of God'*, Brooklyn, NY: Watchtower Bible and Tract Society of New York.

Watch Tower (2010b), '"The Righteous Ones Will Shine as Brightly as the Sun"', *The Watchtower*, 15 March: 19–23.

Watch Tower (2011a), 'Singing Praise to Jehovah', in *2011 Yearbook of Jehovah's Witnesses*, 17–21, Brooklyn, NY: Watchtower Bible and Tract Society of New York.

Watch Tower (2011b), 'Does God Dwell in One Place?', *The Watchtower*, 1 August: 27.

Watch Tower (2013a), 'For Those Loving Jehovah, "There Is No Stumbling Block"', *The Watchtower*, 15 March: 3–7.

Watch Tower (2013b), 'Branch Offices of Jehovah's Witnesses Consolidated', in *Yearbook of Jehovah's Witnesses*, 11–14, Brooklyn, NY: Watchtower Bible and Tract Society of New York.

Watch Tower (2014a), *Draw Close to Jehovah*, Brooklyn, NY: Watch Tower Bible and Tract Society of Pennsylvania.

Watch Tower (2014b), *God's Kingdom Rules*, Brooklyn, NY: Watch Tower Bible and Tract Society of Pennsylvania.

Watch Tower (2014c), *Who Are Doing Jehovah's Will Today?* [brochure], Brooklyn, NY: Watch Tower Bible and Tract Society of Pennsylvania.

Watch Tower (2014d), *What Does the Bible Really Teach?* Brooklyn, NY: Watch Tower Bible and Tract Society of Pennsylvania.

Watch Tower (2014e), *'Keep Yourselves in God's Love'*, Brooklyn, NY: Watch Tower Bible and Tract Society of Pennsylvania.

Watch Tower (2014f), 'Questions from Readers', *The Watchtower*, 15 August: 29.

Watch Tower (2015a), *What Can the Bible Teach Us?*, Wallkill, NY: Watchtower Bible and Tract Society of New York.

Watch Tower (2015b), 'Meetings for Field Service That Accomplish Their Purpose', *Our Kingdom Ministry*, 3 March: 3–6.

Watch Tower (2016a), *Answers to 10 Questions Young People Ask* [brochure], Brooklyn, NY: Watch Tower Bible and Tract Society of Pennsylvania.

Watch Tower (2016b), '"Her Husband Is Well-Known in the City Gates"', *Life and Ministry Meeting Workbook*, 16 November: 2.

Watch Tower (2017), 'Questions from Readers: Might Married Christians View the IUD (intrauterine device) as a Form of Birth Control That Is Compatible with the Scriptures?', *The Watchtower* (study edition), December: 16–17.

Watch Tower (2018a), *Insight on the Scriptures, Volume 1: Aaron – Jehoshua*, Brooklyn, NY: Watch Tower Bible and Tract Society of Pennsylvania.

Watch Tower (2018b), *Insight on the Scriptures, Volume 2: Jehovah – Zuzim and Index*, Brooklyn, NY: Watch Tower Bible and Tract Society of Pennsylvania.

Watch Tower (2018c), *Pure Worship of Jehovah – Restored at Last*, Brooklyn, NY: Watch Tower Bible and Tract Society of Pennsylvania.

Watch Tower (2018d), 'Pleasant Unity and the Memorial', *The Watchtower*, January: 12–16.

Watch Tower (2018e), 'Buy Truth and Never Sell It', *The Watchtower*, November: 4–7.

Watch Tower (2018f), 'Honor "What God Has Yoked Together"', *The Watchtower*, December: 10–14.

Watch Tower (2019a), *Organized to Do Jehovah's Will*, Wallkill, NY: Watchtower Bible and Tract Society of New York.

Watch Tower (2019b), 'What a Simple Meal Teaches Us about a Heavenly King', *The Watchtower*, January: 20–5.

Watch Tower (2019c), 'Love and Justice in the Christian Congregation', *The Watchtower*, May: 2–7.

Watch Tower (2019d), 'Love and Justice in the Face of Wickedness', *The Watchtower*, May: 8–13.

Watch Tower (2019e), 'Providing Comfort for Victims of Abuse', *The Watchtower*, May: 14–20.

Watch Tower (2019f), 'What Will Jehovah Cause You to Become?', *The Watchtower*, October: 20–5.

Watch Tower (2019g), '2019 Service Year Report of Jehovah's Witnesses Worldwide', JW.org. Available online: www.jw.org/en/library/books/2019-service-year-report/2019-grand-totals (accessed 1 March 2021).

Watch Tower (2019h), 'Bible Glossary', JW.org. Available online: www.jw.org/en/library/books/bible-glossary (accessed 1 March 2021).

Watch Tower (2020a), *'Shepherd the Flock of God'*, Wallkill, NY: Christian Congregation of Jehovah's Witnesses.

Watch Tower (2020b), 'Pursue Peace by Fighting Envy', *The Watchtower*, February: 14–19.

Watch Tower (2020c), 'A Small Box That Delivers Spiritual Food', JW.org, 1 September. Available online: www.jw.org/en/library/series/how-your-donations-are-used/A-Small-Box-That-Delivers-Spiritual-Food (accessed 1 March 2021).

Watch Tower (2021a), *Enjoy Life Forever: An Interactive Bible Course*. Available online: www.jw.org/en/library/books/Enjoy-Life-Forever-Introductory-Bible-Lessons (accessed 9 February 2021).

Watch Tower (2021b), 'Jehovah's Witnesses' Scripturally Based Position on Child Protection'. Available online: www.jw.org/en/news/legal/legal-resources/information/packet-jw-scripturally-based-position-child-protection (accessed 20 February 2021).

Watch Tower Society Quotes (n.d.), 'Flip-Flops'. Available online: www.quotes-watchtower.co.uk/flip-flops.html (accessed 1 March 2021).

Wilson, B. (1994), 'Apostates and New Religious Movements'. Available online: https://www.scientologyreligion.org/religious-expertises/apostates-and-new-religious-movements/ (accessed 1 March 2021).

Witness 007 (2012), '"Awake" 1973 Says Witnesses Should Not Play CHESS It's EVIL!!!', Jehovahs-Witness.com, 29 February. Available online: https://www.jehovahs-witness.com/topic/222408/awake-1973-says-witnesses-should-play-chess-evil (accessed 1 March 2021).

Wohl, Robert (1979), *The Generation of 1914*, Cambridge, MA: Harvard University Press.

Xin, Chang, and Human Rights Without Frontiers (2020), '18 Jehovah's Witnesses Sentenced to Years in Jail in Xinjiang', International Institute for Religious Freedom. Available online: https://www.iirf.eu/news/other-news/18-jehovahs-witnesses-sentenced-to-years-in-jail-in-xinjiang (accessed 3 June 2021).

Zieman, Bonnie (2016), *Fading Out of a Cult*, North Charleston, SC: CreateSpace.

About the author

George D. Chryssides is an honorary research fellow at York St John University and the University of Birmingham (UK), and was formerly Head of Religious Studies at the University of Wolverhampton. He is a regular presenter at national and international conferences, and is currently president of the International Society for the Study of New Religions.

He has written extensively on new religious movements, having had a particular interest in Jehovah's Witnesses for over a quarter of a century. His publications include *Jehovah's Witnesses: Continuity and Change* (2016), *Historical Dictionary of Jehovah's Witnesses* (2nd edn 2019), *Minority Religions in Europe and the Middle East* (2019), *The Insider-Outsider Debate* (co-edited with Stephen E. Gregg; 2019) and *The Bloomsbury Handbook to Studying Christians* (co-edited with Stephen E. Gregg; 2020).

Index

CPSIA information can be obtained
at www.ICGtesting.com
Printed in the USA
LVHW082054270422
717384LV00004B/100